AGING BEHIND PRISON WALLS

AGING BEHIND PRISON WALLS

Studies in Trauma and Resilience

TINA MASCHI AND KEITH MORGEN

Columbia University Press
New York

Columbia University Press
Publishers Since 1893
New York   Chichester, West Sussex
cup.columbia.edu

Library of Congress Cataloging-in-Publication Data
Names: Maschi, Tina, author. | Morgen, Keith (Keith J.), author.
Title: Aging behind prison walls : studies in trauma and resilience /
    Tina M. Maschi and Keith Morgen.
Description: New York : Columbia University Press, 2020. | Includes
    bibliographical references and index.
Identifiers: LCCN 2020018181 (print) | LCCN 2020018182 (ebook) |
    ISBN 9780231182584 (hardback) | ISBN 9780231182591 (trade paperback) |
    ISBN 9780231544252 (ebook)
Subjects: LCSH: Older prisoners—United States. | Prisons—Overcrowding—
    United States. | Imprisonment—United States. | Criminal justice,
    Administration of—United States.
Classification: LCC HV9469 .M377 2020 (print) | LCC HV9469 (ebook) |
    DDC 365/.608460973—dc23
LC record available at https://lccn.loc.gov/2020018181
LC ebook record available at https://lccn.loc.gov/2020018182

Columbia University Press books are printed on permanent
and durable acid-free paper.
Printed in the United States of America

Cover image: © Ron Levine / www.ronlevinephotography.com

CONTENTS

AGING BEHIND
PRISON WALLS

INTRODUCTION

Mass Aging in Prison: Crisis or Opportunity?

We cannot solve our problems with the same level of thinking that created them.

—Albert Einstein

There is growing awareness of what was once an invisible crisis: a rapidly growing population of older, sick, and dying people with special needs kept behind lock and key. Prisons were not designed to meet the unique needs of this population and often lack trained staff who could turn a prison into a specialized long-term health-care facility. National and international attention to this rapidly growing "silver tsunami" has increased because of media coverage, articles in academic and professional journals, and community conversations. The experiences of diverse older adults behind prison walls are highlighted in this book and are coupled with their life stories before, during, and after prison. Through news and social media outlets, we now are witnesses, almost daily, to what is happening behind prisons' barbed wire and concrete walls.[1]

Some of the problems faced by the older generation, especially those in minority groups, are related to cumulative disadvantages early in life: untreated health and mental health issues, social isolation, oppression (e.g., ageism, sexism, racism), toxic family stress, lack of access to quality education and community services, and discrimination and structural institutional policy barriers. These cumulative disadvantages are significantly aggravated by the trauma of prolonged incarceration.[2]

Who are these older people in prison? Official statistics show that many incarcerated older adults received long-term or life prison sentences, often for serious violent offenses, when they were juveniles. In plain language, they are disproportionately racial/ethnic minorities, come from communities of poverty, and have histories of traumatic experiences and mental health and substance abuse issues. Other older adults may first enter prison later in life. Some older adults return to prison one or more times for committing similar crimes or because of a parole violation; this is especially common if they are grappling with mental health or substance use issues and lack access to needed health, mental health, and community services.[3] We have classified these inmates into three distinct groups: incarcerated older adults serving long-term or life sentences (who were imprisoned as juveniles or adults age 18–54), those first incarcerated at age 55 or older, and those incarcerated one or more times before reincarceration at age 55 or older.

How did these older adults become involved in the criminal justice system, whether as children, adults, or older adults? And who is responsible for this outcome? Is it the individual, the family, the local community, or society in general? A formerly incarcerated 61-year-old African American man offers his perspective on these questions:

> I think the community has to do a lot to help the younger people staying on the street and give them a reason, provide the resources to not even think about going to jail. Once they get into the criminal justice system that system is not designed to teach you to be a better person out there. So, the community has to do its job not the prison system. If you want to keep a kid on the street, the community has to have the necessary resources both educational, financially, [and] environmentally to make the kid want to not even look in that direction. So, the criminal justice system is not responsible for the upbringing of the kid, the community is. And until the community does its job and stops looking for other people to take care of their young, then you're always going to have a flawed criminal justice system. It starts in the community. It starts at home, then the community, and if all else fails the criminal justice system.

The stories and data about incarcerated older adults shared in the following pages are not only about vulnerability. These stories are also about strength and resilience, self-empowerment, wisdom, and personal growth. Their personal stories describe how individuals are surviving and even thriving despite the stressful conditions of physical confinement. Many formerly incarcerated people from younger generations talk about the positive mentoring they received from older adults while in prison. Inmate hospice volunteers have reported on the therapeutic and curative effects of peer support in caring for an older or dying person in prison. They note how this experience taught them compassion for others in a way that traditional punishment and rehabilitation programs never did. It is the aging prisoner who has awakened the general public to the possibility of a form of justice that cares.[4]

In the spirit of Einstein's wisdom—"We cannot solve our problems with the same level of thinking that created them"—we are making a call to action to usher in a new age of caring justice to replace the old age of criminal justice. The term "caring justice" refers to an individual and group consciousness that focuses on how we value, treat, and care for one another, especially older adults and other marginalized groups, including those with histories of involvement in the criminal justice system. The caring justice perspective transcends dualistic thinking and emphasizes a relational/collectivist approach in which individuals and communities are also responsible and accountable for public safety outcomes. This perspective opens the floodgates of creativity and collaboration, leading communities to find innovative ways to respond to age and justice issues.

This new age of caring justice also has the promise of freeing individuals and the collective to consider alternative approaches to the current overemphasis on relentless retribution and cruel punishment for crime and wrongdoing. A caring justice perspective replaces cruel and unusual punishment with mercy, compassion, unconditional love, transparency (truth), and accountability. With momentum toward this new paradigm, the old paradigm will die a good death. Ushering in a caring justice consciousness will guide criminal justice reform and help us prevent human-made public safety disasters, such as those now found in our prison systems. Caring justice reforms will enable us to provide emergency assistance to older, sick, and dying people behind prison walls, as well as providing assistance to their family members and communities.

Aging Behind Prison Walls: A Look Inside

A look behind prison walls reveals conditions that are extremely difficult for any individual to cope with on a daily basis. Two older inmates share some of the cruel and unusual experiences they have had in prison:

> It's very tough surviving prison. The provoking, the unnecessary treatment, verbal abuse, and violence only adds to the original sentence term to be served. Overcrowded conditions, poor medical service, lack of interaction with Administrative Staff is stammering.
>
> (68-year-old Caucasian woman in prison)

> It was my first week of incarceration in 1979. I was standing in line in the mess hall along with about 150 other prisoners . . . when all of a sudden, a man gets

stabbed from behind with a sword . . . a seven and a half foot sword. The man must have been standing because he was slumped over as if he was touching his toes . . . with the blade through him and the point of the sword stuck in the floor leaving the handle sticking out his back. The kicker was what the officer said. I thought the response would be . . . Everyone on the floor . . . Everyone up against the wall. Instead he yelled for a bed sheet and draped it over the slumped body with the impression of the handle topping the sheet to a point. Bewilderment was all over my face as I looked at the dead body three feet away from me. I couldn't remember if I thought or blurted out the words . . . "What kind of world is this?" The officer looked me right in the eye and said: "Keep the line moving!" Again . . . my rationality kicked in . . . maybe I'm in a different time. . . . I'm definitely in different world. I just wish I wasn't.

(59-year-old incarcerated African American man)

In the pages that follow, we take readers on a journey inside the experiences of older adults through the dark shadowbox of prisons. Prisons are outside the view of the external world, and the environment is often fraught with heavy-handed attempts at control to restrain the chaotic outbursts of abuse and violence. This anything-goes lifestyle is not pleasant for incarcerated people or staff of any age, but it is particularly grueling for many older, sick, frail, and dying individuals. They are at a higher risk of being untreated, undertreated, or mistreated by other inmates and by staff.

Throughout the text, we present data and insights from more than three decades of work with individuals of all ages who have been involved in the criminal justice system. We were inspired to write this book as we sought answers to these three questions:

What is the current situation of aging in prison?
How have we gotten here?
What should be done about it?

We ask you to join us and take a "look inside"—not only inside the prison walls but also inside yourself. Examine your personal reactions, and the reactions of others around you. We encourage you to tap into your heart and mind as you reflect on these questions. Then ask yourself, "What, if anything, do *you* want to do about it?" and "What do *you* think society should do about it?"

Portraits of Aging in Prison

Our increased awareness of the experiences of aging behind bars comes at a time when the U.S. prison population is shrinking. By the end of 2016, fewer people were held in state and federal prisons than in any year since 2004.[5] But one group in prisons is still surging, older people. By 2030, people over the age of 55 will make up one-third (33 percent) of the overall U.S. prison population. This trend has been developing for decades: from 1999 to 2016, the number of people 55 or older in state and federal prisons increased by 280 percent, whereas the number of incarcerated younger adults grew by only 3 percent. Incarcerated older adults now represent 11 percent of the total prison population. Many individuals also die in prison, especially older adults. More than 3,000 (5 percent) people die in U.S. prisons each year, and most are age 50 or older.[6]

The global rise in older people in prison has been attributed to two central causes: increases in the aging population coupled with the long-term aftermath of stricter sentencing and parole policies from the 1970s and 1980s.[7] Incarcerated older people also may have longer criminal histories than their younger counterparts, so some of these life sentences may be the result of enhanced prison terms for people who have had "multiple strikes." In 2013, about one-third (31 percent) of state prisoners age 65 or older were serving life sentences.

Official statistics offer some insight into the pipeline to prison for older people. Bureau of Justice Statistics cite two major factors that contributed to the aging of incarcerated people between 1993 and 2013: a greater number of individuals were sentenced to and were serving longer periods in state prison, predominantly for violent offenses, and general admissions of older people increased.[8] These official statistics suggest that the pipeline to prison has an open entrance valve to the mass incarceration of older people along with an almost closed exit valve. Geriatric and compassionate release are rarely used because of various laws, policies, and practices, especially bureaucratic processes, that often deny or delay release, leading to older adults becoming frailer or even dying in prison.[9]

The age-related special needs of older adults can be quite complex. Many correctional facilities are ill-prepared to care for their acute and long-term needs, such as their physical and mental health and addictions. As we detail in later chapters, older people in prison have higher rates of chronic illnesses or disabilities, such as heart and lung disease, cancer, HIV/AIDS, and cognitive impairment/dementia, compared to incarcerated younger adults and their older community counterparts. Past poor health behaviors (e.g., addictions, living in poverty, homelessness, and chronic exposure to violence) coupled with the stressful conditions of the prison environment place older adults at increased risk for age-related mental health problems, especially dementia and early mortality.[10]

After their release, older adults commonly report social isolation. They often have no or limited contact with informal or formal caregivers, such as family, friends, and professionals. In a previous study of 677 older adults in a northeastern prison, we found that contact with prison workers, community professionals, or volunteers and family was generally low. Most participants reported having contact with medical staff (66 percent), incarcerated people (43 percent), and community-based religious volunteers (43 percent), but they had even less contact with professionals, such as social workers (37 percent), psychologists (32 percent), psychiatrists (26 percent), probation or parole officers (10 percent), and teachers (8 percent). Many participants also commonly reported minimal contact with family or friends during the past three months. Over two-thirds had no contact with their marital or life partner (67 percent) or parents (69 percent). The majority reported no contact with their children (60 percent) or their grandchildren (77 percent). Almost half (49 percent) reported they had no contact with siblings. This has significant implications for maintaining health and well-being before prison and the adjustment needed after release.[11]

The corrections facilities also grapple with how to manage the complex health, mental health, addictions, social, and legal needs in a system that was not designed as a specialized long-term-care facility for frail elders or for the seriously and terminally ill. Some correctional systems have some level of programming while in prison and after release, but many still do not. For those that do offer services, several fall short of the age-specific needs of older people related to physical health, mental health, family, and social supports.[12] A caring justice approach to age and criminal justice matters can address the issues this 55-year-old African American incarcerated adult foresees about soon being released from prison:

> You don't need a survey to know you have a lot of men over 50 getting ready to go home, with no money. No place to stay. And no one trying to understand this part of the problem. I earn $15 a month. I go home in nine months. I have no family to turn to. I don't want to come back to prison, after doing seven years. I am trying to stay positive. I pray. I go to see the psych for one on one, and I try to look on the bright side. But the reality is, when I hit the street, I am on my own. Tell me what good your survey will do me, or people like me?

Older people face significant challenges as they finish their sentences and reenter society. Among those challenges are ill health, cognitive impairment, limited ability to work, alienation from friends and family, and discrimination based on their age, offense history, or other minority statuses.[13] When older adults are released from prison, the crisis of care extends to the community, and variables such as being old, formerly incarcerated, and the associated stigma often create barriers to obtaining needed medical and mental health treatment as well as social and legal services. For able-bodied older adults, employment or job training are essential factors for successful community reintegration, yet their criminal history may create barriers to attaining employment, housing, or even placement in nursing homes or hospices. Such obstacles place formerly incarcerated older adults at risk of recidivating and returning to prison.[14]

This type of adverse treatment places the well-being of older adults released from prison at risk when returning to their communities. For example, older adults who served long prison sentences may experience institutionalization or significant psychological distress, including symptoms of posttraumatic stress disorder.[15]

Barriers and Facilitators to Successful Reintegration Reported by Community Correctional Staff (N=78)

Barriers to Successful Reintegration	Facilitators to Successful Reintegration
1. Finding employment	1. Family, employment, social security, transportation services
2. Not finding a job	2. Family members
3. No family they can count on or be able to see	3. Family being part of their life
4. Not being able to find a job for those that are still able to work	4. Family support
5. Finding a place to live	5. Without family support it is a little harder for a person who honestly has a desire to get on the right path
6. Homelessness	6. Their mental or emotional maturity
7. Lack of family support	7. Having positive communication
8. Lack of support system to provide moral support and assurance that everything will work out	8. Staying on top of them and guiding them where they have to go
9. Family problems	9. Motivation, understanding
10. Substance abuse	10. Following program guidelines
11. Not able to adjust to the program standards	11. Because our individuals have done so much time in prison, they are thankful to be on parole and strive to do what is required because they realize that they don't have many years left. Once they get settled with a place to live and some assistance, they are happy and completing parole becomes easy.
12. Noncompliance with authority figures	12. Integration, asking for helpful feedback
13. Issues with trust/respect	13. Putting them in healthy role model situations in the community

In one of our previous studies on community reintegration, professionals, mostly parole officers, reported barriers and facilitators to the successful reintegration of older adults from prison (see the text box). Community correctional staff described the factors that influenced the reunification process of older adults. Professionals most commonly reported structural barriers, which included employment and housing (i.e., homelessness), as posing challenges to success in their work with older adults. They also reported personal and social barriers that include histories of substance abuse and lack of family and other social supports. One staff member said, "When the family is not supportive, it makes it a little harder for a person who honestly has a desire to get on the right path." Staff also reported factors they perceived as facilitating successful reintegration. These included access to employment, social security, and transportation services. Social facilitators included family support ("family being part of their life") and having a relationship with staff to provide guidance, structure, motivation, and understanding. Staff also described the beneficial effects for older adults who had developed "higher levels of "mental/ emotional maturity" and used interpersonal skills that reflected "positive communication," and who had the potential to become mentors. One staff participant observed that formerly incarcerated older adults, especially those who had served long sentences, needed to be provided "with opportunities to be healthy role models." Overall, the staff perceived internal and external supports or resources as helpful in facilitating the successful reunification of older adults with their families and communities. Balancing autonomy and empowerment with support, including leadership and mentorship opportunities, was described as essential.[16]

Some older adults who are released from prison may have limited functional capacities and may need assistance with activities of daily living, such as taking care of personal hygiene and clothing. Other seriously or terminally ill older adults may need long-term institutional care, such as placement in a nursing home. However, barriers to placement in nursing homes and hospices may exist because of the stigma and discrimination against individuals with criminal histories, especially those with more serious offenses, such as arson and sex offenses. Some terminally ill older adults may need hospice placement in the community to address their palliative and end-of-life care.[17]

Some older adults or terminally ill people released from prison may return home to their families. Family members often experience stress when their loved ones are denied or experience delay in getting needed medical supplies or benefits. The following vignettes highlight the experiences of the sick and dying in prison and the impact this has on their family members. They also illustrate the difference between families that do not and those that do have access to financial and social supports to care for their dying loved ones at home.

Mr. C is a 59-year-old African American male who has served thirty-three years in a New York state prison for a sex offense. He is married and has no children. His wife visited him monthly for the first three decades. Three years ago, he was diagnosed with cognitive impairment (dementia), asthma, obesity, and COPD and placed in a regional medical unit. In the past year, his condition progressed, and he became dependent on oxygen and a wheelchair (he is unable to walk long distances because of his weight and COPD). He was approved for medical parole because he was considered significantly incapacitated. The parole board saw him within eight weeks and approved his medical parole release. His wife requested home placement. The medical parole coordinator of the institutional discharge planning unit (DPU) facilitated the care-transition process and was in contact with the patient and his wife. In the written discharge or transitional care plan, his wife committed to driving him home from prison and finding a primary care doctor and a cancer specialist for follow-up care. She also agreed to obtain durable medical equipment for their home. The medical parole co-ordinator completed the Medicaid application. Upon his release date, Mr. C's Medicaid was pending and would not be activated until after his release. His wife could not afford to pay for services until his Medicaid benefits were activated. The visiting nurse association (VNA) also would agree to accept the case only after Medicaid was activated. Because his family lacked the financial supports needed, Mr. C went home with only a wheelchair. He was home for eight days with no oxygen, no hospital bed, and no visiting nurse service.

✳ ✳ ✳

Mr. O is a 51-year-old Caucasian male serving a ten-year sentence for a drug offense in a New York state prison. Six years into his sentence, he was diagnosed with an advanced stage of lung cancer. The family, his elderly parents and sister, regularly visited him two times a week in the regional medical unit and had ongoing contact with medical staff. In the past year, Mr. O became completely bedridden and needed to be tube fed. The family requested that a medical parole application be completed. The medical parole coordinator of the institutional DPU facilitated the application. The correctional medical doctor diagnosed his disease as a terminal illness and gave him six months or less to live. The parole board held a special hearing because his physical condition was rapidly deteriorating. His medical parole was approved within four weeks. The medical parole coordinator also was in contact with the patient, the family, and community supports in development of the discharge plan. Mr. O's discharge plan included caregiving and financial supports and home placement. Before his release, his elderly parents were able to arrange for community doctor appointments and obtain necessary home-care equipment. His parents also were able to pay up-front for any services until Medicaid became active, which could take up to one month. During the care-transition process, the medical parole coordinator provided coaching three times or more a week with the family. The development of the discharge plan included details on how family members would assist in home placement, including nighttime coverage from the sister. The medical parole coordinator also secured a visiting nurse who would make the hospice referral when it became necessary.

Who Is Old in Prison?

The definition of old age in prison varies by geographic location and setting, and it is often different from the traditional notions of old age in the local community. For example, correctional systems may classify older adults as those 50 or 55 years old even though the age individuals in the community are defined as older or elderly differs across countries. Many global societies, such as the United States, perceive 65 years of age or above as older because full pension or social security benefits are tied to that age. However, the age at which an incarcerated person is classified as old is often much younger compared to their community dwelling adults. For example, incarcerated people in the United States may be classified as "older adult" or "elderly" at an average age of 55.[18] The United Kingdom (England, Scotland, Wales, and Northern Ireland) designates the "elderly" in prison as age 50 and older, and Canada has a two-tiered system in which "older" in prison is age 50 to 64 years and "elderly" is age 65 and above.[19]

The younger age classification of "older" in many correctional systems compared to the wider culture is generally attributed to differences found in chronological versus biological age between incarcerated adults and community dwelling older adults in their geographic location. The 50-year-old lowest age classification as "elderly" in corrections may reflect the average incarcerated person's accelerated decrements in health status, which are equivalent to community dwelling adults who are fifteen years older.[20] Accelerated aging is corroborated by evidence from international prison studies showing that older adults in prison have significantly higher rates of physical and mental health decline compared to younger prisoners or to older adults of a similar age in the community.[21] The rapid decline in health of incarcerated older adults has been attributed largely to their high-risk personal histories, chronic health conditions, poor health practices such as poor diets and smoking, and alcohol and substance abuse, coupled with the stressful conditions of prison confinement, which include prolonged exposure to overcrowding, social isolation and deprivation, a sedentary lifestyle and poor nutrition, and prison violence.[22] These combined personal, social, and environmental risk factors significantly increase the likelihood of the early onset of serious physical and mental illnesses, including dementia, among older adults in prison.[23] A more in-depth exploration of health and accelerated aging in prison is provided in chapter 5.

Age, Nature, and Culture in Prisons

To contemplate the lived experiences of older people in prison, it is helpful to understand the nature and culture of prisons. Two older adults shared their perspective on aging behind prison walls.

> Prison is a hard place. Pure Hell! As long as you are in khaki, you are considered nonhuman. The elder suffer the most because there isn't much for them, us. I have the starts of osteoporosis and seeing how some people young and old are treated makes me suffer and deal with it. Overall it's horrible and I wouldn't wish this on my worst enemy.
>
> (66-year-old woman in prison)

> When I had my last surgery in prison, um, there was a 93-year-old man, white guy, he was a nice guy. He was in there, I believe, for, um, assault. He's been in there for like seventeen years or eighteen years, but this guy is in a hospital. He cannot even hold his bowels, so I'm like what is a guy like this going to do? What is he going to do? He cannot, he can barely walk. He's been in a hospital, in a hospital or infirmary, for a year. What is he going to do? You'll see guys in there that just sit there staring into space.
>
> (50-year-old African American man describing a fellow inmate)

There are reasons for the challenges older people experience in prison. The early architects of U.S. criminal justice policy targeted punishment, deterrence, and incapacitation as the primary underpinnings for prisons. This philosophy was codified in law, and prisons were built as a concrete reminder. Most prisons, especially many U.S. prisons, were not designed for the comfortable long-term confinement of adults, especially those with age-related physical and mental health needs. Rather, prisons were designed as stark environments that are uncomfortable. Residents experience minimal natural light and live in small cells, in which they must stay for long periods of time, often twenty to twenty-three hours a day.[24] In addition, incarcerated individuals are often deprived of fresh air and healthy food. Based on this dark and dank description, it is not so far-fetched that anyone or anything (including plants) would lose their vitality. With the exception of a reformed prison, the prison environment requires inhabitants to tap their own inner resources to thrive; other inmates may just barely be able to survive the experience and have an early onset or exacerbation of health and mental health issues.[25]

The culture of prisons is commonly characterized by control, order, and obedience. One of the most important and basic rules of survival in prison is to follow directions to avoid disciplinary infractions and remain as physically independent as possible. Therefore, being obedient is often essential, not only for the survival of incarcerated people but also to avoid institutional charges that may result in secure confinement. Even the healthiest of individuals must be vigilant and rapidly respond to authority and to prisoner leaders in the prison environment.[26] However, this task may range from confusing to incomprehensible for older people with different levels of cognitive impairment. The ability of individuals experiencing the loss of short- and long-term memory or impairment in other areas (e.g., reasoning, personality, language, visual processes, executive functions, behaviors, and relationships) to fit into the regimen of control, order, and obedience may be significantly reduced.[27]

Older adults in prison are at higher risk for developing dementia than are their younger counterparts. Typical behavior of early to late stages of dementia, such as not being able to follow directions, pacing about a cell, or aggressive behavior, may cause disruptions in the movement of the general prison population or in congregate living quarters.[28] These behaviors related to dementia, coupled with a highly volatile prison environment, may put older individuals at risk of becoming victims or perpetrators of violence.[29] Equally important, older adults with dementia who cannot follow prison rules run the risk of receiving institutional charges that may result in placement in secure confinement, which in turn may significantly compromise their physical and mental well-being.[30]

Prisons are characterized as providing a frightening and traumatizing environment, and aggression, violence, and bullying are integrated into their fabric. Both the young and the old and those who have physical or mental disabilities are increasingly vulnerable to victimization by other prisoners or staff.[31] Vulnerable groups are the most common targets of harassment and bullying, and both inmates and staff may make fun of them in an attempt to provoke a response of self-defense.[32] A violent self-defense response may result in a disciplinary action. Youth, women, LGBTQ+ people, and the elderly also may experience sexual victimization by other prisoners because they are less able to defend themselves.[33] The challenges of prison affect everyone, but it is especially difficult for older people and other vulnerable groups to successfully navigate these challenges. Is this what the general public had in mind when they entrusted the administration of justice to the government and to corrections professionals? Are U.S. citizens comfortable with the unequal measures of punishment facing those we are incarcerated? Could our tax dollars be spent in a way that would value life and produce cost savings for all those involved directly in crime: victims, offenders, and their communities? Is there another way?

Final Reflections

The good news is that there are other ways to look at the criminal justice system and the solutions that flow from it. Over the past two decades, a growing caring justice response has led to the development of positive programming for aging people across the criminal justice system, especially for those in prisons and in community corrections. In some countries, governmental and nongovernmental organizations have moved to identify and respond to this crisis. These programs recognize that older adults often derive little value from prison programming designed to target the needs of the younger people in prison: education, vocational training, employment, and programs aimed at reducing high-risk offending behavior.[34] The United States and some other countries with large prison populations have begun to adopt more palliative care services. For example, peer support programs, such as the Gold Coat program in California, employ a well-trained team of interdisciplinary professionals who train and supervise fellow inmates who take care of the sick and dying in prison.[35] Some of these practices and innovations are described in detail in part II of this book.

We challenge you to think outside of the shadows and darkened social structures of the prison box and visualize communities of care that actually do care. Can you conceptualize prisons as houses of transformation that are part of the community rather than being invisible, separate, and abusive institutions? At reentry, community release goals could go beyond community reintegration to include reunification of older adults with their families and the local environment. There are many definitions of community, but the definitions most relevant to the current discussion include (1) a group of people living in the same location; (2) a feeling of fellowship with others as a result of sharing common attitudes, interests, and goals; and (3) a unified body of individuals.[36] In this sense, community is a physical, psychological, emotional, social, and spiritual place and state. Here is the way a formerly incarcerated older person describes his internal and external experience of connecting with community. It begins with connecting with himself, then connecting with the process and with the larger web of life:

> I mean, at the end of the day it's about doing what I can do to help myself. It's a process, it really is. To me it is a system within itself. Doing what I can do for myself, then my family, then that immediate community that I may be in, and

then subsequently, ultimately the greater community, because, I mean, actually my mind says import, export. My mind says, I'm seeing my future, my mind says where can I go? Okay, can I go there? How can I take what's going on here in America and take it and perhaps be of service to these folks that's over here and these folks that's over here, these folks that's here and bring a full circle, absolutely, obviously. I'm talking about food, of course, clean drinking water, you know, that's from the nonprofit aspect of it as well anyway.

The economic and human costs of current practices and policies are already astounding, and they will only become more dramatic. In the United States, federal and state governments spend a combined $77 billion annually to operate correctional facilities.[37] About 20 percent, or $16 billion, is spent on health care for older adults in prison.[38] It costs approximately three times more ($68,000) per year to care for people age 50 and older than to care for younger people ($34,000) in prison.[39]

The human and moral costs are also high. After more than thirty years of stricter criminal justice policies that have adversely affected many marginalized groups,[40] including older adults, it is past time for us fellow community members to reflect on the many costs involved in people aging in prison. It is our wakeup alarm, and public concern is mounting. We are at a crossroads; we can continue down this road, or we can redefine this crisis as an opportunity to reinvent ourselves and our connection to our families and communities. This problem was created by all of us, and together we can find solutions so people of all ages will be safe in their communities and in prison.

We encourage you to ask yourself and then others: How did we get here? Is this the situation we would want for our family members or for other people's family members with a loved one who was a victim or a perpetrator of a crime? Is this the kind of common humanity we want our children to inherit or how we want to be treated as grandparents? Can we envision alternative strategies that reinforce personal accountability coupled with compassionate care for both those victimized and those who committed offenses? Can we forge new solutions that foster intergenerational family and community justice for all? Communities must deliberate on the costs and benefits of their approach to matters of care and justice. Do you support a community approach and a justice system that promotes healthy and safe communities (1) for all people of all ages, (2) only for some people and communities and not others, or perhaps (3) for no person or community?

How do we co-construct our own road maps that foster holistic well-being and justice across the life course for everyone? Both the problems and the solutions to providing quality care exist within the community, and corrections and prisons each represent a part of it. As illustrated in figure 0.1, the primary community roadway is the Unity Circle, and its secondary roadway

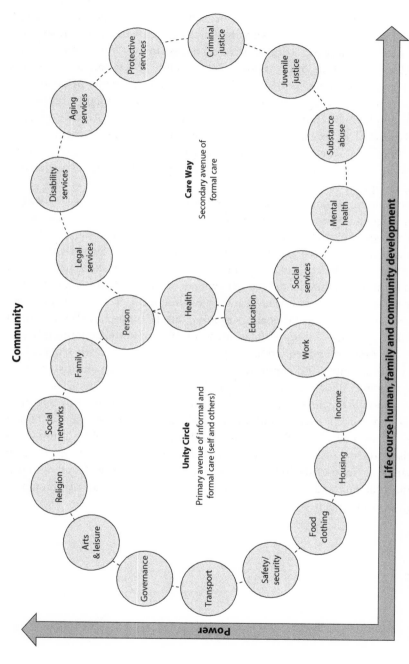

Community

Care Way
Secondary avenue of formal care

Unity Circle
Primary avenue of informal and formal care (self and others)

Protective services · Criminal justice · Aging services · Juvenile justice · Disability services · Substance abuse · Legal services · Mental health · Person · Health · Social services · Family · Education · Social networks · Work · Religion · Income · Arts & leisure · Housing · Governance · Food clothing · Transport · Safety/security

Power

Life course human, family and community development

0.1 Co-constructing a community for the health, well-being, and safety of individuals of all ages and their families is Care Way. Unity Circle is populated by informal care networks (e.g., family, peers, and other social networks) and foundational supports (e.g., food, housing, and transportation). All individuals are entitled to two primary sectors of care in the Unity Circle: universal access to education and to health care. The Unity Circle of community is the source of self-care and informal caregiving; it is where individuals learn socially responsible behavior and accountability. Access to education is a key factor in opening possibilities for future employment and obtaining a meaningful vocation. Access to health care is critical for prevention, clinical intervention, and treatment. People enter Care Way when they need professional assistance such as physical or mental health services or substance abuse treatment. The criminal justice system is an option of last resort.[41]

In chapter 6, we detail the construction of community for people of all ages. This model can be used to conceptualize and plan more effective prevention and intervention strategies that benefit all community members, including older adults who are released from prison. When we asked formerly incarcerated older adults what would help them succeed in transitioning from prison to the community, they shared the following needs: access to foundational supports for food, clothing, housing, and employment services or linkages; specialized health and mental health supports; family support and other social supports; guidance and representation; and transformational community justice.[42] As these recommendations suggest, formerly incarcerated older adults long for community and connection and want to rejoin the fabric of society. The question is: Should communities do their part to help make this happen?

This book is organized into two parts. The first seven chapters profile individual and social/structural conditions that have led to the aging in prison crisis. We also detail the characteristics and experiences of older adults prior to prison, during prison, and after their release. In part II we shift our focus to the caring justice partnership paradigm, presenting a new way of looking at this age-old problem, and we apply this framework to some innovative programming ideas and practices.

PART I

MASS AGING IN PRISON

How Did We Get Here?

CHAPTER 1

AN OUNCE OF PREVENTION IS WORTH A POUND OF CURE

The only source of knowledge is experience.

—Albert Einstein

This chapter begins with a description of the intersectional disparities commonly found among older adults in the criminal justice system that placed them at risk of criminal justice involvement. Next we take readers directly inside the prison system to experience the thoughts, feelings, and observations of James O in his own words, written while he was incarcerated. James was 55 years old at the time, and he had served seven years of a nine-year sentence for a serious crime. James guides readers on a reflective and emotional journey to better understand his life and how his experiences and choices led to his incarceration and experience of prison and how he has managed not only to survive but also to thrive despite the challenges. We conclude with an analysis of the factors that may have influenced his pathway to prison, his experience of prison, and his perceptions for the future.

Pathways to Prison for Older Adults

Research and theory suggest that the pathways to prison for older adults may vary in one or more cumulative health, social, and justice disparities (figure 1.1).

Birth	➡	Cumulative Determinants	➡	Mass Aging and Dying in Prison

Individual level factors	Social/structural factors
Age	SES-Poverty
Race/ethnicity	Education/employment
Gender	Intergenerational incarceration
Sexual orientation	Homelessness
Religion	Oppression, stigma, attitudes, bias, discrimination
Physical disabilities	Family
Mental disabilities	Peers

1.1 Cumulative social determinants of health, social equality, and justice

Cumulative determinants that may influence individual outcomes include age, race/ethnicity, gender, sexual orientation, educational level, socioeconomic status (SES), and level of access to services and justice. Older people have been discriminated against historically in all societal arenas: discrimination in the workplace, violence and abuse in homes and institutions, and lack of access to quality health and social care when age-related decline in functional abilities is inevitable.[1] An expanding body of evidence documents the rapidly growing tidal wave of older adults in prison who are disproportionately represented by disenfranchised groups, such as race/ethnicity minorities, persons living in poverty, and working class people.

Ageism is a significant issue affecting justice for older adults in prison and in the community. As research studies and advocacy reports commonly note, older people in the criminal justice system experience neglect and mistreatment by other incarcerated individuals and by correctional officers and other staff members.[2] Intersectional minority discrimination is another global trend related to ageism, and the United Nations has identified minority discrimination based on racial/ethnic groups, immigration or disability status, gender, sexual orientation, class, and educational status. The United Nations designates these minority groups as special needs populations because they also are discriminated against in many global criminal justice systems.[3] Racial/ethnic minorities and those in the lower class are more likely to be arrested, prosecuted, and imprisoned for longer terms than are members of the majority population. Therefore, of the 10.35 million people in prisons around the world

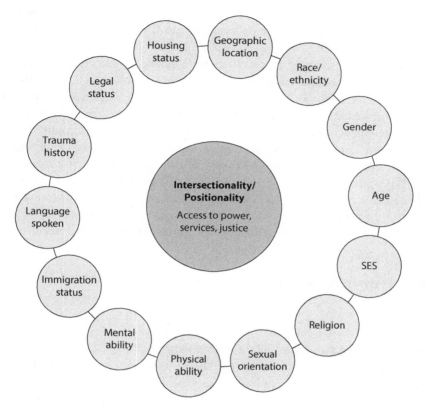

1.2 Diversity in intersectional identities and social locations

(144 per 100,000 people worldwide), minorities and the economically disadvantaged are disproportionately more likely to grow old in prison and to
struggle with multiple discriminations after release from prison. [4]

Global prison and community correctional trends suggest that age, race,
class, and other forms of discrimination (figure 1.2) are drivers of growth in
the graying world prison population. Other drivers include social determinants of health and justice, stricter criminal justice policies and practices
(such as mandatory minimum sentences), truth in sentencing laws, and strict
bail practices. A growing body of research suggests that social, cultural, and
economic conditions have influenced the rise in age of the prison population.[5]
A common trend across the world toward long-term incarceration as punishment for people who use drugs and life and long-term prison sentences for
violent offenders mean that many individuals will reach old age before their
release from prison.[6]

Aging in prison is the current outcome of these policies, but much less is known about the personal life pathways to and through the criminal justice system that led to this outcome. We explore the pathways to prison throughout the life course by focusing on narratives from older adults in prison. We begin with the life history oral narrative of James O, a 55-year-old man incarcerated in the United States in a northeastern prison. James shares his personal story that led him down his later-in-life pathway to prison and his in-depth observations of the prison environment. He provides a compelling firsthand account of coping with life in prison and suggests some ways to improve the criminal justice system. This life history narrative was slightly abridged to protect his confidentiality, and narrative markers were added to assist the reader in easily identifying his life experiences from childhood to older adult, both before and after involvement in the criminal justice system.[7] This life history narrative was part of the qualitative data collected from the mixed methods Hartford Prison Study.[8]

Why I Am in Prison: Oral History of James O

Childhood

Early Childhood and the Social Environment

My name is James O, and I was born in the Kensington section of Philadelphia (figure 1.3). Back then it was a blue-collar, Irish-German neighborhood of row houses and many factories. It was a rough area of the city, but it was also a close-knit community with very little serious crime. Most of the adult males were roofers, construction workers, machinists, police officers, and firefighters. Boys of my age were expected to follow suit. I entered a vocational high school and studied machine construction/tool and dye making but found myself more interested in the academic classes. I decided that I wanted to earn a living with my mind instead of my hands, much to the consternation of my family.

Family Discord, Separation, and Loss

I was one of seven children, born in the middle. My father (for whom I named) was a bus driver. He had a severe gambling habit and left my mother when I was about 5 years old to live with a woman who was willing and had the means to finance his gambling. He made no attempt to be involved in our lives and tried to withhold child support to coerce my mother into agreeing to a divorce. She had only an eighth-grade education and was compelled to hold down two or three jobs as a cook or housekeeper to provide for us. To her everlasting credit, she never acquiesced to pressure from my father to put all of us in a home and live for herself.

1.3 James O. in prison

By age 10, I found myself the oldest surviving child. An older brother and sister were killed in an automobile accident, and another older sister died of an illness. A younger sister, born prematurely, died as an infant before my father left. As the eldest, I became responsible for my younger brother and sister when our mother was working. I didn't have much of a childhood after that.

Adolescence

Teenage Military Escape

As soon as I turned 17 years old, I convinced my mother to allow me to quit school and join the army. I knew I could finish school at a later date and that my family could use the money I would be sending home. I also wanted to be the first in my family to attend college and knew that I'd only be able to do so via the GI Bill. I had to reassure my mother that I would enlist for a military job that would provide training for a civilian career and keep me from being sent to Vietnam. Unbeknownst to her, I made arrangements with the recruiter to volunteer for the Airborne (paratroopers), Infantry, and Vietnam.

I wanted to experience what it was like to jump out of a plane, and the Airborne had a reputation of being elite troops. I wanted Infantry and Vietnam for a couple of reasons. My father had used his first marriage to avoid being sent overseas during World War II, staying stateside as an Army MP. The war was the major event for my generation, and I wanted to experience it firsthand as a combat soldier. I would also receive extra money for being a paratrooper and for serving in a combat zone.

After Basic, Advanced Infantry, and Parachute training, I was sent to the 101st Airborne Division, operating close to the demilitarized zone that separated North and South Vietnam. We were the last army combat troops to leave Vietnam. During my tour in Vietnam I learned about teamwork, leadership, brotherhood, survival, and how to deal with the sudden loss of friends. I also learned to kill.

War Backlash, Flashbacks, and Rewards

When I came home, my elation at having survived was quickly offset by the treatment I received in the United States. Although I will be forever bitter about it (I have not seen a Jane Fonda movie to this day), I have and always will refuse to use Vietnam as a crutch or as an excuse for any of my personal failings. I'm glad to see today's vets being thanked for their sacrifices and hailed as the heroes that they are. As for me, I have been able to put the war behind me. The dreams have all but disappeared, and I only revisit my experience on Memorial Day each year as I remember the guys who didn't come back.

I had two opportunities to make a career of the army. I was offered the chance to attend West Point because I had scored so high on the tests I had taken during basic training and on the GED test. I was also offered a spot on the army's Parachute Team (Golden Knights) when I returned from overseas. I became an avid skydiver when I was assigned to the 82nd Airborne Division at Ft. Bragg, North Carolina, and I made 354 jumps. I turned down both opportunities, and I often wonder how different my life would have been had I accepted either.

Adulthood

Love, Work, and Family

I met my first wife just before my enlistment ended. We married in 1975 and moved to the inner city in the north because I was unable to find a job in the southeast. I found a job as a night watchman and went to college during the day on the GI Bill. My oldest daughter was born in 1976. Unfortunately, with a full-time job and a full slate of classes, I wasn't home much. My wife was a country girl and couldn't adjust to city life. She became extremely homesick, and she was also angry that I left the army. We were divorced in 1978. I stayed in touch with my daughter until she was 13 years old, when my ex-wife took her to Germany to live with her husband, a career soldier.

Most of my working life was spend in retail loss prevention management. I also spent seven years working in the city as a recruiter, trainer, and sales manager. I met and married wives two and three through work and have a daughter from each marriage. I was more than ten years older than my wives, and both marriages ultimately failed, one after three years, the other after seven years.

All of my daughters reside far from me, and my oldest daughter has a daughter of her own. I've never seen my granddaughter. I hope to be able to get them all together with me one day. I haven't heard from any of them since 2007, but I know that they found each other via Facebook and that they continue to communicate with each other. I think they are ashamed of my incarceration. The only news I have of them now comes from my nephew, who is also on Facebook.

The Tipping Point to Prison

Three years after my last divorce, I met a woman who developed a rare form of sarcoma. I was living in a small town in the suburbs at the time and had a job that paid really well. I took care of her and her son for a year. In 1999, I moved into her house in the rural southern part of the state. I thought I had finally found happiness, but in 2003 I discovered that she was cheating on me with an old boyfriend. I was working two full-time jobs to provide for her and her son, and I was shocked and hurt by her betrayal. I began to experience trouble sleeping and turned to drinking as a form of self-medication. I was still living at her house (as a paying tenant) when I committed my offense. I had reached rock bottom. My drinking had steadily worsened, and I was physically exhausted and under emotional stress. This culminated in a blackout, during which I committed an act that ran contrary to everything I've ever believed and shocked everyone who knows me. To this day, I am horrified and ashamed of what happened. So that is why I'm in prison.

Aging in the Criminal Justice System

Irony of Justice

My prison experience has been the darkest six and a half years of my life, but upon honest reflection I have come to realize that it may have saved my life. My drinking had put me in a downward spiral from which I had little chance of escape. For the first time, I had lost control of my life, and I shudder when I think of where I might have ended up. Of course, I didn't have that view when I was first introduced to the criminal justice system. I had never even had a serious traffic ticket before this, so I had no idea of what to expect other than what I had seen on TV and in the movies.

Arrest, Shame, and Humiliation

I will never forget the shame and humiliation of being arrested. I had to call upon every ounce of inner strength I possessed to get through the first forty-eight hours. It was the most surreal experience I've ever had. One moment I was worried about finances and finding a new place to live and in the next I was facing prison for an offense that I scarcely recalled and steeling myself for any eventuality that might arise. Having grown up in a fairly rough neighborhood and being a former paratrooper, I know how to defend myself, but it had been a long time since I was compelled to do so. Luckily, I wasn't really bothered by anyone in jail.

Court and the Public "Nondefender"

I had a public defender because I had been living hand-to-mouth and couldn't afford a lawyer. It was about two weeks before I met my public defender, and I remember being relieved when I was first summoned to meet with him. I thought I would finally have a chance to speak with someone who wouldn't be antagonistic toward me. I also remember how deflated I was after our initial conversation.

When I was escorted into the room, he peered at me over a large stack of case files. As soon as I sat down opposite him, he said, "you're looking at thirty years for this." I was shaken when the magnitude of the situation I was facing came crashing down on me. I began to sense that my future depended on this very young, disheveled, overworked person, and his obvious apathy did not bode well for me. He made two half-hearted attempts to get my bail reduced, but failed. He also entered a "not guilty" plea on my behalf. He later came to me with a plea bargain of fifteen years. I declined, and he seemed to concur.

Questionable Legal and Treatment Practices

As I was awaiting further developments, I was summoned to meet the county jail psychiatrist (or psychologist) for an evaluation. After a long interview, she said she was going to recommend that I be placed in a twenty-eight-day alcohol rehabilitative program. She was true to her word and had me take part in a telephone interview with the director of the program. She had also gotten the Veterans Administration (VA) to agree to pay for it. I was accepted in the program and was told that a bed would be available within a week. I was to complete twenty-eight days of inpatient care, followed by five years of outpatient care and probation. All that was required was the judge's signature. I was ecstatic that something good was finally going to happen. The jail psychologist even appeared in court on my behalf to affirm her recommendation. The judge seemed satisfied and had pen in hand when the prosecutor objected, stating that the matter was still being "investigated." The arrangement was set aside, pending the outcome of the investigation. My public defender was mute, and the matter was never revisited.

I met with my public defender a few days later, and he told me that the court had called in a prominent psychologist from the state to interview me. My lawyer made no attempt to hide the fact that he was dubious about the result he expected from this interview. He went on to say that the psychologist (Dr. Q) was an ivy-league-trained expert who was often used by the prosecution.

I was interviewed by Dr. Q a day or two later. I was told that the interview would take fifteen to twenty minutes, but it lasted two and a half hours. Dr. Q kept shaking his head in disgust as I related my story, and he said that he found my charges to be incredulous. He said I did not belong in prison and assured me that he would appear in court to testify on my behalf. I was elated, and I truly believed that this nightmare was about to finally end.

I had to wait a week before the public defender called me for a meeting. He said he had good news: Dr. Q had written a lengthy, favorable report saying that in his opinion I could not have been capable of forming criminal intent that day because of "diminished capacity." He diagnosed me as having a medical condition of alcohol intoxication, with additional diagnoses of alcohol abuse, alcohol dependence, dysthymic disorder, and adjustment disorder. Naturally I was flush with excitement. This quickly dissipated when the public defender shrugged and said, "diminished capacity is a very difficult defense. The prosecutor will just bring in another expert who will refute Dr. Q's findings." Nothing more was said about it.

Cajoled Sentence

Not long after that I was notified of a status conference regarding my case. It was subsequently postponed twice. Finally, I was informed that the prosecutor was offering a plea bargain of nine years. I said I would need time to think about it. Seven months had passed since my arrest, and I was weary of the emotional roller coaster. The Christmas holiday had arrived, and the status conference was postponed until January. I called my family and told them I couldn't go on any longer and would probably accept the plea bargain.

When January finally arrived, I met with the public defender and told him I would accept the deal. I had been cajoled by him, the judge, even a bailiff to the point where I just wanted it to be over. When I appeared at the status conference and made it known that I agreed to the deal, the prosecutor, public defender, and judge had a sidebar conversation, after which it was announced that the first degree offense would be downgraded to a second degree offense, with all other charges dismissed.

Nine years is two years above the presumptive sentence of seven years for a second degree offense, so I hoped the judge might exercise his discretion and give me the presumptive term at my sentencing. When that day came, he said that he rarely had a defendant appear before him who was so genuinely remorseful, and he went on to cite my complete lack of a prior criminal record. He followed this by saying that the court couldn't make exceptions, so I got nine years with an 85 percent mandatory minimum, plus three years of supervised parole upon release. The most significant aggravating factor against me was that my crime was "committed under cover of darkness." I quickly pointed out that it happened in broad daylight, but the public defender paid no attention to this discrepancy.

As I waited to be taken to prison, I became increasingly disturbed by this. I also read of a 21-year-old with an extensive criminal record who committed the same offense except that someone had been killed. He was given *eight years* in a plea bargain! I immediately filed an appeal of my sentence as being excessive.

Wait List Limbo

My experience with the county jail was coming to an end. While there, I began to do push-ups, dips, and pull-ups on a daily basis. I also attended Alcohol Anonymous once a week. Most important, I rekindled a relationship with an ex-girlfriend, which did more for my emotional well-being than anything else.

It took a month for the state Department of Corrections to come for me and transport me to the central reception facility. On the way there, they stopped at my county jail to pick up a load of inmates. The route they took was the same route I used to take to work. I was filled with profound sadness as I looked out at the familiar scenery.

I was informed at reception that I would be going to a medium-security prison in a southern part of the state, but I spent three months (April–July) at the reception facility because of a backup there. Most guys were in and out of reception in a week or two. It was freezing cold in April, oven-hot in July, and it was overrun with roaches and mice, so I was happy to finally be moved to this prison.

While at prison reception, I was given a physical and was told that my blood work was "perfect." When I finally got to the prison, I was assigned to a two-man cell. My cellmate was a skinhead, about 35 years old, and three months away from finishing his third adult bid.

Introduction to the Infirm and Tormented Souls in Prison

I had made up my mind to make prison as positive an experience as I could. I took a voluntary Test for Adult Basic Education (TABE) and requested enrollment in three vocational training programs. I was subsequently placed on a waiting list for all three. I was initially assigned to a job in the Infirmary Enhanced Care Unit (ECU) as a porter. The infirmary is often very depressing. They have a couple of padded cells there, and the screams of tormented souls could be heard throughout many shifts. There was also a row of five or six cells that housed terminally ill inmates, which we called the "death rooms." These prisoners had been brought in from prisons around the state, and many were fairly young. The medical "professionals" had minimal interaction with them; they were largely cared for by palliative-care inmate volunteers. When one of the terminal cases passed away, an ambulance would eventually arrive to take the body out of the prison. The guards and medical staff would not help "bag and tag" the body, so it was left to us porters to assist in this task.

The apathy of the guards toward dying inmates was unconscionable. One inmate about 30 years old had a wife and two small children who were given permission for a special visit because he was near death. As shift change approached, a nurse entered the room, and the family had to stand outside of the door. A female guard yelled to the nurse, "Isn't he dead yet? I don't want to have to stay late to do the paperwork." The two little girls were sobbing in no time.

We also had an inmate who turned 100 years old there. He was completely bedridden. He passed away eventually, but I was left wondering how society was being served by that. In the six months I worked there, six or seven inmates passed away. Hepatitis and diabetes cases abounded, with many amputations.

A Love of Teaching

After six months, I had a chance conversation with a blind inmate whose job was to teach braille to other blind inmates. When I happened to mention that I had attended college, he asked if I would be interested in a job as a teacher's aide. I said yes and was soon interviewed by a civilian teacher who had a pre-GED class. This teacher was also responsible for the education effort at the infirmary. He gave me a teacher's assistant position. I spent Monday through Thursday mornings at the ECU, conducting pre-GED classes, and I worked the afternoons and both sessions on Fridays in the facility classroom. I grew to love teaching. I'd had some experience teaching in a classroom setting as a corporate trainer, so I knew a little about teaching adults. I had a lot of success in this job.

When my first cellmate left after three months, I was able to arrange to have a guy my age replace him. He was my cellmate for more than three years, and we never had a single argument despite the close quarters and all of the inherent problems that come with that.

After I reached the halfway point of my sentence, I became eligible for consideration for transfer to the minimum-security unit, which is situated outside the prison fences. I had no disciplinary actions, so I was approved and moved to the "min camp" in 2008.

Ethnography of Prison

During the more than three years I spent "behind the wall," I saw a few fights, but nothing serious. Most altercations involved the street gangs, and they were brought under control quickly by the guards. I did not see or hear of any sexual assaults. Inmates who were unable to control their sexual urges were often able to satisfy them by making a deal with an openly gay inmate. (There were always a couple of them on each wing.)

I was delighted when I was moved to the "camp." There was no razor wire on the fences. Psychologically, that is huge. Part of the prison parking lot borders the camp, and a road runs past it. We can see people coming and going to work, civilians power-walk past the camp, bicyclists go by occasionally—normalcy. It represents the first real step toward home. Morale soars. On the inside, I could only see our rec yard and a tree line that surrounds most of the prison. I spent over three years watching a single sapling grow into a tree.

There was much more recreation time in the camp. If not at work, an inmate could go outside from 8:30 a.m. to 9:00 p.m., except for mealtimes and physical counts. A fully equipped gym was attached to the rec yard. I was able to do a vigorous workout six days a week and was soon in the best physical shape I had been in since the army. I was able to lift pound for pound with guys twenty years younger than me.

The housing situation took some getting used to. There are two wings on the first floor and two on the second floor. Each wing has six rooms containing thirteen beds, arranged around a large dayroom/dining area in a horseshoe shape, two rooms per side. The steam tables are at the open end of the horseshoe. After more than three years of dealing with just one other personality, being in a dorm setting with twelve others can be disconcerting at first. There are two showers, but one is a handicapped stall and is used to store cleaning supplies and a trash receptacle. There are two sinks and a urinal, plus a single toilet that is situated behind a shower curtain for privacy. This setup is conducive for causing arguments, and I've had many out here, mostly involving noise, baby powder, or conversations with which I didn't agree. Despite the higher number of arguments, the number of fights is small because most guys are waiting to leave via parole or transfer to a halfway house. They don't want to spoil their chances.

Staff Violations of Dignity, Respect, and Safety

One big difference between the camp and life on the inside is the attitude of the guards. Inside the prison, most of the guards were professional in their interaction with inmates. They were stern but fair and tended not to sweat minor things. Guards in the camp tend to be the direct opposite. They know that most guys are out here to get closer to home, and they just want to finish without any trouble. Camp guards often exploit that, talking to guys in a condescending manner and constantly threatening to send them back inside for the slightest infraction, real or imagined. I don't understand why they make such a concerted attempt to embitter guys who are getting close to being released back into society. If you treat someone like an animal all of the time, you get an animal. Stripping an inmate of his dignity and self-esteem virtually guarantees that he will lash out at society sooner or later.

Some guards resort to childish stunts to antagonize inmates. All of the announcements are made on a public address system. I recall one incident in which a guard mumbled something that sounded like "recreation out." As inmates from the second floor descended the stairs to go out to the yard, they were met by several guards who wrote them up for "being out of place."

One guard has a work detail assigned to him that reports for work at 7:30 a.m. The building they work in has an inmate bathroom, but he doesn't unlock it for the first two hours. Any inmate who requests that it be opened is told, "Ask me again and you'll hear two clicks" (handcuffs and a trip to detention). This guard often mumbles his directions incoherently, and if an inmate asks for clarification, he is threatened with lockup. How can that not embitter people?

When I first came to the camp, three adult cats and three kittens lived in the woods adjacent to the rec yard. Many inmates brought them food and milk and kind of adopted them. It was a slice of normalcy. One guard who hated cats would kick them if he saw them in the yard, and he would lock up any inmate he saw giving the cats food or petting them. The cats soon learned to differentiate between guards and inmates, clearly preferring the latter. All of the cats were named, of course.

Toward the end of summer 2008 one of the adult cats was run over by a doc patrol van. Then someone put out real cat food laced with poison. One adult and all three kittens died horrible deaths. This upset all of the inmates.

A civilian employee heard about it and recovered the bodies. A bag of cat food and poison was found in a locked room. The guard who hated cats was visibly shaken and told all of his inmate workers that they'd better not say anything to animal control or to the administration.

Two inmates jumped the fence and escaped recently. The guards were embarrassed because it took two hours for them to notice the inmates were gone. As a result, rec time has been considerably reduced, and the guards seem bent on sending as many guys back inside the prison as they can.

Holiday Shakedown

One other thing we have to deal with is major holidays. Either right before or immediately following a major holiday, we are invariably subjected to harsher than normal treatment and shakedowns. I once heard a guard admit that they are trained to make us as miserable as they possibly can. I guess they view this as a deterrent to recidivism, but it doesn't work. Inmates like me aren't going to return no matter how we are treated, and career criminals will come back no matter how they are treated. A new breed of inmate is rapidly filling the prisons: Street gang members have no sense of morals, do not value human life, and gain points, status, respect, and move up in rank through violent acts. Gang members are expected to do a certain amount of prison time, and they are everywhere. They get extra respect for harming guards, and someday this is going to backfire on the Department of Corrections in a very big way.

Sources of Stress in Confinement

Denial of Health and Well-Being

The prison diet is a major health concern; the quality of most of the food is poor at best. With the bleak economy, the amount of food we are given has decreased steadily. As bad as that may be, the food we do receive is not doled out in a fair manner. If the meal is a decent one, large and even double portions are given to gang members and Muslims. The reason? The servers are all gang members and Muslims. In addition to undersized portions, any undercooked food, end pieces of bread, or anything that is undesirable is certain to end up on the tray of an older, white inmate. As a result, I've been compelled to supplement my diet with goods purchased from the prison commissary. The problem is that most of the food available for purchase is high in sodium, sugar, cholesterol, and trans fat or saturated fat. For the first time in my life, my cholesterol levels are high, and I'm compelled to take a statin (Zocor's generic equivalent), which is something I really dislike having to do. With the reduced rec time, I can't work my levels down through exercise, so I have no choice.

Another health concern comes from overcrowding (there are two beds in each room without power outlets, indicating that beds were not originally intended to be there) and unsanitary conditions. Overcrowding may worsen because the administration has been considering adding three more beds per room. These rooms have approximately 485 square feet of living space for thirteen inmates. Three more beds, plus lockers, would allow 30 square feet per inmate. There are not enough brooms, mops, scrub brushes, and cleaning supplies to go around, so we are required to share with other rooms. No matter how hard we might try to maintain a sanitary living environment, we still wind up spreading dirt and germs from other rooms through our area. The plumbing is atrocious for a prison built in the late 1990s. MRSA is a *major* concern. Many inmates are drug addicts who have little or no idea of the importance of good hygiene.

Even more disconcerting is the fact that the same brooms and mops used in the rooms (and, more significant in the *bathrooms*) are used to clean the dayroom, which doubles as the dining area! As annoying as all of this stuff is, I realize that it is part and parcel of prison life. I put myself in this situation, the fault is mine, and I don't believe prison should be a pleasant experience. I just question the necessity of policies that undermine good health.

Denial of Safety

Prison populations are being flooded with gang members, and specialized "gang units" have been eliminated because of budgetary concerns. Gang members have been placed among the general population, along with all of their attendant baggage. Cell phones and drugs are smuggled into prisons, and fights are becoming commonplace. Extortion of weaker inmates is on the rise, and some of the guards are even gang members. There is a lot of recruiting. Younger inmates almost *have* to join a gang or the Muslims to have any hope of surviving prison. Gang initiations are beginning to involve harming other inmates, much as they harm innocent civilians on the outside. Rules and regulations are disregarded by these fools who have deluded themselves into thinking they are running things—then the Department of Corrections starts to crack down and reassert its authority. Unfortunately, those of us who abide by the rules and are trying to do right get punished along with them. We have lost countless rights and privileges since the number of gang members increased significantly in 2009.

Social Care-lessness

I can't talk to social services or the chaplain about things that bother me because I know how they handle personal problems here. In 2008, I was taken to a meeting with a prison social worker in a small room occupied by her, a sergeant, and two other guards. I was grilled about my family and made to provide the names of all my siblings. When I got to my half-brother George, I had to provide his wife's name. Once I did that, the guards moved closer and the social worker said, "your sister-in-law needs to talk to you." She called my sister-in-law, who told me between sobs that George had passed away. The guards were staring at me intently to see how I would react. In truth, I had been expecting it; he had been ill for over a year. I consoled my sister-in-law as best I could until I was told to terminate the call.

As soon as I hung up, the sergeant told me that I couldn't attend the funeral because it was out of state. I was then placed in a dirty holding cell, where I sat until a psychologist came and asked if I wanted to escape, hurt myself, or hurt someone else. Satisfied with my answers, he left, and I sat there alone until a guard came and escorted me inside the prison. I was told that my minimum-security status had been changed to medium, thus requiring that I be moved back inside from the camp. I had only the clothes on my back: no towel, no toiletries. I had no job and was housed on a tier where I didn't know anyone.

I had nothing to do but think about my brother's passing. Apparently, we are considered a flight risk and may be dangerous when we lose someone, so we are removed from friends who would have been consoling and dropped among strangers. I will forever feel bitter about how that was handled.

Coping and Creativity in Confinement

In this section, James describes how he maintains cognitive, physical, emotional, social, and spiritual well-being while in prison by engaging in activities and practices that foster wellness.

Survival of the Physically and Mentally Fittest

Prisons have their own code of values and social mores. New inmates who can't or won't recognize this and adjust accordingly are in for a long, miserable existence. As a paratrooper, I was trained to operate behind enemy lines. This carried with it the high probability of being captured. I use a lot of the techniques I learned about surviving as a POW to survive in prison. Staying physically fit and mentally active are important prison survival skills.

I was able to obtain a teacher's aide position in a horticulture class at the camp. I got the position because of a great reference email sent by the civilian teacher I worked for on the inside to his counterparts out here in the camp. Although the job I have now does not involve as much interaction with the students, I have learned a great deal about horticulture. I took and passed a state pesticide applicator licensing exam, which could lead to a job someday.

To stay mentally sharp I learned to read and write braille from the blind teacher's assistant in the infirmary. In exchange for teaching me braille, I taught him how to type on a computer. I plan to see if I could possibly work with blind veterans when I am released. I'm a voracious reader, and I've become hooked on sudoku. I also devised a mathematical system for predicting the outcomes of college and pro football games, which has endeared me to a lot of inmates who "gamble" on them. I've also written an outline of my experiences in Vietnam, and I'm up to twenty-three chapters now. I've also been working on learning conversational Italian. I play chess but hate the prison version.

My ability to stay in good physical shape has been seriously impeded by the reduction in outside rec time that followed the recent escape of two inmates. I work until 2:30 p.m., and the last movement for outdoor rec is called ten or fifteen minutes before that. Consequently, I only get access to the yard and the gym on weekends, instead of six days a week.

Cognitive Self-Empowerment

Perhaps my most effective tool in coping with prison life has been my military background. The army taught me how to adjust to hostile, stressful environments and to remain calm in the face of extreme adversity. It also taught me to be resourceful and self-sufficient. I drew a pair of jump wings on my workout sweatshirt to remind me that I've survived extreme adversity before and that I was once a part of an elite military force. I once served with the best young men America had to offer.

A side benefit of being a vet is that the gang members respect (and fear) anyone with military training. They are especially respectful and wary of Vietnam veterans, thanks to Hollywood. They see us as walking time bombs (Rambo) who are experts in hand-to-hand combat (Chuck Norris). I certainly don't try to dissuade them from these beliefs because I'm one of only a few white inmates who is addressed as "mister" or "sir."

Giving and Receiving Love and Social Support

Coping with all of this is considerably easier if an inmate has a solid support group on the outside. Letters and visits remind us that there are still people who love us and don't view us as the scum of the earth. I was fortunate to have someone who wrote me a letter every single day for the first six years, who talked to me on the phone twice a week, who traveled here twice a year for a two-hour visit, and who was ready to help me in any way she could. Unfortunately, she has been stricken with a severe case of multiple sclerosis and is now severely debilitated. We had plans for her to move to New Jersey when I was within a year of my release date. We were going to live together, and if that went as well as expected, we planned to marry. Instead, we have had no contact since April, and I am unable to help her in any way.

Spiritual Practices

I am a Christian, but I don't attend services here. Muslims, God-body, and 5 percenters go out of their way to mock Christians and their beliefs. I content myself with a nightly prayer, although lately they seem to be falling on deaf ears. I continue to believe that things happen for a reason. I've also been studying the beliefs and principles of Buddhism, and I practice meditation. I agree with much of what Buddhism has to say as a philosophy, but Christianity is still my religion.

Recommendations for Policy Reforms

Education and Vocational Training

With the current budget crisis, prison education has taken a serious hit, especially the vocational courses. I think this is a mistake.

Veteran Housing Units

California has an experimental housing unit in one prison populated entirely by inmates who are veterans. According to the article I read, the unit is maintained in immaculate condition and has had virtually no disciplinary issues. The inmates police themselves. I would love to be housed in such a unit, and I tend to gravitate toward and associate with inmates who are fellow veterans. Many of us take pride in our military service, and it is a part of our life. Returning to disciplined, respectful surroundings is a welcome respite from the ignorance, inconsideration, and stupidity encountered daily in prison. A measure of self-respect, self-esteem, and dignity goes a very long way, and I think it would be worth looking into that kind of policy rather than continuing the current policy of stripping inmates of all of these things. I truly believe that the current policy makes it extremely difficult for inmates to adjust when they are released into society.

Specialized Geriatric Units

The Department of Corrections should also consider creating entire housing units populated by older inmates, especially first timers who have been free of disciplinary charges for a prescribed period of time.

Discharge Planning

Inmates need more help to make a successful transition back into society. A released inmate who has no reason for hope is doomed to fail. I am a prime example of someone facing these worries. On January 9, 2011, I will have less than a year to go. I experienced the shrinking employment opportunities that were available to older persons before my arrest. Now, in addition to my age, I will have to contend with being a convicted felon, a notion that is still surreal to me.

A year ago, I was beginning to be excited that the end of this nightmare was finally within sight. I knew I would be coming out to a home with a person I loved and who truly loved me. Now all of that has come crashing down, and no one is left in my home state to provide any support during this transition. I am facing the prospect being jobless, homeless, and dependent on a state that would rather I didn't exist and a society that will refuse to acknowledge that I have paid my debt to it. I want nothing more than to have a decent job, a decent car to get to that job, a decent place to live, and to be left alone to live out the remainder of my life in peace. I'm not a bad person, and I have been hurt more by my separation from society than by anything the Department of Corrections has put me through. I long to be a productive part of society, not a burden to it. For the first time in my life, I am afraid of the future. Instead of elation at the prospect of being released, I'm beginning to dread it. The light at the end of this long, dark tunnel suddenly has the potential of being an oncoming freight train.

Life History Analysis

Life History Reviewed

The major factors that led to James's incarceration in later life were described as a series of "mixed blessings," positive and negative experiences with his family and community from childhood through adolescence (figure 1.4). Early life experiences with trauma, stress, grief, loss, and social and economic injustices put James at risk socially and psychologically. He grew up in poverty, in a rough, blue-collar, inner city neighborhood; he had limited educational opportunities and experienced family death, separation, and loss during childhood. In his young adult years, James experienced military combat, the tragic death of his friends, and post–Vietnam War discrimination. His "tipping point" was the betrayal of his seriously ill girlfriend, which led to a downward spiral into alcoholism and depression. At age 47, James committed a second degree violent offense.

The lack of access to justice and to needed mental health and addictions treatment were harmful to James. He also questioned the practices of criminal justice, health, and social care professionals and their unwillingness or

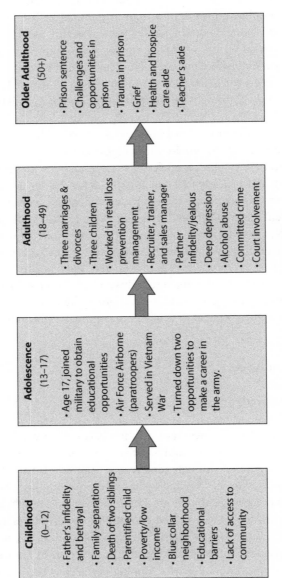

Childhood
(0–12)

- Father's infidelity and betrayal
- Family separation
- Death of two siblings
- Parentified child
- Poverty/low income
- Blue collar neighborhood
- Educational barriers
- Lack of access to community

Adolescence
(13–17)

- Age 17, joined military to obtain educational opportunities
- Air Force Airborne (paratroopers)
- Served in Vietnam War
- Turned down two opportunities to make a career in the army.

Adulthood
(18–49)

- Three marriages & divorces
- Three children
- Worked in retail loss prevention management
- Recruiter, trainer, and sales manager
- Partner infidelity/jealous
- Deep depression
- Alcohol abuse
- Committed crime
- Court involvement

Older Adulthood
(50+)

- Prison sentence
- Challenges and opportunities in prison
- Trauma in prison
- Grief
- Health and hospice care aide
- Teacher's aide

1.4 Major life experiences of James O. from childhood through older adulthood

lack of ability to deal with his psychosocial, emotional, and legal issues. These failures and lack of assistance were present from the time he entered the system until discharge planning for release was completed. James also noted that many correctional staff behaviors promote a culture of fear and negativity, which contribute to the extremely stressful conditions of confinement. To counteract these adverse experiences, James used his personal cognitive, emotional, physical, social, spiritual, and participatory (self-empowerment) coping skills to sustain him in even the most dire prison circumstances.[9]

"What If" Prevention and Intervention Scenarios

Based on James story, we can identify times when people might have interacted with James to circumvent his pathway to prison. For example, what if, in early childhood, James's family had known how to access needed social, vocational, and educational training to address their poverty, addiction, family divorce, death, loss, and other traumas? What if his family had received counseling regarding gambling addiction, mental health deficits, and infidelity? Might that have helped James to better navigate his own romantic and family relationships later in life?

What if James had knowledge of and access to a school guidance counselor? Might his decision to accept a blue-collar occupation rather than attend college and pursue a higher education have been different? Might that have shifted the later life outcome of prison?

What if James had been knowledgeable of and had access to adequate mental health services and to veterans' support groups after returning from Vietnam? Might he have been able to process his PTSD symptoms, deal with his chronic grief over the loss of friends in combat, and advocate for more respectful treatment to counter an antiwar movement that made the community climate difficult for returning veterans? What if he also received family counseling to address his marital issues and learn strategies to reunite with his children despite their physical distance? Might that have significantly altered his life path?

What if James had been able to get treatment for depression and substance abuse and had relationship counseling after the betrayal and infidelity of his girlfriend, or what if he attended self-help groups to manage these concerns? Might his access to these supports have resulted in a very different response and outcome for James?

What if James had better legal representation when he entered the criminal justice system? Might he have received a fairer trial with a different outcome? What if the judge upholding the strict sentencing policies of the 1980s was more sensitized to the underlying issues of this first-time offender? What if courts offered a diversion or alternative to incarceration program or residential treatment for people like James? Might James have received compassionate care instead of the maximum allowable sentence for his second degree offense?

What if correctional and social service professionals were trained in compassionate care and safety? What if prisons set aside special units for veterans? Might James's prison experience have been less stressful and traumatic?

What if corrections facilities adopted high-quality educational and vocational training programs? What if corrections also had programs that foster sources of resilience, such as encouraging family contact and support and teaching cognitive, physical, emotional, social, and spiritual coping skills? Might incarcerated people of all ages benefit from learning better ways to triumph over challenging life experiences? Might society at large also benefit when these inmates are released?

Final Reflections

Once we begin to recognize the complex life histories of incarcerated older people, we can identify points along the way when individuals and communities could have done better. James's experiences in life were not his alone; they also reflect his interactions with his social world, including his community. Individuals, families, communities, and interdisciplinary professionals are all faced with unique challenges to prevent, assess, and intervene at many points along the way. If individuals of any age lack access to quality physical and mental health care, education, and employment, they will continue to fuel the tragic prison pipeline that culminates in stockpiling the old, the sick, and the dying.

A public health parable provides a relevant metaphor for the current effects of trauma and disparities that individuals experience from childhood to older adulthood.[10] In the public health parable, babies are found floating down a river. Some villagers travel upstream to prevent as many babies as possible from falling into the dangerous waters. Other villagers remain downstream to intervene and catch the floating babies. We must use this two-pronged approach of prevention and intervention to end the proliferation of risk factors and to promote protective factors throughout the life course. Over their lifetime, some of the "saved babies" reach adolescence without being taught to swim, and they fall off the bridge and into troubled waters again. Some villagers travel downstream and save these youth once again, and some for the first time. As adolescents become young adults, some defy the warnings of the dangerous river and fall into turbulent waters another time. This time no villagers are waiting to save them, and they must struggle toward shore in their own way. No one in the village is paying attention as these troubled adults continue to rise and begin to flood the village.

We are like the villagers who have the opportunity to "do nothing" or to thoughtfully "do something." We can continue to ignore the problems, or we can save our communities and those in it who cannot "swim" on their own. Each of us has an opportunity to choose the ending of this story.

CHAPTER 2

INTERSECTING PERSPECTIVES ON AGING, DIVERSITY, DIFFERENCE, AND JUSTICE

We must not only learn to tolerate our differences. We must welcome them as the richness and diversity which can lead to true intelligence.

—Albert Einstein

I n this chapter, we synthesize interdisciplinary perspectives regarding the individual, societal, and structural factors that have influenced the increase in the aging prison population. We begin with two case studies of older people in prison. Next, we explore critical perspectives, such as intersectionality and oppression theories, to illustrate how power imbalance and hierarchical social structural dynamics infused in institutions, policies, and laws have contributed to the increasing number of aging people in prison. We present a life course systems power perspective that integrates the three dimensions of the life course of individuals across their interactions with their social and power environments. We explore pathways to prison and review life course perspectives (e.g., life course stressors, trauma, resilience, and cumulative inequality), illustrating how these experiences can influence incarceration rates and length of sentencing for older people. Next we explore person–in-environment interactions and the influence of social environments on behavior. Through the lens of ecological systems, person-in-environment, and social support theories and perspectives, we illustrate how systems, such as families and service providers, can contribute by providing access to justice and child welfare services, victim services, and mental health services, at some point in the lives of aging people in prison. Next we put theory into practice through a life course history power analysis of Pedro, an older Latino adult in prison. We discuss how this information can be used by individuals and communities to guide multilevel prevention, assessment, and intervention efforts that will benefit older adults in prison and their families and communities.

THE CASE OF PEDRO

Pedro is a 56-year-old heterosexual male from Puerto Rico and the youngest of nine children. He has a history of trauma that includes the unexpected death of his father at age 5, childhood sexual victimization prostitution, and substance abuse (heroin addiction). His criminal offending includes drug dealing, and he has been incarcerated two times. From ages 7 to 12 the whole family lived in poverty and worked at the sugar cane plantations. When Pedro's father died and sugar cane processing became industrialized in Puerto Rico, Pedro's mother lost her job, and the family survived with the help neighbors' donations and a small vegetable garden. At age 16, Pedro and his family immigrated to the United States. At age 17, Pedro committed armed robbery to support his heroin addiction and was sentenced to twenty years in prison. During his prison term, he continued to use drugs. He violated parole within twenty-four months of release and was charged with a sexual offense of a minor and possession of controlled dangerous substances and is now serving a forty-five-year sentence. He has spent eight of the past twenty-seven years in prison in solitary confinement. He perceives prison as "an overcrowded monster" designed to hold, degrade, and punish people. He views the staff as disinterested and disengaged and is despondent over the limited access to counseling and educational rehabilitative services. Pedro was diagnosed with cancer six months ago and is projected to receive parole in fourteen years; he will be in his late seventies. He has not had any contact with family in more than five years and reports feeling depressed. Even though Pedro grew up in a Catholic family, he says he does not have any religious beliefs.

THE CASE OF DAWN

Dawn, a 64-year-old Caucasian Catholic woman, is incarcerated in a maximum-security facility for women. She identifies herself as bisexual. As a child, she experienced the divorce of her parents, abandonment by her mother, and sexual, physical, and verbal abuse by her father, whom she described as having serious mental health issues. At age 25, Dawn married a man ten years younger, had two children, and divorced. This is her first criminal conviction, and she is serving a ten-year prison sentence (85 percent minimum) for conspiracy and the attempted murder of her abusive husband, which she describes as self-defense. Dawn believes this sentence as unfair and unjust because of mitigating circumstances. She has a medical history of hypertension, vision impairment, and osteoporosis; it is difficult for her to walk or use a top bunk bed. Dawn's extensive dental problems have resulted in a premature need for dentures. She describes her current prison experience as "degrading, especially the way correctional officers treat inmates." Although she reports feelings of depression and despair, she copes with her prison experience by "finding meaning" in it through spirituality. Despite her ill health, Dawn is resistant to using prison health care services. Her projected parole date is in two years, when she will be 66 years old. Because of the distance, Dawn has not had any in-person visits with her family members since her incarceration, but she corresponds monthly by mail and every three months by phone with her two adult children and four grandchildren. She misses her family immensely.

Diversity Among Older Adults in Prison

Pedro and Dawn represent the tip of the iceberg of a very diverse group of older adults in prison. Gender, education, socioeconomic status, disability, sexual orientation, and legal or immigration status are among the differences common to older inmates, and the influence of these factors varies according to racial/ethnic background, gender, and chronological age. Most incarcerated people report having experienced one or more traumatic life experiences, and the level of access varies for services and supports needed to resolve issues of mental health, substance abuse, and physical health.

What distinguishes incarcerated older adults from their younger counterparts is the accumulation of trauma and stress of prison life and other types of trauma unique to old age. Although their crimes may vary by age at which they first occurred, the level of seriousness of the crime, and the length of criminal offending, older adults generally are found to have a lower recidivism rate when compared to their younger counterparts.

We can create a large-scale portrait of diversity of older adults in prison using the 2016 National Corrections Reporting Program (NCRP) new admissions data. We profile diversity using age, gender, race/ethnicity, educational level, and criminal justice history. Over a twenty-year period (1996–2016), adults age 55+ represented the lowest number of new admissions of all cohorts. However, new admissions of older adults steadily grew from 2005 through 2016.[1]

Gender. The prison population is overwhelmingly male (86.4 percent); females represent 13.6 percent of the total population. Adult males (5.7 percent) and adult females (3.2 percent) 55+ represent a small number of total admissions; however, when combined with adults 45–54 (males 21.4 percent and females 16.0 percent), admissions in the 45+ age category mirrors the admission size for the 18–24 age cohort. The age-related gender needs of older adults should be an area of focus to better understand their unique experiences and service needs while in prison and after release. The number of older adults that identify as other than male or female is not represented in these data.[2]

Racial/Ethnic Diversity

Diversity among older adults in prison is suggestive of the disproportional incarceration rates of racial/ethnic minorities. Similar to other age ranges, adults 55+ admitted to prison in 2016 were primarily white/non-Hispanic (50.1 percent) followed by black/non-Hispanic group (36.3 percent), Hispanic (11 percent), and other racial/ethnic groups (2.6 percent). It is important to note that there is a disproportionate prison admission rate for racial/ethnic minorities such as black/non-Hispanic people. Even though the adults age 55+ admitted to prison in 2016 were primarily white/non-Hispanic (50.1 percent) or black/non-Hispanic (36.3 percent), racial and ethnic disparities in the nation's prison population becomes evident when imprisonment rates are taken into consideration (i.e., the number of prisoners per 100,000 people). For instance, in 2017, there were 272 white incarcerated individuals for every 100,000 white adults and 823 Hispanic incarcerated individuals for every 100,000 Hispanic adults; the imprisonment rate for black incarcerated adults was 1,549 per 100,000 black adults, nearly six times the imprisonment rate for whites and almost double the rate for Hispanics.[3]

Level of Education

NCRP 2016 admissions data show that a small population of adults age 55+ represent the most educated (any college) within their age group (32.2 percent). The majority (67.8 percent) of those 55+ attained a high school diploma/GED (48.8 percent) and had some college experience (11.1 percent). However, one in three age 45–54 (33.7 percent) and 55+ (32.2 percent) still do not have a high school diploma or GED. Older adults with education/training can benefit from work assignments such as peer mentors, teachers, and teachers' aides, and these opportunities also aid them during their reentry process. Those without a high school diploma need equal access to education. Corrections and community support groups should provide opportunities for educational advancement regardless of age and incarceration status.[4]

New Court Commitment and Parole Revocation (Recidivism)

NCRP 2016 admissions data reveal rates at which adults ages 45–54 and 55+ were incarcerated on a new admission (45–54 = 13.1 percent; 55+ = 5.2 percent), a parole revocation (45–54 = 14.9 percent; 55+ = 5.7 percent), or some other type of new admission (45–54 = 14.4 percent; 55+ = 5.0 percent). The parole return/revocation rate was lower in the 55+ (5.7 percent) and 45–54 (13.1 percent) age groups than for their younger counterparts ages 18–24 (20.8 percent), 35–44 (23.4 percent), and 25–34 (37.5 percent). These data suggest that older adults are at reduced risk than those in younger age cohorts for incarceration whether it be a new commitment or parole return/revocation. However, it is difficult to determine individual, family, and community factors that may have contributed to the entrance or return to prison, including the effects of residual institutionalization.[5]

Current Offense Type

When compared with younger age cohorts, adults age 55+ were less likely to be incarcerated for violent (5.9 percent), property (4.4 percent), drug (4.9 percent), or public order offenses (6.5 percent). A similar pattern was found among adults ages 45–54 incarcerated for violent offenses (12.3 percent), property offenses (13.6 percent), drugs (4.9 percent), and public order offenses (6.5 percent). Admissions in 2016 for those 55+ were relatively evenly distributed between violent (29.7 percent), property (22.6 percent), drug (22.7 percent), and public order offenses (24.5 percent). Admissions in the 18–24 age range presented with the smallest proportion of drug offenses (15.2 percent).[6]

Length of Sentence

The NCRP data show that those individuals serving life, life without parole (LWOP), life plus additional years, or death represented 16.6 percent of the maximum sentence length for all age groups. Those in the 25–34 age group (28.1 percent) had the highest percentage of life sentences followed by the 35–44 age group (22.1 percent), 45–54 age group (18.5 percent), and 18–24 age group (16.6 percent). Adults aged 55+ had the lowest number of life sentences (14.7 percent). However, a sizable number of older people were destined to die in prison, possibly within the next ten to twenty years.[7]

Inmates in 2016 who were serving 10 to 24.9 years or over 25 years would all be aging in prison and would reenter society in later life with a criminal justice history. The largest age grouping with a 25+ year sentence and those most likely to reach 50–55 years old while in prison were the 25–34 age group (26.7 percent), followed by the 35–44 age group (24.4 percent), the 45–54 age group (21.3 percent), and the 18–24 age group (15.0 percent). Adults 55+ represented the lowest number with 25+ year sentences (12.6 percent). Within the 55+ age group, the most common maximum sentences were for 2–4.9 years (29.4 percent), 5–9.9 years (20.8 percent), less than one year (17.8 percent), and 10–24.9 years (16.6 percent).[8]

The high number of long-term and life sentences illustrate the use of incarceration as a criminal justice sanction in the United States rather than employing less restrictive sanctions. This trend affects individuals, families, and communities as well as state and federal correctional facilities. U.S. prisons were not designed to be long-term geriatric care facilities or to have specialized intake and mental health and substance abuse services for a geriatric population. Pushing our societal ills, such as poverty, violence, and other health and justice disparities, out of sight and out of mind and throwing away the key has not and will not work no matter how long and hard we try. This is especially concerning given that many state and federal institutions have a significant number of older people.[9]

State-by-State Custody Data

We focus on the five states with the highest total admissions, California, Florida, Illinois, Pennsylvania, and Texas (N=4,769,893); and the five states with the lowest total admissions, Hawaii, Maine, Montana, New Hampshire, and Wyoming (N=82,545). Of the top five prison admissions states, California's aging prison population (55+) was 2.6 percent, followed by Florida at 3.2 percent, Illinois at 2.2 percent, Pennsylvania at 3.2 percent, and Texas at 6.8 percent. Of the five states with the lowest total prison admissions, New Hampshire had the lowest (55+) at 3.4 percent, followed by Wyoming at 4.5 percent, Maine at 3.2 percent, Montana at 7.6 percent, and Hawaii at 3.5 percent. Although older adult (55+) admissions represent (by far) the fewest admissions in 2016, when combined with the 45–54 age range, the older population becomes much more substantial. In all fifty states, those in the 45–54 age range were sentenced to maximum incarceration times of 5–9.9 years (22.3 percent) or 10–24.9 years (15.6 percent), which explains why the older adult population has expanded not just in prison admissions but also in the overall year-to-year prison population totals.[10]

In summary, the NCRP paints an accurate picture of the diversity in the U.S. prison population based on age, gender, race/ethnicity, and criminal justice history. Those who are older or who are destined to become older in prison because of their long prison sentences are more likely to be men of lower educational attainment and racial/ethnic minorities with serious and long-term offense histories. Although men represent the overwhelming majority, the plight of women, especially older women, also requires the need for gender-identity awareness and gender-specific responses to those involved in the criminal justice system. The NCRP data lack information on LGBTQ+ and gender identity status, so there is a significant gap in the ability of the correctional system to identify and respond to their special needs. To respond effectively to an aging prison population, a closer examination of how intersectional identities influence the identification and treatment of diverse populations is critical. This is especially true among the older prison population with multiple needs.[11]

A Life Course Model

What Can Communities Do About It?

An important first step is to understand the problem. Figure 2.1 illustrates the process and outcome factors, such as diversity and difference, life experiences (positive or traumatic), social contexts, coping, resilience, health, overall well-being, and justice across the life course of individuals, families, and communities. This model can be used by individuals, groups, and communities for personal and collective development for community problems, including health disparities and community violence. It also can be used for prevention, assessment, and intervention that influence the process and outcomes of the aging prison population in communities.

Why Should Communities Focus on Incarcerated Older Adults?

Older adults' high-risk, life course trajectories present unique challenges for individuals, families, organizations, and communities that want to prevent, assess, and intervene with and on their behalf. Enhancing social relations compromised by a history of marginalization and victimization; addressing the principles of risks, needs, and responsivity;[12] and instilling community-based supports attuned to cultural and gender differences can have a stabilizing effect, particularly after release from prison, decreasing the likelihood of reoffending, especially for sexual or violent offenses. Communities are safest when trained professionals and peer supports are available to work with older individuals in the criminal justice system. It is important for community members to advocate to ensure that their geriatric trained community service network has interagency cooperation to best address the often overlooked population of older adults at risk of prison, already in prison, and after their release.

In the next sections, we unpack the life course systems power model. We begin with intersectionality and oppression theories, which address diversity and difference, key factors in understanding how other personal and group

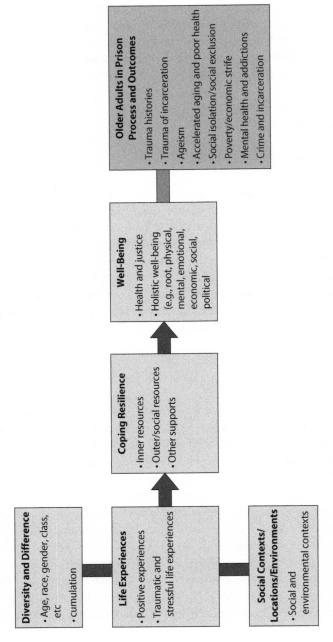

2.1 Life course systems power model showing factors that influence outcomes for individuals

social identities and social contexts influence life experiences, coping adaptation, and well-being. We illustrate how these factors may influence older adults' pathways from freedom in the community to confinement in prison. We conclude with an explanation and application of the synthesized interdisciplinary life course systems power perspective and an individual case analysis of Pedro. Throughout this chapter, we apply the ideas of diversity and difference, life experiences, and social relationships to aging people in prison. We encourage you to think about these concepts as they apply to how, if at all, it shifts your perception of yourself and of people aging in prison.

Intersectionality Theory

Intersectionality is grounded in black feminist epistemological underpinnings, which value the self-conscious struggle to empower women and men to actualize a humanist vision of community. A major theoretical assumption is that individuals have multiple, layered identities that are derived from social relations, history, and the operation of structures of power.

Intersectionality theory can be used to explain how differences among the aging prison population have influenced their involvement in the criminal justice system and why older adults might be experiencing health and justice disparities, especially related to later life imprisonment. An intersectionality approach considers the dynamics of oppression, power, and privilege between individuals and within society. The term "intersectionality" generally refers to the different layers of social stratification, such as race, class, gender identity, sexual orientation, age, religion, and disability status. These different social identities are interlocked and interdependent, and socially constructed categories of oppression and privilege interact to *create unique life experiences*.[13] Each individual is unique, and being older and in prison is just one part of a person's identity. To aid in understanding this theory, we have provided definitions of some key terms (see text box).

Key Terms Related to Diversity and Intersectionality

Term	Brief Description
Diversity	Variations between and within social groups based on gender, age, race/ethnicity, nationality, skin color, language, religion, ability/disability, sexual orientation, social class, immigration status, and region of the country.

Term	Brief Description
Culture	A system of shared values, beliefs, ideas, and learned patterns of behavior.
Ethnic group	A group identity based on ancestry, nationality, or race/ethnicity that shares a common experience and a common set of beliefs and identities passed down through the generations.
Power	The ability to impose one's will on others, even if those others resist in some way.
Privilege	Special rights or advantages available only to a particular person or group of people that may be earned (deserving) or unearned (undeserved).
Oppression	Unjust use of power and authority by one group over another.
Bias	Preference for a particular perspective, ideology, or result that interferes with the person's ability to be impartial, without prejudice, or objective.
Prejudice	Adhering to stereotyped beliefs and negative attitudes about an individual, group, or phenomenon without proof or systematic evidence.
Stigma	Attitudes and beliefs about those perceived to be different that lead people to reject, avoid, or fear them.
Discrimination	Prejudgment and negative treatment of people based on identifiable characteristics such as race, gender, religion, or ethnicity (involves physical actions).
Intersectionality	Conceptualizing the differing forms of oppression as mutually dependent and intersecting.
Positionality	An individual's location in the social world from which a partial view of privilege and subordination are derived.
Social inequality	Unequal access to valued resources, services, and societal positions and how individuals or groups are ranked by others.
Inclusion or exclusion	Groups underserved in community services or disproportionately overrepresented in institutions, and the invisibility of subgroups within larger groups.
Marginalization	Political, economic, and social exclusion in society experienced by minority groups.
Criminalization	Perceiving, labeling, and treating individuals who are different from the dominant group as disgraceful and likely to engage in practices and behaviors that break the law.
Social location	The intersection of multiple identities that form interlocking structures of oppression and determine who gets in and who is left out or marginalized.

Age	Gender
Race	LGBTQ
Class	Other
Micro	**Individual**
Mezzo	**Group**
Macro	**Society**

2.2 Levels of identity in intersectionality theory

Racism, sexism, classism, and heterosexism are independent factors, but they also form a complex set of interlocking and self-perpetuating relations of domination and subordination. Individuals belong to more than one community and can simultaneously experience oppression and privilege. Structural inequality is always present, but treatment may change because of the context and the individual's social location.

Intersectional identities vary among older adults in prison (figure 2.2). The micro (individual) level is the location in which each person resides (e.g., age, race, gender) regardless of social location (e.g., community or prison). The micro level is defined as day-to-day interactions, such as contact and communication between older adults in prison and staff, and the social position of each within interlocking structures of oppression that may include sexism, racism, and ageism. For example, minority older adults may be subject to racism if a high proportion of people of color incarcerated later in life are less likely to be paroled than their majority white counterparts.[14]

The mezzo level is represented by institutions and organizations that provide essential services to society (e.g., education, health care, law enforcement, corrections, and state and local government). Although populated by individuals, organizations take on a life of their own and can be a mechanism of oppression. At the mezzo level, there are copious examples of older people reporting discrimination in education, health care, employment, and the criminal justice system prior to being in prison.

The macro level represents society's power as a transmitter of social and structural discrimination, including racism, sexism, patriarchy, heterosexism, and capitalism. Mechanisms of oppression and discrimination may be codified in laws and policies, such as stricter sentencing policies (e.g., mandatory minimum sentences and three strikes and you're out laws). Intersectional identities commonly found among aging people in prison place them at risk of social structural level adverse life experiences, social inequality, lack of inclusion, marginalization, and criminalization.

In the community, the continued lack of access to culturally responsive quality services for racial/ethnic minorities, women, LGBTQ+ people, and older people places them at increased risk for criminal justice involvement. It is important to understand your own as well as the other person's social location to capture the complexity of people's experiences, including actions, choices, and outcomes. For example, James O was identified as a person with mental health and substance abuse issues who committed a crime (see chapter 1). Even though he needed mental health and addictions services and was willing to receive them, the services were not provided, and he was sent to prison.

Community service providers can become aware of intersectional identities and their impact on incarcerated and formerly incarcerated older adults through the intersectional assessment tool (table 2.1). This tool enables service providers to gain feedback regarding a client's unique perspective and how the client (Pedro) sees himself. Service providers and clients can then work together to define needed supports.

Key terms related to diversity, such as culture, ethnic group, and intersectionality, emphasize similarities within groups as well as differences between groups (e.g., white or black, women or men, and lower or upper class). Negative judgments or behaviors are not explicitly suggested by recognizing the similarities or differences within and between groups, but the reality of power differentials creates a system of domination, subordination, and oppression by the majority group over minority groups. Key terms related to this power differential include privilege, oppression, bias, prejudice, stigma, and discrimination. Many older adults involved in the criminal justice system have two or more of these intersectional social identities, so intersectionality and positionality are significant concepts for understanding and responding to their needs in a culturally responsive manner (see figure. 1.2).

Oppression Theory and Levels of Oppression

Oppression is "the unjust use of power and authority by one group over another."[15] Racism, sexism, and classism encompass a complex interplay of psychological, sociopolitical, economic, interpersonal, and institutional processes. Oppression is characterized by awarding privilege, advantage, and visibility to a dominant group (e.g., elite, white, adult, ruling, heterosexual, able-bodied, males). In contrast, subordinate groups are treated as inferior, second-class citizens; they are oppressed, disadvantaged, and invisible. The dominant group represents the norm, and older adults in prison are judged against this almost unattainable norm. The mechanism of oppression is maintained by a dominant ideology (belief) that polarizes superiority and inferiority and targets the oppressed group through structural violence. When members of the subordinate group accept this dominant narrative, they have internalized a view

TABLE 2.1 Intersectional assessment tool

Case Example, Pedro

Identity categories	Client demographic profile	Client feedback on areas of strength or of concern	Client interest in supports in this area
Race/ethnicity	Puerto Rican		
Class	Poor		
Gender identity	Male		
Sexual orientation	Heterosexual		
Age	56		
Religion	No belief system		
7. Disability status	Mental health/substance abuse	Needs counseling and educational/ rehabilitative services	Referral to arts program and connection to library services
Criminal justice history	Armed robbery(twenty-year sentence); sexual offense of a minor and possession of controlled dangerous substances (forty-five-year sentence		
Other (list all that apply)	Childhood sexual victimization Prostitution		Referral to trauma therapy and substance abuse program
	Substance abuse		
	Solitary confinement Cancer		
	Lack of family contact		

Source: Adapted from Maschi, Weber, & Kaye, 2019

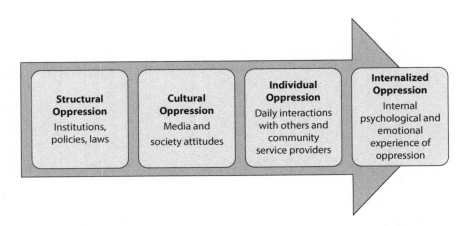

2.3 Levels of the oppression framework

of themselves as unworthy, undignified, valueless, powerless, and inferior to a dominant authority. Oppressive thought and practices are woven throughout the fabric of society and institutionalized through power and control, social norms, laws and policies, and by separating minority groups and pitting them against one another.[16]

The oppression framework consists of four levels: structural, cultural, individual (personal/interpersonal), and internalized (figure 2.3). These levels of oppression are relevant to understanding the experiences of justice by older adults and the social, institutional, community, and structural interactions they have with individuals, groups, and systems.

Structural oppression is transmitted via institutions (e.g., economic and social institutions), organizations (e.g., mental health, aging, and criminal justice service providers), structures (e.g., local, state, and federal governments), laws, and policies. Structural oppression can be found wherever society disproportionately allocates good jobs, health care, and housing to the dominant group. The subordinate group is left with an unfair share of unemployment, poor health care, homelessness, poverty, incarceration, and low social status. Social inequalities are sanctioned, and physical and psychological violence may be imposed on subordinate groups with little or no social or legal consequences.[17] Many of these social inequalities exist in the aging prison population as well. Perhaps most noteworthy has been the adverse influence of stricter sentencing policies imposed in the 1970s and 1980s, sending large groups of people to prison to serve long-term and life sentences. Many of those individuals are currently aging in prison. Structural level oppression is also characterized by the disproportionate number of racial/ethnic minorities, particularly African American and Latinx populations, in the criminal justice system. Although most incarcerated adults and older adults are male (93 percent), racial/ethnic minority women are being incarcerated at a much faster rate than males and have unique health and mental health issues. [18] Race-neutral laws have become a less overt way of perpetuating racial dispar- ity; policies such as drug-free zones and habitual offender laws continue to produce different outcomes by race.[19]

Cultural oppression can be found in the common attitudes and judg- ments of a society. Culture provides a common set of values and norms, including shared patterns of seeing, thinking, and acting. Culture is a living phenomenon, and its political nature translates into an expressive and inter- actional activity that influences social learning and communicates the desired social order.

Communication includes verbal and nonverbal language and symbolism. In cultural oppression, a dominant message promotes, universalizes, and imposes itself on everyone, oppressing, suppressing, and repressing messages from other cultures.[20] The dominant culture propagates its message through educational institutions, churches, mass media, the publishing industry, and other agents. News, entertainment, and other mass media broadcast messages, images, and products overtly and subliminally reinforce the dominant group's privileged status. This barrage of messages continually reproduces the world- view, language, and symbolism of the majority group, often leading to the belief that subordinate groups are the "other."

Dominant group members strive to normalize their worldview, propagate their official definition of reality, underscore their inclusion and exclusion crite- ria, and obtain social control.[21] Stereotyped images of subordinate social groups are biased, oversimplified, and generalized, and these images are imposed by the dominant group. Stereotypes often defy logic and are negative and hurtful, but they are accepted as reality and rarely questioned.

The complexity of culture manifests itself in three forms for people aging in prison: (1) incarcerated adults are subject to their country's overall culture; (2) based on age, race/ethnicity, and sexual orientation, they may participate in their minority background's culture; and (3) they are subjected to the culture of prisons. Dehumanizing language such as "prisoners" or "crim- inals" are cultural expressions of oppression. More humanizing language, such as referring to older people in prison as incarcerated older people or simply older people is more respectful and accurate. Alternative narratives about the older prison population that counteract the dominant messaging has recently been coming through social media in the form of positive news stories about older people in prison: Who they are, what are they experienc- ing? Incorporating critical theories of diversity, difference, and oppression are key to getting to the root causes of the rise and rapid growth of the aging prison population.

Individual oppression (or personal/interpersonal oppression) consists of an individual's experiences among people in his or her immediate micro level network. This contact can be with family members, neighbors, strangers, or professionals. Individual oppression is characterized by the transmission of thoughts, attitudes, and behaviors that depict negative prejudgments of subordinate groups, and it is usually based on stereotypes. It occurs overtly or covertly and may or may not be intentional. It may manifest in the form of conscious acts of microaggressions, overt aggression, or hatred, including violence. It also may manifest as unconscious acts of aversion and avoidance.[22] Individual oppression in the criminal justice system may occur between an older adult and another incarcerated person, a correctional officer, or another staff member. Examples include the exchange of biased statements based on race, gender, age, sexual orientation, or incarceration status between a younger and an older incarcerated adult or between a correctional officer and an older incarcerated adult.

Internalized oppression occurs when the individual's psyche (internal experience) does not match the individual's interpretation of the reciprocal relationship with the environment made up of social, cultural, political, and economic factors. Individuals play an active role in mediating the effects of these disparate perspectives. Oppressive social conditions include discrimination, powerlessness, subordination, exclusion, exploitation, scapegoating, and low social status. Those conditions also block opportunities and have a psychological impact on individuals. Bulhan notes that the psychological functioning of oppressed people ranges from compromised perceptions of self-worth to diminished emotional and social well-being.[23] Internalized oppression is commonly associated with self-hatred, helplessness and despair, mutual distrust and hostility, feelings of inferiority, and psychological distress. However, the line between individual and internalized oppression is often blurred:

> I was crippled when I was younger because my family member beat and molested me. I was tied to the basement poles, beaten always, told repeatedly you're a jail bird just like your father. This was so tightly put into my head it blurred everything I saw.
>
> (65-year-old man in prison)

Individuals and groups lack access to power and resources for a number of reasons (see text box). Feminist philosopher Marion Young describes how exploitation, marginalization, powerlessness, cultural imperialism, and violence are used to subordinate oppressed groups.[24] Additional faces of oppression include voicelessness and criminalization.[25]

The Seven Faces of Oppression

Exploitation refers to the dominant group benefiting from the subordinate group's work. The work of the subordinate group is denied or undervalued (e.g., unpaid, slave labor, grossly underpaid). Subordinate groups also may be exposed to poor working conditions, unfair wages, or oversight of their contributions (e.g., past and present slavery and female family caregivers).

Marginalization refers to the establishment of second-class citizens based on difference. The marginalized subordinate group is socially excluded from full participation in society, which adversely affects their rights and opportunity to full physical, social, and psychological development.

Powerlessness refers to a dominant group's denial of access by the subordinate group to resources and assets. They also are excluded from important decision-making processes.

Cultural imperialism refers to the dominant group's imposition of their worldview onto the subordinate group. The subordinate group is marked as the "other," which makes them different and deviant.

Violence refers to the dominant groups' systematic violence against the subordinate or oppressed group at both the individual and structural level. Acts of violence could include harassment, threats, or humiliation. The dominant group is often indifferent to this violence.[26]

Voicelessness refers to silencing the subordinate group at the individual, structural, and cultural levels of oppression. The dominant narratives are shared by and are about the dominant group.

Criminalization refers to the dominant narrative that projects the identity of criminals onto subordinate groups to delegitimize them. An example of this is the criminalization of stigmatized groups, such as black men or individuals with mental health problems.

In the next section, we infuse the understanding of diversity and difference as explained through the lens of critical theories of intersectionality and oppression within the life course systems perspective.

A Life Course Systems Power Perspective

The life course systems power model maps the ever-changing dynamics of the individual, social, and political/structural systems across time (life course), space (social and system interactions), and height (power dynamics). It moves beyond two-dimensional explanations that focus on one point in time, such as a photograph of an older adult in prison. It offers a three-dimensional explanation of the processes that have led to the current outcome, capturing the movement through time like a motion picture. The life course systems power perspective documents the trajectory of individuals, their families and communities, and their access to well-being and to power, services, and justice across time.[27]

The life course systems power perspective is consistent with the social determinants of health model, which examines social determinants of health and factors associated with varying degrees of well-being, especially factors related to health and behavioral health disparities among marginalized groups (e.g., diverse elders). The prerequisites for health and overall well-being include shelter, food, education, income, a stable ecosystem, sustainable resources, social justice, equity, and peace. In extending this perspective to incarcerated older adults, our examination includes the social determinants of both health and justice.[28]

To understand the experiences of older adults prior to, during, and after prison, a holistic assessment of each person in a social and environmental context is essential. Integrating access to power (e.g., intersectionality and levels of oppression) with life course stress and resilience and access to care systems (e.g., ecological/person-in-environment/social support) is a way to capture the changing dynamics in the lives of aging people in prison and their families and communities.[29]

A life course systems power analysis assesses the personal, systems, and power issues that affect individuals or groups at risk or involved in the criminal justice system (figure 2.4). The process and current outcomes for older adults in prison and can be evaluated for clinical, organizational, community, and policy assessment, prevention, and intervention efforts.[30] A prevention and intervention plan that addresses the cases of Pedro and Dawn may require an integrated clinical, case management, and advocacy response. Some key terms related to the life course systems power model are provided in the text box.

Life Course Systems Power Model: Key Terms

Person: The individual and his or her subjective experiences and life events are the central focus.

Human agency: The creative life force drive to fulfill one's life purpose, potentials, and goals.

Well-being: A holistic state of wellness that includes physical, cognitive, emotional, social, spiritual, economic, and political well-being.

Life course process and outcomes: Co-occurring or sequential individual or collective experiences (birth to death).

Cumulative determinants: Biopsychosocial and structural determinants (i.e., risk or resiliency factors or advantages or disadvantages) that influence personal, collective, or generational experiences throughout the life course.

Social environment or contexts: Social conditions or external contexts.

Values and ethics: Personal, professional, and societal values, beliefs, and perceptions, such as human rights (dignity and respect for all persons).

Power dynamics: Equality or oppression (internalized, interpersonal, structural, cultural) levels that influence relationships between the dominant group and subordinate groups.

Historical time: Personal or collective experiences and subjective responses to multilevel trauma, stress, or loss events.

Practice/stakeholder contexts: Care sectors and societal intersections of family, peer caregivers, and professional services.

Integrated interdisciplinary perspective: Assessment of life course perspectives regarding trauma and resilience, social justice capabilities, ecological systems, and critical (intersectionality, oppression) person-in-environment factors.

Evidence-based and evidence-informed practices: Justice and person-centered mixed (quantitative and qualitative) methods of research and evaluation using evidence to develop and monitor the process and outcomes of prevention, assessment, and interventions.

Life Course Analysis (Length of the Model)

The life course perspective focuses on the whole person and his or her dynamically changing subjective experiences and meaning-making regarding life course events (e.g., objective event [victim of sexual assault] and subjective response [adaptive or maladaptive]) and well-being. Human agency is a core component in life course and social justice theories.[31] Human agency is the central driver of an individual's intentions and pursuit of his or her life's purpose, passion, and goals. In connections to and with others, a sense of well-being and connectedness develops.[32] Earlier life traumas and prison experience present a challenge for Pedro and Dawn in their pursuit of life course human agency.

Well-being is a state of multidimensional well-being, not just the absence of disease.[33] We also infuse domains of well-being that are consistent with

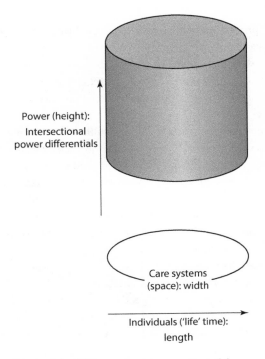

Power (height):
Intersectional
power differentials

Care systems
(space): width

Individuals ('life' time):
length

2.4 The three dimensions of the life course systems power model

Maslow's hierarchy of needs and basic human rights (table 2.2): safe housing, food security, financial security, health and wellness, happiness, personal safety, social inclusion, family and social connection, personal power, and freedom.[34] The domains of well-being correlate with human/personal development and growth, and we highlight community service as a way to address these needs and rights.

When conditions are optimal throughout the life course, individuals express their human agency through concern for self and others, and they sustain high subjective levels of well-being and meaning-making. However, under suboptimal conditions or when confronted with social and environmental barriers (e.g., poverty, low educational attainment, adverse neighborhood conditions, long prison sentences), human agency may diminish, manifesting as illness (e.g., somatic symptoms) or offending behavior.[35] As the two case examples show, Pedro and Dawn have had adverse life experiences, including prison placement, that they describe as challenging to their health and well-being.

TABLE 2.2 Maslow's hierarchy of needs, basic human rights, and community services that address these needs and rights

Level of Needs (highest to most basic)	Characteristics of Needs	Human Rights	Community Services That Address These Needs and Rights
5. Self-actualization	Self-awareness, personal growth, self-assertiveness, and fulfilling one's potential	Mental well-being and education	Education, mental health services, politics, advocacy work
4. Esteem	Personal worth and recognition for achievements	Mental well-being and freedom of thought and conscience	Education, mental health services, community programs, politics
3. Social	Important social relationships (family friends, and social groups)	Freedom of association	Community child and family agencies, mental health services, community prevention programs
2. Safety and security	Freedom from violence in the home or community, shelter, access to health, education, and work	Safety and security, education and work, freedom from arbitrary arrest, detention, or exile, and fair and public hearings by an impartial tribunal	Child welfare agencies, domestic violence shelters, medical hospitals, social services, education, correctional settings, family and community, violence victims' services, unemployment service, victim advocate programs, community organizing
1. Physical	Bodily needs for food, water, and sleep	Economic freedom, social security, shelter, life and liberty	Social services, homeless shelters, hospitals, case management agencies, advocacy organizations, legal aid

Life Course Stress and Resilience

Integration of the life course perspective with stress processing theories provides a useful lens to study the accumulation of trauma and stressful experiences on criminal behavior among incarcerated older adults.[36] Elder argues that significant life events, which can be interpersonal (e.g., experiencing physical or sexual victimization) or historical (e.g., being a combat soldier in a war) events, influence the life course trajectories of individuals.[37] Stress process theory emphasizes the temporal sequencing of significant life events that influence individuals' behavior, including life course criminal behavior.[38] Individuals who experience stable life patterns (a stable family, school, and work life) and fair treatment in life develop stable life course trajectories, including health and well-being, and are at low risk of committing a crime. Individuals who experience one or more periods of chaos or change (traumatic, stressful, or discriminatory experiences common to many incarcerated elders) are exposed to a heighted risk of adverse effects, including in old age. General strain theory posits that trauma and stressful life events heighten the risk of maladaptive coping responses (maladaptive thoughts and feelings) and delinquent or criminal behaviors, including recidivism.[39]

Cumulative inequality theory also incorporates aspects of oppression and discrimination.[40] It focuses on psychosocial, structural, contextual factors, which include intersectional identities and locations such as being a member of a racial/ethnic minority or a socioeconomically disadvantaged group or living in an impoverished neighborhood. The accumulation of stressors may affect an individual's overall well-being, including increasing the risk of criminal justice involvement.[41] This theory also has a coping resilience element; it takes into account human agency (acting on personal goals), psychological and social support, and other factors that assist individuals, families, and groups in preventing or overcoming challenging experiences such as trauma and racial discrimination. Cumulative inequality theory also conceptualizes the pathways to health and justice disparities among disadvantaged groups in society, such as elder racial/ethnic minorities in prison.

The capabilities framework is based on the work of Amyrata Sen and Martha Nussbaum (figure 2.5). This perspective focuses on the fair distribution of capabilities; that is, the resources and power to exercise self-determination and to achieve well-being.[42] This approach recognizes the global imbalance of power and expands on the need for distributive justice, which is based on social work values of self-determination, human dignity, and well-being. McGrath Morris points out the congruence between the capability's perspective and other theories that focus on strengths, person-in-environment, and empowerment.[43] Nussbaum's work has been used to guide advocacy work when circumstances are "outside of

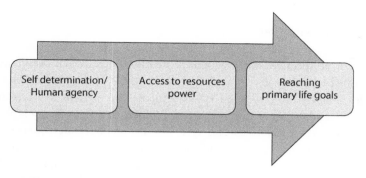

2.5 The capabilities perspective and approach

one's control and do not permit some people, especially women and persons of color, to develop their capabilities." Securing primary goods is an essential part of the process for achieving social justice, but it is not the goal. "Capability is based on what a person wants to achieve and what power he or she has to convert primary goods to reach her or his desired goals." The capabilities perspective begins at the individual level and imagines what a person can do and become.[44]

Contemporary philosopher Martha Nussbaum developed a list of capabilities that represent the benchmarks for a minimally decent life: life, bodily health, bodily integrity, senses, imagination and thought, emotions, practical reason, affiliation, other species, play, and control over one's environment.[45] Materials and resources are used to create and facilitate the development of human capabilities, and rights are viewed as entitlements for capabilities.

Systems Analysis (Width of the Model)

Family, services, and legal systems often change during an individual's life course. Access to services and justice may facilitate or impede an individual's right to human agency and his or her ability to achieve life goals. When societal conditions are suboptimal, which is the case of most U.S. state correctional systems, the health and well-being of older adults may be significantly compromised.[46] Other social contexts include society's values and ethics, interdisciplinary perspectives, and the use of evidence-based and evidence-informed practices. Values and ethics can be personal, professional, or societal.[47] A central value and ethical principle of human rights philosophy is honoring the dignity and worth of all persons and having respect for all persons, including people in prison.[48] Pedro and Dawn describe a lack of honoring human rights, access to evidence-based services, and justice during the course of their criminal justice experiences.

Ecological Systems (Person-in-Environment)

Theories or perspectives that may illuminate the complex relationship between incarcerated and formerly incarcerated older adults, their families, and communities include the ecological systems theory, the person-in-environment perspective, and the social support theory. Ecological systems theory is based on the work of developmental psychologist Urie Bronfennbrenner,[49] and this theory asserts that individual level and social/environmental factors affect human psychosocial development. The ecological system consists of many levels: the micro level (individual biological level), the mesosystem (family, peers, and school), the exosystem (external social settings), and the macrosystem (culture). Reciprocal interactions take place among the different subsystems, such as older adults with histories of incarceration, their families and local communities, and society at large, and a change in one subsystem will bring about changes in other parts of the system.[50] For example, an older person with a criminal offense history may make amends and become of service to others. Similarly, if communities provided access to housing, employment, social, and other services, the risk of an older person becoming involved in the criminal justice system would be reduced.

The person-in-environment perspective is a competence model put forth by Hooyman and Kiyak that specifically addresses aging and life course development.[51] A person's living energy unfolds across the life course in dynamic and reciprocal interactions with the social environment—community, neighborhood, and society. In the best conditions, individuals have access to rights and needs, self-mastery or control, and are highly adaptable to changes in circumstances. Age-related physical and mental decline is a natural process, and the physical and mental health of older adults released from prison may be significantly compromised because of poor health histories compounded by the trauma of incarceration. Older people released from prison often face challenges navigating the social and environmental context and balancing their capabilities for maximum health and well-being, especially after serving long prison sentences. Older adults released from prison may experience environmental stress because of discrimination based on their age and formerly incarcerated status. Community care providers may not offer services or have the capacity to address the diverse needs of these formerly incarcerated older adults and their families.[52]

Social support theory focuses on factors that influence successful community reintegration. Informational support from formal and informal networks of care providers guide incarcerated and formerly incarcerated older adults in navigating their transition from prison to the community. Instrumental support provides concrete services such as food, clothing, or access to housing for older adults released from prison. Emotional support by family and care providers can make these adults feel loved and cared for and foster a sense of dignity and self-worth. This often overlooked aspect of support can influence successful reintegration of older adults released from prison.[53]

Power Analysis (Height of the Model)

It is important to assess the history of power and privilege throughout the life course, especially for older adults who have experienced victimization and committed crimes. Power dynamics across the life course may be balanced (equitable) or imbalanced (oppressive). This social environment factor may facilitate or hinder individuals throughout the life course. It may serve to open doors to advancement in society or result in accumulating disparities across the life course. Individuals or groups can be oppressed at the personal (everyday interactions), structural (institutional), or cultural (societal attitudes, media) level. For example, cumulative life course disparities often result in criminal behavior by oppressed persons that result in disproportionately strict sentencing and confinement of minority populations and create barriers to their release on parole.[54]

Interdisciplinary perspectives are commonly fragmented when addressing aging people in prison. The social workers' perspective may vary from a medical model to a more contextual philosophy of practice. Assessment and intervention should address these varying perspectives. In a life course systems power analysis, a holistic and integrated theoretical base is essential to adequately address the process and outcomes of the crisis.[55] Finally, evidence-based and evidence-informed practices need to be evaluated to adequately capture the process and outcomes of interventions for older adults in prison.[56]

Critical Theories (Diversity, Difference, and Power)

Intersectionality and oppression are critical theories that address power dynamics and inform the life course systems power model. Reflect on how intersectionality applies in your own life and how it influences your personal and professional contacts and general approach to the world (see figure 2.2 and figure 2.3). Intersectionality documents hierarchies of access to power and privilege, justice, and services based on diversity and difference.[57]

Intersectionality theory also offers a social change mechanism, challenging the contradictions between the beliefs, values, and subsequent practices and policies that arise from the privileged experiences of dominant groups and the devalued reality often experienced by subordinate and marginalized

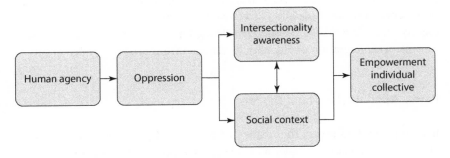

2.6 Intersectionality theory of change for individuals and society

populations (figure 2.6). An intersectional perspective emphasizes human agency (independence and autonomy) and empowerment. Awareness of differences among individuals and groups can be grounded and negotiated to realize a fairer and more just society. The means by which differences find expression influence the social construction of group politics and individual and collective advocacy.[58] Applying an empowerment/partnership model as opposed to a disempowerment approach may lead to better health and justice outcomes for older adults in prison. The practice of deep reflection, such as keeping a daily reflection journal, can empower community members to become life-long learners and to advocate not only for themselves but also for those around them.

Restorative Justice and Risk, Need, and Responsivity

Embedded in the life course systems power analysis are restorative justice models that emphasize strengthening pro-social bonds, community-based management and systems of care for offenders, and enhanced protective measures against sexual and nonsexual criminal reoffending. Protective factors in restorative justice approaches (such as circles of accountability and support)[59] focus on offender reintegration that includes fostering interrelationships and community engagement and support as well as mutual accountability in addressing the needs of older adults in prison. Principles of risk, need, and responsivity (RNR)[60] coincide with the shift from punishment/criminalization to a rehabilitation model that is more attentive to social and psychological risk and protective factors in designing interventions (figure 2.7). RNR underscores respectful and collaborative working relationships between clients and correctional agencies that promote the use of effective assessments and interventions, resulting in lower recidivism rates.[61] RNR is based on three therapeutic principles that match services to the individual's risk level (risk

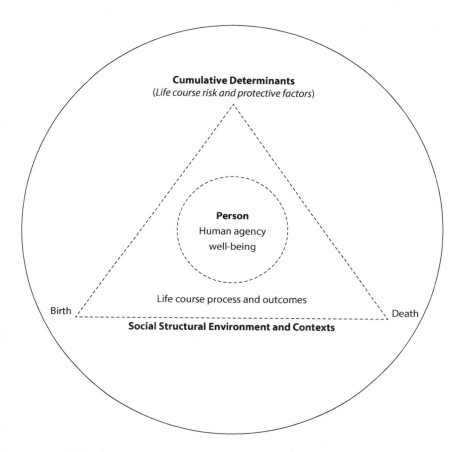

2.7 A social context model of human development and well-being for multilevel prevention, assessment, and intervention

principle), address criminogenic (e.g., sexual drive, the sequelae of traumatic stress, and social rejection) and noncriminogenic needs (need principle), and tailor interventions based on an individual's motivation, learning style, agency, identity, and systems context (responsivity principle).

Life Course Systems Power Analysis

In this section, we conduct a life course systems power analysis using the case of Pedro. We use the life calendar assessment tool for an individual created by Maschi and Kaye[62] to assess the three dimensions of Pedro's life course trajectory and to document the changing dynamics within and across life course experiences, systems of care interactions, and power dynamics (table 2.3).

TABLE 2.3 Life History Calendar: Pedro

Event Year / Age	1963 / Birth	1968 / 5	1970–1975 / 7–12	1979 / 16	1980 / 17	1990 / 27	1992 / 29	2011 / 48	2014 / 51	2019 / 56
Developmental stage	Infancy	Childhood	Middle childhood	Adolescence	Adolescence	Adulthood	Adulthood	Middle adulthood	Middle adulthood	Middle adulthood
Family	Youngest of nine children	Death of father	Childhood sexual victimization	Immigrated to the United States (NYC)	Some family contact	Some family contact	Some family contact	Some family contact	Last contact with family	No family contact
Religion/spirituality	Raised Catholic	Raised Catholic	Raised Catholic	No religious beliefs	No religious beliefs	No religious beliefs	No religious beliefs	No religious beliefs	No religious beliefs	No religious beliefs
Peers/social networks		Peer support with their own limited resources		Negative peer influence	Negative peer influence	No peer support				
Neighborhood/community/location		Poor/collectivist neighborhood		Underserved/individualistic community	Underserved/individualistic community					
Self-perceptions					I had to support my addiction somehow					Despondent w/ lack of resources in prison
Emotional well-being		Grief and loss	Trauma experience	Cultural adjustment	Addiction/trauma	Addiction/trauma		Trauma experience		Depression
Health status		Malnutrition	Malnutrition	Substance abuse (heroin addiction)	Substance abuse (heroin addiction)					Cancer/Depression
Economic well-being	Poverty	Poverty	Poverty	Poverty	Poverty					
Housing	Lack of adequate housing	Lack of adequate housing	Lack of adequate housing							
Safety, security, basic needs	Lack of basic needs	Lack of basic needs	Unsafe home environment	Unsafe community	Unsafe prison environment	Unsafe community	Unsafe prison environment	Unsafe prison environment	Unsafe prison environment	Unsafe prison environment

Education	No access to education	No access to education	No access to education	No access to education	Limited access	Limited access	Limited access	Limited access	Limited access
Employment	Parents and older siblings worked in the sugar cane plantations	Unemployed mother, surviving with the help of neighbors and small vegetable garden							
Access to health care	No access to adequate health care	No access to adequate health care	No access to adequate health care	No access to adequate health care	Limited access to counseling services	Limited access to counseling services	Limited access to counseling services	Limited access to counseling services	Limited access to counseling services
Access to services, supports, justice				Limited access to rehabilitative services	Limited access to rehabilitative services	Limited access to rehabilitative services	Limited access to rehabilitative services	Limited access to rehabilitative services	Limited access to rehabilitative services
Historical events	Industrialization process/ deterioration of sugar cane plantations	Industrialization process/ deterioration of sugar cane plantations							
Other			Prostitution	Drug dealing	Armed robbery		Sexual offense of a minor and possession of substances		
Other					Twenty-year sentence in prison	Parole	Forty-five-year sentence in prison	Solitary confinement	

Source: Adapted from Tina Maschi and Adriana Kaye, "Responding to the Crisis of Aging People in Prison: Promising Corrections and Community Practices," *Advancing Corrections: Journal of the International Corrections and Prisoners Association* 7 (2019): 151–60.

The life course history calendar classifies information regarding the event year, age or occurrence, developmental stage, family, religion/spirituality, peers/ social networks, neighborhood/community/location, emotional well-being, health status, economic well-being, housing, safety, security, and basic needs, access to health care, access to services, supports, and justice, historical events, and other factors. It is generally written in chronological order, providing a description of the life history followed by a critical analysis of themes related to life experiences, system of care interactions, and power dynamics.

Pedro's Description of Life Events. Pedro's life was characterized by the loss of his father, sexual victimization, and prostitution during childhood (5–12 years old). During adolescence (16–17 years old), Pedro immigrated to the United States (NYC), got involved in drug dealing, was addicted to heroin, and was sentenced to twenty years in prison for armed robbery. Most of Pedro's adulthood was spent in jail. He was released on parole when he was 27 years old, but he recidivated at age 29 and was sentenced to forty-five years in prison for a sexual offense of a minor and possession of controlled dangerous substances. In prison he has spent eight out of twenty-seven years in solitary confinement and has not had any family contact in the last five years.

Critical Analysis

Life experiences. Pedro's life experiences have been stressful and traumatic since birth. He has experienced structural, cultural, individual, and internalized oppression, major losses, sexual abuse, substance abuse, jail, solitary confinement, depression, and cancer. The effects of these adverse life experiences have been accumulating and have manifested through mental and physical illnesses. His past and current life experiences influence his personal worldview and his mental and emotional well-being.

System of care interactions. Pedro has had multiple experiences in the community, beginning in childhood with consistent access to education and other needed community services. In his current situation in prison, Pedro perceives the staff as disengaged and uninterested. Ideally, Pedro would actively participate in wraparound services, with a team of clinical physical and mental health providers, case managers, lawyers, and advocates working together to determine the best treatment modalities and rehabilitative path for him.

Power dynamics. In prison Pedro has limited access to resources such as physical and mental health treatment, and rehabilitative services. His extensive time in solitary confinement has resulted in further deterioration of his mental and physical health.

Treatment Recommendations

Consult with Pedro to establish his interest in clinical or supportive services. These services may include individual/group counseling or self-help support groups. Provide trauma-informed care, substance abuse treatment, education, and healing through arts, meditation, yoga, and other alternative therapeutic approaches. Consider stress/anger management, personal growth, and addictions support groups.

Interdisciplinary wraparound services that include physical and mental health providers, case managers, lawyers, and advocates are needed to develop a comprehensive treatment plan for Pedro while in prison that can be continued after his release. Pedro will collaborate with these experts to determine the best treatment modalities and rehabilitative path for him. Pedro may also be interested in consulting the prison ombudsman to document his mistreatment in prison or for assistance with outreach to his family members or other community supports.

Suggested Interventions

Measures of prevention and intervention at the cultural, structural, personal, and internalized levels are listed in the text box. By targeting these areas when working with individuals, groups, communities, and organizations, we can begin to dismantle the oppression experienced by older people in U.S. prisons and aging people in prisons across the world.

Life Course Systems Power Prevention, Assessment, and Intervention Plan

---

Cultural Prevention Strategies
Media and societal attitudes
Scope: local, national, and
   international
Target population: international
   and national

- Build a humanistic restorative culture
- Use mass media to promote humanistic language, alternative cultures, and discourse
- Public awareness campaigns (reduce stigma, oppression, negative attitudes, and biases)
- Evaluate target social determinants of health and justice

Interventions with Populations at Risk Personal, internalized, oppression intervention Scope: local and national Target population: individuals at risk of receiving a long prison sentence	• Community level interventions for those at risk of victimization or criminal justice involvement and older adults, their families, and communities • Restorative justice, empowerment practices through grassroots innovations and coalition building • Individual, group, and community empowerment interventions • Self-care, self-help, and other social and community support groups
Interventions with Population Directly Affected Personal (individual and group) Daily family and community practices; everyday practices and informal networks Scope: local and national Target population: clinical and justice-involved aging and older people in prison	• Target clinical populations and formal services • Holistic assessment • Holistic, integrated intergenerational care, trauma-informed care coordination, and culturally responsive education • Individual, group, and community clinical and empowerment interventions • Self-care, self-help, and other social and community support groups • Local community education and forum
Building the Structural Power Base Institutional structures. laws, and policies Political involvement at each level (intersects with all levels) **Structural Intervention** Scope: local, national, international Target population: individuals, groups, organizations, and communities	• Transformative practices with social, economic, justice, or political systems • Develop alternative institutions and services • Group organizing (incarcerated and formerly incarcerated older adults and their families and communities; crime victims and their families and communities) • Community and institutional engagement • Community organizing • Adopt an intersectional framework for policy development and analysis • Local, national, international advocacy (e.g., engage in policy development or policy reform, such as compassionate/geriatric release)
Evidence-Based and Evidence-Informed Assessment and Interventions Research and evaluation at each intervention level (intersects with all levels)	• Quantitative and qualitative research • Intersectoral collaboration within aging, criminal justice, and community service providers • Development of geriatric services that address short- and long-term needs • Evaluation of interventions at all levels

Final Reflections

This chapter explored the dimensions of diversity and difference, power, privilege, and oppression as they relate to the aging prison population in the social context of their communities and society in general. Our perceptions influence our actions toward one another, including individually or collectively turning a blind eye and a deaf ear to the increasing number of older adults who are sick and dying in prison. Even if you do nothing to help aging people in prison, you can learn from their experience of diversity and difference. Exploring your own intersectional identities may influence how you feel about power, privilege, and oppression and lead you to reexamine your personal biases about people who are different from you.

Many older adults in prison learn to love and forgive themselves despite the false perceptions and projections of others that try to limit who they can become. If you learn to love yourself, you will help create a better world in which the pathway to prison will fade away for many others. If you choose to do something about prison reform, Jane Addams would cheer you on: "Action is indeed the sole medium of expression for ethics." A commitment to justice values and the ethics of service to others is the springboard. There is much left to do.

When learning about the ugly side of human nature, such as viewing a dying person in prison who is chained to a bed, it is common to grieve for our imperfect humanity. If you choose to contribute to your community and make it safe and fair for people of all ages, including those caught up in the justice system, you will benefit from the opportunity to form affiliations with like-minded others who believe that actions can transform the world.

CHAPTER 3

TRAUMA AND DIVERSITY AMONG OLDER ADULTS IN PRISON

There is no greater agony than bearing an untold story inside you.

—Maya Angelou

In this chapter, we investigate the role of cumulative adverse life experiences—traumatic and stressful life experiences and diversity and difference as mechanisms of oppression in the form of structural and systemic violence—as they relate to diverse older adults before, during, and after prison. The Hartford Prison Study at a northeastern prison system found that seven out of ten incarcerated older adults (N=677) reported experiencing one or more prior traumatic or stressful life experience and a high level of lingering subjective psychological distress. Incarcerated older adults commonly reported interpersonal traumas, such as being a victim of or a witness to physical or sexual assault, or stressful life experiences, such as divorce, separation, or losing a loved one. These events occurred across the systems of care and were facilitated by individuals or groups that had power over them. These care systems included their homes, neighborhoods, community services (e.g., foster care and health care), and prison. Narratives of older people illustrate the trauma and stress of aging in the oppressive environment of prison such as this description by a 54-year-old African American man after thirty-six years of incarceration. He was convicted of murder in

1976 and received a life sentence. He was 19 years old at the time and had no prior record.

> My life experiences are very slender given the fact of my incarceration before exhausting my teenage years. Any combination or totality of my life experiences developed and/or accumulated prior to my beginning of incarceration of course remains with me throughout my life. The current criminal justice systems are motivated and codified upon factors, such as race, economic status, some religion (more so religion in this time following 911), gender, political agenda, et al. The End.

We conclude with a life course systems power analysis at the institutional level (prison) and suggest interventions to reclaim the culture and climate of health and well-being for older adults and people of all ages in secure care settings.

Older adults in prison are a diverse group with many intersectional social identities based on their race/ethnicity, gender, class, age, disability, immigration status, and more.[1] Many of the personal social identities of individuals are formative aspects of the developing self as they learn to negotiate their social environment. These social identities precede the social identity of being an older adult in prison who must integrate social identity and location into their personal selves and worldview. These intersectional identities may affect their access to the social determinants of health, well-being, and justice. Social determinants of health and mental health include gender and race (e.g., a higher risk for males and racial ethnic minorities), history of earlier onset or prolonged mental illness, prior access to mental health assessment and treatment, housing status (e.g., history of homelessness or solitary confinement), education status, and employment history. The frequency, magnitude, and duration of past interpersonal trauma and chronic stress (i.e., life course cumulative trauma), level of family and social support, spirituality/religious practices, and criminal justice history all affect their social identity.[2]

Second-class citizenship status places subordinate group members (women, racial/ethnic minorities, lower class/poor, and older adults) at a heightened risk of retraumatization, structural or systematic violence, and interpersonal violence. Johan Galtung[3] described structural violence or trauma as a form of violence in which some social structure (e.g., laws or policies) or social institution (e.g., education or correctional system) prevents people from meeting their basic needs. Cultural or institutionalized biases, stereotyping, prejudices, and discriminatory practices affect members of subordinate groups in the form of ageism, classism, ethnocentrism, racism, sexism, ableism, and criminalization (labeling someone a prisoner or offender). Iris Young states that the dominant group engages in systematic violence or trauma at the individual and social/structural levels,

3.1

Source: ©Ron Levine/www.ronlevinephotography.com

targeting subordinate/oppressed groups. Interpersonal level acts of structural and systematic violence may include intentional verbal harassment, intimidation, threats, humiliation, and physical violence.[4]

Many older incarcerated adults report some type of personal or social structural trauma or violence beginning in childhood and continuing in prison:

> I witness lots of violence and death. Both sides, prisoner on prisoner and DOC on prisoner. I've experienced a life I was familiar with witnessing as a child, the bloodshed of human beings.

Research reveals a high rate of traumatic life experiences, such abuse, neglect, mistreatment, stress, and multisystemic trauma, across the life span of older adults in prison.[5] The prevalence of these life experiences may vary within sub-groups of community-dwelling adults, such as by gender and race. More men (61 percent) than women (51 percent) report having at least one traumatic life experience at some point in their life.[6] Girls/women are more likely to experience sexual assault, whereas boys/men are more likely to experience physical assault and early mortality.[7]

There is growing evidence of race-based trauma.[8] Racial discrimination and victimization, especially as a result of a hate crime, are traumatic for both those who are victimized and those who have witnessed or learned about them. These race-based events have been linked to PTSD symptoms, and some communities of color have higher rates of PTSD than the general population.[9]

The number of traumatic experiences reported in care settings are higher among older adults who use health-care services or are involved in the health system.[10] For example, 70 to 90 percent of adults who receive behavioral health-care services or are in prisons report a history of trauma.[11] Studies of incarcerated older adults showed that 70 percent report having three or more cumulative traumas or stressful life experiences.[12]

The LGBTQ+ community is another group at risk of trauma and oppression, including criminalization, criminal justice involvement, and prison trauma and abuse. Incarcerated adults who identified as gay, lesbian, or bisexual had the highest rates of sexual victimization by other incarcerated people (12.2 percent in prison and 8.5 percent in jail). LGBTQ+ people in prison (5.4 percent) and in jails (4.3 percent) have reported being victimized by staff as well. Incarcerated people with mental health needs who identified as nonheterosexual reported the highest rates of inmate-on-inmate sexual victimization (14.7 percent in jail and 21 percent in prison). Transgender women in male prisons are at high risk and were thirteen times more likely to experience sexual violence in a California study.[13] Incarcerated LGBTQ+ people also have health-care concerns that include sexually transmitted infections (STIs) including HIV/AIDS, and mental health and substance use disorders. The health care of transgender incarcerated individuals is often an administrative matter that results in medical neglect. Some denial of services are due to institutional policies preventing hormone- or transition-related care.[14]

In the least ideal scenario, the traumatic experiences of individuals are left undetected and unaddressed in the criminal justice system. These unresolved traumatic experiences may have adverse long-term effects on individuals' capacity to cope and heal, especially at an older age. Trauma survivors may experience distress in their physical, psychological, emotional, social, behavioral, and spiritual well-being. They also are at risk of revictimization, especially in later life when older adults become frail and more dependent on family and professional caregivers. Older adults also may experience traumatization in formal care settings, such as nursing homes or prisons.[15]

Research on the aftermath of childhood trauma shows that unresolved childhood trauma, such as being a victim or a witness to violence, is related to poor mental and physical health and behavioral well-being in later life.[16] Social determinants, such as age, gender, race/ethnicity, class, religion, sexual orientation, and marital status, are related to the types of traumatic events experienced. The positive news is that the data suggest that trauma survivors who live in a trauma-informed care environment and learn to tap into their adaptive coping resources are much more likely to become resilient to the lingering effects of trauma on their overall health and well-being. A safe care environment should be provided for survivors to move from trauma to a stage of well-being and posttraumatic growth.

Unraveling Trauma and Stressful Life Experiences

> It was hard to get yourself mentally ready for the morning because you never knew what was going to happen that day, and that's a real terrible feeling, like, what's going to happen to me today. Every day was, like, I got to keep up. I got to keep up. I got to look left. I got to look right because people were just being abused all throughout my stay.
>
> (formerly incarcerated LGBTQ+ older adult)

What exactly is trauma and stress? The Substance Abuse and Mental Health Services Administration[17] defines individual trauma as an event, series of events, or set of circumstances experienced by an individual as physically or emotionally harmful or life-threatening that results in long-term adverse effects on the individual's functioning and mental, physical, social, emotional, or spiritual well-being (figure 3.2). In other words, traumatic life experiences are unusual extreme stressors that involve the threat of or actual serious physical or psychological harm to oneself, a family member, or a close friend. Examples include being

3.2 Trauma equals the sum of the event, plus the experience and the effect. That is, when an unusual event occurs (such as a shooting or an accident), an individual, group, or community directly or indirectly experiences it, and it has an adverse psychological or emotional effect (subjective trauma response). The result can be described as a traumatic experience.

Source: Substance Abuse and Mental Health Services Administration.

the victim of physical or sexual assault in childhood or adulthood, witnessing a traumatic event such as family or community trauma, shootings, war combat, a mass disaster, or an accident. Witnessing or learning about a serious injury or sudden death of a family member or close friend is also considered a traumatic experience. Traumatic exposures often result in psychological distress and can result in posttraumatic stress disorder (PTSD) in some people.[18]

Generally, lifetime traumatic events are broad in scope, range in intensity, and may have a dosage effect. People's objective experiences of trauma range from a singular event that took place in childhood or adulthood to a series of traumatic and stressful life experiences that occur across the life course. A person's subjective response to traumatic events may be psychological, emotional, physiological, social, or behavioral. Survivors of traumatic experiences may continue to be affected in a variety of ways at different stages of the life span.[19]

It is important to understand the difference between traumatic and stressful life experiences. Stressful experiences are less severe and more common environmental events that tax the adaptive capacities of individuals and cause distress or concern in most people. Examples of stressful life experiences include divorce or separation, job loss, social isolation, current or prior incarceration, and so forth. People manifest their distress in a variety of ways, including physical, emotional, psychological, social, spiritual, and behavioral problems.[20] For example, an untreated trauma survivor may commit acts of delinquency and crime to relieve stress.[21]

Multigenerational Trauma and Oppression

Intergenerational trauma is an important aspect of understanding the cultural dynamics of trauma and oppression that affect aging people in prison. Maria Yellow Horse Brave Heart defined historical trauma in her work with tribal communities as an "accumulation of emotional and psychological wounding throughout the life span and across generations" that emerges from massive group trauma experiences. African Americans also have experienced historical and generational trauma in the form of forced slavery, segregation, and institutionalized racism. Daily experiences of microaggressions and other forms of racial biases and discrimination, such as multigenerational incarceration, may internalize oppression or racism among individuals from diverse groups with a history of multigenerational trauma. Joy DeGruy states that historical trauma may contribute to physical, psychological, and spiritual trauma.[22] If so, the complex multigenerational trauma felt by diverse groups in the criminal justice system should address the multidimensional ramifications of systemic trauma.

Multigenerational trauma is experienced by a cultural, racial, or ethnic group that has been systematically oppressed because of their second-class status (e.g., slavery, Holocaust, forced migration, brutal Native American colonization).

Some groups may have no historical trauma effects, but others may experience poor physical and behavioral health. These effects can include low self-esteem, depression, self-destructive behavior, marked propensity to violent or aggressive behavior, substance abuse and addiction, and elevated rates of suicide and cardiovascular disease. A society that discounts or does not address grief and mental health and emotional needs can trigger internalized oppression and acute issues of domestic violence or alcohol abuse not directly related to historical trauma.[23]

When reflecting on the effects of oppression among diverse older adults in prison, historical or intergenerational trauma is a critical consideration. Personal and social/structural level trauma vibrate throughout societies and are handed down from generation to generation. The First Nations and aboriginal peoples in Canada created the concept of historic trauma in the 1980s to explain the perceived unending cycle of trauma and chronic stress in their communities. Their intergenerational experiences of this human-made disaster—genocide, cultural loss, and forcible withdrawal from family and communities—have resulted in unresolved psychological strain that continues to be acted out and re-created in contemporary aboriginal culture.[24] Similarly, Michelle Alexander's groundbreaking book on mass incarceration documents how stricter sentencing in the New Jim Crow era has resulted in African American men and women being disproportionally incarcerated, thus remaining in a form of bondage and slave labor.[25] This 58-year-old incarcerated African American man offers a similar perspective on multigenerational and historical trauma and its impacts:

Dear Doctor, I hope you will understand some of the things I am trying to say. My imprisonment and its effect on my life has been dramatic. Since this is my first encounter with the law, what makes this experience so overwhelming is that is happening at an age where I was looking forward to retiring and enjoy some of the benefits of old age even though I have children of school age, also grandkids. I was sentence to six (6) years imprisonment in 2010; that's when my nightmare begins. From the time that I was arrested to my incarceration here, I am more convinced about how biased the judicial system is, especially against minority groups, black, Latino, the poor. I believe that if a white male had committed (accuse) a similar felony there is a likelihood (75 percent) that he would have been treated differently and less harsh. A white or rich individual would have walked away with a slap on the wrist, some judges blatantly show racism in their decisions toward the poor + minority. Those of us who depend on the public defender to represent us in the courts. These are the people who are flooding the prisons. Some of us are not aware of our predicament. I am not saying that some of us don't deserve to be here (if U do the crime U have to do the time), what I am saying is let's be fair from the top to the bottom: the police lie, the prosecutors lie, the system lies, 80 percent of the prisoners here are appealing their conviction. I discovered that the prisons have become a business for the states.

Neurobiology of Trauma

It is important to understand how trauma and stress affect the brain and the body, and why people might react the way they do (figure 3.3). Three parts of the brain are important in understanding how trauma affect us: the brain stem, the limbic region, and the cortex.

The **brain stem**, sometimes referred to as the survival or old brain, is the part of the brain that develops and controls human arousal and automatic

3.3 "He would go into black moods. Very black moods where he wouldn't speak to me for two or three weeks. He would stay out in the garage and only come in for meals. He started hitting on my daughter. That's what done it. She was 28. I'm not one that displays my feelings that much, but that morning I just snapped. I couldn't take it any longer, I couldn't think of a way out. I was very hungry." (incarcerated 52-year-old woman, sentenced to second-degree murder)

Source: ©Ron Levine/www.ronlevinephotography.com

responses for survival. The **limbic region** includes the amygdala (the brain's alarm system) and the hippocampus and connects the high and low parts of the brain. The hippocampus facilitates the experience and expression of memory and emotion. The last part of the brain to develop is the **cortex.** It is responsible for cognition and thinking, such as self-reflection. The prefrontal cortex assists with concentration and other higher brain functions.[26]

There are several important structures within the limbic system: the amygdala, hippocampus, thalamus, hypothalamus, basal ganglia, and cingulate gyrus. All the structures of the limbic system work together to regulate some of the brain's most important processes. Emotions and sensory perceptions are a function of the limbic system. When a person experiences a traumatic event, adrenalin rushes through the body, and the memory is imprinted on the amygdala. The amygdala holds the emotional significance of the event (the intensity and impulse of emotion) and stores images of the trauma as sensory fragments of how the five senses experienced the trauma: sight, smells, sounds, tastes, or touch. These are subjective memories, the opposite of a narrative or a story.

After a traumatic or stressful life experience, the brain can easily be triggered by sensory input and misinterpret normal circumstances as dangerous. For example, an older adult in prison who was abused by a parental authority figure may react to staff who exhibit similar behaviors. The sensory fragments are misinterpreted, and the brain loses its ability to discriminate between what is threatening and what is normal. People who feel threatened may react aggressively, thinking that they are acting in self-defense.[27]

Processing and Reason

When confronted with a stressful or dangerous situation, people react in one of three ways: fight (self-defense), flight (run away), or freeze (become immobile). When a person perceives the onset of a stressful/dangerous situation, the brain sends messages to the autonomic nervous system to prepare the body to respond to the stressor/danger. The autonomic nervous system consists of two branches: the sympathetic nervous system and the parasympathetic nervous system. The **sympathetic nervous system** increases arousal via the release of a chemical called adrenalin, and it signals the sympathetic nervous system to continue or increase activity over time.[28] Adrenalin is eventually neutralized, and as the body becomes exhausted, the **parasympathetic nervous system** restores the body to a normal state. The arousal state does not continue in perpetuity, nor does it intensify to harmful stress levels.[29]

The **prefrontal cortex** is responsible for processing, reasoning, and making meaning of language, but it may shut down under stress, creating a profound imprinted stress response. When the brain becomes disorganized and overwhelmed by the traumatic experience, the higher reasoning and language structures of the brain shut down. Since logic and judgment can be affected, this may explain why some untreated trauma survivors commit crimes.[30]

Two brain-body pathways play a critical role in reactions to stress. When facing a threatening situation, the hypothalamus excites the sympathetic nervous system, which results in rapid heartbeat and other physical changes associated with the experience of fear or anxiety. The release of epinephrine (adrenaline) and norepinephrine (noradrenaline) further produce arousal reactions throughout the body. The hypothalamic-pituitary-adrenal pathway also plays a key role. When the body faces stressors, the hypothalamus signals the pituitary gland to release adrenocorticotropic hormone (ACTH), a major stress hormone. ACTH then triggers the adrenal cortex to release stress hormones called corticosteroids.[31] The relationship between untreated childhood trauma/stress and addictions and criminal behavior is a public safety concern, as this narrative of an incarcerated older adult illustrates.

My life began as a normal child with two loving parents who worked hard to provide. At age 10 things started to change with mom + dad drinking alcohol more and more. Reflecting back, it seemed as though the pressures of 4 children, bills, work, and infidelity became too much. My father cheated on my mother; she found out from me because I caught him and then told her. She took it hard and although they didn't separate they fought over it constantly and would become violent on occasion especially when drinking. The violence became worse and worse. Mom would fight with him violently but would always get the worse end of it. My father has over a two-year period (my age 10 to 12) beat mom, causing a broken arm, nose broke two times, black eyes, split lips, and lots of bruises. At age 12 I would step in front of him and try to protect mom by taking the blows. I eventually would fight him back. My younger brother and I both would plot on him to keep him from hurting her. They finally separated at my age of 13. That's when living with only mom I turned to friends who got high and I used LSD for the first time, first drug and loved it. I found a way to get out of reality and escape to another world of laughter and pleasure that I could no longer find normally as a 13-year-old child should.

Research consistently shows high levels of lifetime traumatic and stressful life experiences among incarcerated juveniles, adults, and older adults. The literature also suggests that both traumatic and stressful life experiences are associated with criminal behavior and criminal justice involvement among diverse age groups.[32] More than 90 percent of incarcerated people of all ages report histories of traumatic and stressful life experiences.[33]

In a nationally representative sample of 984,000 incarcerated people of all ages, one out of five reported being a victim of violence (i.e., physical or sexual assault) during multiple developmental periods. Gender differences were also found. More male prisoners reported being maltreated during childhood or adolescence (14.4 percent age 17 and younger) than in adulthood (4.3 percent over the age of 18). Female prisoners were likely to report high rates of victimization in both childhood (36.7 percent) and adulthood (45.0 percent). Incarcerated men and women also reported multiple stressors, including parental substance abuse (29.4 percent, 75.7 percent, respectively), out of home placement (43.6 percent, 86.7 percent, respectively), and a family member who was incarcerated (20 percent, 64 percent, respectively).[34] Violent victimization histories were associated with higher levels of violent crime and substance use.[35]

Racially diverse groups also have high rates of interpersonal, structural, and historical trauma experiences. Several studies of youth and young adults from diverse racial/ethnic backgrounds provide empirical support for the relationship of life course cumulative trauma and stressful life experiences and nonviolent, property, and violent offending.[36] Johnson explored the relationship of childhood trauma among a marginalized sample of Florida juveniles with a nonmarginalized group. Youth who had experienced three or more traumas had a 200 to 370 percent increased chance of being arrested for a violent felony when compared to youth who had experienced a single traumatic event. Racial discrepancies revealed a 300 percent increased risk for violent felony arrests for blacks when compared to whites with the same number of traumas. These findings suggest that racial biases and discrimination may influence the disproportionate justice system involvement of racial/ethnic minorities, despite similar histories of traumatic experiences and criminal offense patterns.[37]

The prison environment is also recognized as a source of traumatic experiences and stressor events, especially for older adults. Hochstetler, Murphy, and Simons[38] found that prior victimization experiences predicted revictimization in prison, so incarcerated older adults who are untreated trauma survivors are at a heightened risk in prison. For example, our study found that incarcerated older adults in prison experienced a variety of traumatic and stressful life experiences. These prison traumas include bullying and harassment and verbal abuse by correctional officers or other inmates, physical and sexual victimization, health trauma related to lack of access to health care, and social traumas, such as being separated from family, friends, and the overall community. Older incarcerated adults also experienced institutional and policy trauma in response to strict and rigid rules that were dehumanizing, as well as continued denial of parole.[39]

Hartford Prison Study: Diversity and Trauma Among Older Adults in Prison

The Hartford Prison Study was funded by the John A. Hartford Foundation and the Gerontological Society of America (principal investigator,

Tina Maschi, PhD, 2010).It is a cross-sectional correlation study that used survey mail methods to gather information on the health and well-being of 677 older adults residing in a northeastern prison in 2010. Responses included narratives like this one from an incarcerated older white Catholic woman:

> I am a 59-year-old woman who has spent my life sheltered. When I was 12 years old my parents separated and eventually divorced. During this time, I was a mother, wife, sister, and housekeeper. To make a long story short, my dad was a very strict Catholic with 7 children (6 girls, me being the third oldest, 1 brother who is the youngest), an abusive and mentally, emotionally, and physically alcoholic. He not only beat my mother but also us children. My dad was very deranged. He drew a gun on my mom, which warranted her to leave us children. Eventually we all, through torture and drama, left or was physically removed and reunited with my mom. To this day, my mom is very depressed, shamed, guilty, and remorseful for leaving us children. I believe she will suffer the rest of her life since she has already suffered 74 years of it. With me in here, I feel I have caused her more guilt and shame. My dad has since passed away (6/21/09). My relationship with him was limited, by his choice. Since I have been in prison, I realized I chose men exactly like my father.

Histories of cumulative trauma and stress are important considerations among older people in prison, including racial/ethnic minorities, women, and persons with mental or physical disabilities.[40] Life history trajectories suggest that power imbalances, family discord, and the lack of access to services and justice often precede imprisonment. When untreated trauma survivors experience the trauma of incarceration, it may exacerbate unresolved emotional or mental distress and disenfranchised and complicated grief.[41] The trauma of incarceration is echoed by 59-year-old Mary, who talks about her experience of being an older woman in prison.

> Prison is a hard place. Pure Hell! . . . As long as you are in khaki, you are considered nonhuman. . . . I miss my family and want to go home so bad. I don't feel there is enough mental health available on a regular basis or the comfortable feeling of just expressing yourself without the fear of being put in lockdown. The elder suffer the most because there isn't much for them, us. The medical here makes no sense. Until you have an ailment, you are put off and time holds you back. I have the starts of osteoporosis and seeing how some people young and old are treated makes me suffer and deal with it. I look at it that I will deal with it when I get home. In the meantime, I hurt and deal with it. Prayer and God is what gets me through every day, moment, second I am here. Overall it's horrible, and I wouldn't wish this on my worst enemy.

In the following sections, we present more data on the Hartford Prison Study related to trauma, stressful life experiences, and diversity among older adults in prison.

Intersectional Diversity Portrait of Older Adults in a Northeastern U.S. Prison

The intersectional diversity portrait reveals that the 677 incarcerated older adults who participated in the study were from diverse backgrounds. Their ages were evenly distributed between young-old and old: 45 percent were age 50–54 and 44 percent were age 55–64, and 9 percent were age 65 and older. Their racial backgrounds also were diverse: African American (45 percent), white (35 percent), Hispanic/Latinx (11 percent), and other racial/ethnic groups, such as Asian/Pacific Islander and Native American (9 percent). The overwhelming majority (96 percent) were men, with women making up 4 percent of the sample. There was religious diversity among the older adults, with the majority reporting their religion as Christian (62 percent), followed by Islamic/Muslim (13 percent), atheist/agnostic (13 percent), or some other religion (12 percent). Thirty percent of the participants had been in the military.

Socioeconomic Status and Class

Socioeconomic status (SES) and class also differed among older adults, including education, income, and prior occupation. Nine out of ten reported having a high school diploma (74 percent) or a college degree (16 percent). Only 10 percent had not yet earned a high school diploma or GED. About half (49 percent) of the older adults reported that their income was $20,000 or less prior to prison, and 70 percent described themselves as unskilled laborers.

Family and Relational Constellations

Family and relationship constellations also differed among participants. Only about one-quarter were currently married (14 percent) or partnered (11 percent); the others were single (29 percent), divorced (29 percent), separated (7 percent), or widowed (8 percent). Most older adults reported being a parent (80 percent) and a grandparent (61 percent), with one or more children under age 18 (23 percent) or one or more grandchildren under age 18 (56 percent). About half (48 percent) of the older adults reported having at least one other incarcerated family member.

Clinical Portrait

A clinical profile of the older adults revealed physical health, mental health, and addictions issues. Roughly 41 percent reported one or more serious chronic physical health problem or another health issue, such as hearing and vision problems or difficulty walking. Twenty-one percent of the older adults reported having a serious physical illness, such as cancer, HIV/AIDS, or lung disease, and 28 percent reported having a mental health diagnosis. More older adults reported having a drug addiction (44 percent) than an alcohol addiction (25 percent), and 72 percent reported being involved in religious activities because of their addiction (e.g., AA or NA). Thirty-three percent reported being in mental health treatment.

Criminal Justice History Portrait

Their criminal offense histories also were diverse: delinquent offenses (35 percent), violent offenses (64 percent), sex offenses (25 percent), drug-related offenses (46 percent), violation of probation (44 percent), and parole violations (42 percent). Sixty-six percent reported a history of two or more prior incarcerations.

The length of time served in prison ranged from one to five years (38 percent), to six to nineteen years (28 percent), to twenty or more years (24 percent); 5 percent will serve a sentence of fifty-one years to life. About one out of ten older adults reported spending one or more days in solitary confinement in the past year: 1–10 days (2 percent), 11–150 days (3 percent), and 151–365 days (4 percent). Their expected prison release date varied as well: within one year (22 percent), two to five years (37 percent), six to ten years (13 percent), eleven to fifty years (12 percent), and fifty-one years to life (5 percent). Over two-thirds of these older adults expected to be released to communities located in urban/suburban neighborhoods.

Access to and Use of Prison Services

Most older adults reported using prison medical services (86 percent) in the past three months, and about three-quarters found these services helpful. Approximately one-fifth of the respondents reported using inpatient/outpatient mental health services, and two-thirds found these services helpful. Only 25 percent reported participating in substance abuse services, but most (74.1 percent) found these services helpful. Slightly more older adults

(32 percent) reported participating in Alcoholics or Narcotics Anonymous, and the majority (83 percent) found these programs to be helpful. Most older adults (65 percent) reported attending religious services, and almost all (94 percent) reported those as being helpful. Close to three out of four participated in recreational activities, and 89 percent found them helpful.

Incarcerated Older Adults Experiences of Trauma and Stress

- Adults age 50+ averaged three lifetime traumatic or stressful life events and current subjective distress
- 80 percent report being witnesses or victims of family or community violence, including war
- 60 percent report an unexpected death of someone close
- 60 percent report abuse and stress in prison
- 40 percent were diagnosed with a serious physical or mental illness and were retraumatized in health-care settings
- 25 percent had been a caregiver of a person with a serious illness
- 28 percent reported forced separation from a child
- 5 percent have a child with a handicap

History of Traumatic and Stressful Life Experiences

The Hartford Prison Study data revealed that many people in prison have experienced life challenges related to their marginalized or disadvantaged statuses based on personal or social structural characteristics and personal and historical trauma histories. Their stories reveal an accumulation or aggravation of life course disadvantages, such as being born in poverty; experiencing childhood, adolescence, and adulthood trauma or exploitation; and juvenile and criminal involvement. They also lacked access to community services that could address their concerns about housing, employment, mental and emotional health, substance abuse, and family issues.

The Life Stressors Checklist–Revised (LSC-R) self-report questionnaire was used to gather histories of traumatic and stressful life experiences prior to and while in prison. The older adults reported on whether an event occurred, the age at which it occurred, and its subjective impact then and now. Most respondents (seven out of ten) reported experiencing one or more direct traumatic or stressful life experience. A significant number of older adults reported a history of physical, sexual, or emotional abuse or neglect in childhood:

emotional abuse or neglect (36 percent), physically attacked before the age of 16 (34 percent), or sexually assaulted (19 percent) or touched (22 percent) before the age of 16. In the overwhelming majority of cases, older adults reported still being moderately to extremely affected by these experiences in the past year: emotional abuse or neglect (73 percent), physically attacked before the age of 16 (59 percent), sexually assaulted (69 percent), or touched (65 percent). At least half of the older adults reported indirect exposure to violence or witnessed violence at some time in their lives. Particularly noteworthy is that 48 percent reported being exposed to family violence before the age of 16, with most older adults reporting that they believed someone would get hurt (74 percent), felt horror at the time (88 percent), or felt moderately to extremely affected by it in the past year (58 percent).

Older adults also reported stressful life experiences related to grief, loss, and separation. These experiences included the unexpected death of someone close (60 percent), someone close died but not unexpectedly (70 percent), forced separation from a child (28 percent), and separation or divorce (53 percent). Almost two-thirds of older adults reported still feeling moderately to extremely affected by their loss or separation. Older adults also reported that physical and mental health concerns were stressful life experiences. Older adults reported being diagnosed with a serious physical or mental illness (41 percent; 27 percent) on average in their mid to late thirties. Interestingly, most older adults reported a subjective reaction in which they felt horror at the time of the diagnosis of serious physical or mental illness (82 percent; 86 percent) and were still being moderately or extremely affected by it in the past year (68 percent; 70 percent). Older adults also reported stress over being a caregiver of a person with a serious illness (25 percent) or having serious money problems (52 percent).

Stress over prison and institutional care was commonly reported among older adults. These events included a history of foster care or adoption (10 percent), prior jail term (68 percent), having a close family member or friend in prison (45 percent), or experiencing abuse/stress in prison (53 percent).

Sources of Stress Reported by Incarcerated Older Adults

Health Status

- Thrombosis in left leg, anti-embolism socks
- Pains in chest and diagnosed leakage in graph
- When I found out I had cancer and hepatitis C
- Stent in aorta

- Gender dysphoria (transgender)
- Coming to prison all my life infected with HIV, and dying in prison
- Having diabetes, lack of treatment
- Asthma attack
- Heart problems
- My health, my heart
- Raped, hepatitis B
- Hepatitis C
- Strokes
- Going blind in prison
- Deaf
- Cancer
- Heart attacks
- HIV/AIDS, pneumonia, cancer
- Personal medical issues
- Five-year hunger strikes, twelve hospitalizations

Health Care

- Dying in prison from poor health care
- Diabetic treatment
- Poor health care
- Prison medical's failure to treat my heart problems
- Abandoned by family, friends
- Failure of medical department to treat my injuries and illnesses
- Getting my medication

Prison Environment

- Solitary confinement
- Raped
- Killing in prison yard or mess hall
- Disciplinary charges used to lock me up in closed custody illegally
- Guards killing inmates—abuse, heart attack
- I was assaulted by a young mental patient
- Corrections officers abusing their authority
- Beaten by corrections officers, guards

3.4 "It's hard. It's hard in here. Because after so long you lose support of your family. I have children, but the last I've heard from them was in 2005. I'm in here for 'helping my family.' I learnt my lesson. That won't happen again . . . but y'see they don't help me. . . . I just take care of myself the best that I can." (incarcerated woman, 77, sentenced for murder)

Trauma and Stress in Prison

Our mixed methods analysis of the Hartford Prison Study data provided an eye-opening look inside the conditions of confinement as perceived by incarcerated older adults from diverse backgrounds. Our data was from the Life Stressors Checklist items:

> Have you ever experienced abuse or other stress while in prison (yes or no)?
> If yes, what was the event?

More than half (53 percent) of the sample (N=677) reported experiencing abuse and stress in prison, and 86 percent of them felt moderately to extremely affected by it in the past year.

We also used qualitative data from open-ended questions on two items on the Prison Stress and Coping Scale–Short (PSCS-S):

> What are the types of things that caused you stress while in prison in the
> past month?
> What kind of things did you do in the past month, if anything at all, to help
> with your stress?

A subsample of 201 participants provided firsthand, detailed descriptions of current experiences of prison trauma, stress, and coping (during the past month).

Particularly noteworthy is the occurrence of abuse/stress in prison; the average age of older adults when the event first occurred was 47 (SD=13.3), and 74 percent of these older adults believed someone would get hurt, 94 percent felt horror, and 86 percent still felt moderately to extremely affected by prison abuse/stress in the past year.

A subsample of 200 older adults described prison trauma and oppression as both an external and an internal experience. The most prominent descriptions of external prison trauma and stress were categorized as interpersonal, social, cultural, and structural; internalized descriptions were based on negative self-talk. We address these categories in the following sections.

Interpersonal Trauma and Oppression

Interpersonal trauma and oppression are described as one-on-one events, such as interpersonal abuse, neglect, bullying, or harassment. About one-third of older adults reported experiencing interpersonal oppression from correctional or medical staff or other inmates that included demeaning attitudes and unjust actions. Of the 31 percent of older adults who reported interpersonal trauma, 43 percent reported that these experiences occurred with staff, 18 percent with other incarcerated persons, and 15 percent reported experiencing oppressive attitudes, beliefs, and practices in their interactions with both staff and other incarcerated persons.

The firsthand accounts of older adults shed light on the harsh reality of life as an incarcerated older person. Some older adults described others' condescending attitudes, such as "bias from guards/security officers" and "harassment from officers." Others reported "being picked on for petty things," "constant shakedowns," and "canceled recreation." Older adults reported a high level of stress living with the reality that "you could be set up by an officer at any given time, just because he doesn't like you," "being punished for other people's actions," or "being accused of things you didn't do and have your job taken away." Significant distress was associated with "male guards feeling on my body." One participant reported witnessing "corrections officers stomping inmates into comas."

Older adults also shared feelings of distress associated with interactions with other incarcerated people. Peer-to-peer stress included "ignorance of inmates," "immature inmates, arguments," "being among fellow prisoners who have no honor, little integrity, and who revel in depravity (just like the guards)," "bias from gang members," "aggression from other inmates," "getting into fights with other inmates" and "being robbed." One older participant feared for his safety and said, "I am 72 years old, and I am afraid of getting raped again."

Social Trauma and Oppression

Almost half (45 percent) of the older adults reported social trauma and oppression, predominantly regarding separation from family and the community. One man said, "I am confined like an animal and kept away from family." Others reported feeling stressed about "being here away from my family and not having freedoms," "being transferred to a prison where my loved ones couldn't visit because of the distance," or lack of contact with family: "I cannot contact family, I think about my children, grandkids, children in DYFS." One respondent noted: "It is hard for me cause my son's mother is not with me now. She's on my mind, and I think about my kids and new granddaughter." Poor mail delivery, lack of phones, and families often stressed due to lack of resources or other members incarcerated were common complaints.

Cultural Trauma and Oppression

Cultural trauma and oppression caused stress for about 15 percent of older inmates. Cultural or societal attitudes toward incarcerated people were reenacted by staff and by other incarcerated people. In particular, the prison culture fosters the "subhuman status of being labeled prisoners," which is conveyed by prison staff and found in society as well. The stigma of incarceration and the loss of identity is communicated by responses such as "you're identified as a number, and not as a human being" and "as long as you're in khaki, you are considered nonhuman." One participant noted, "you can't get an answer from Department of Corrections or from social workers" and "corrections officers disrespect inmates and beat them up."

Structural Trauma and Oppression

Twenty-nine percent of these older adults reported structural trauma and oppression. Almost two-thirds reported that the trauma and stress were the result of laws, policies, and institutional regulations. Several older adults reported that staff often created and enforced their own informal rules but failed to enforce existing institutional policies, such as responding to prison abuse. One participant made the following observation about correctional officers: "they seem to lack a 'higher power' to address prison abuse and neglect."

Older adults described feelings of powerlessness, particularly in response to unjust laws and policies and lack of family support as they attempted to navigate the legal process: "My family is not downloading the files from the Internet to help me with my appeal."

One-third of older adults reported trauma and stress related to poor nutrition and inadequate health care in the prison. One respondent wrote, "food nutrition poor; variety-poor-balance-none-lack of use of utilities-water-no water to drink for two days, food, meat not cooked, not getting out to yard enough," and "everyone chain smokes around me all the time." Other responses often referred to medical neglect: "there is indifference to my need for medical care," "medical department ignoring medical complaints," "there's a failure of medical personnel, malpractice, a failure to treat, negligence, abuse, denial of vital medication, heart meds," "a failure to follow specialists' recommendations for treatment of hypertension and pain," "there's mismanagement of prison and neglect of serious health issues," "I have constant back pain, scoliosis, lumbar/thoracic spine," and "I get no medical attention when my tooth throbs." Female adults shared that health-care services were inadequate for the special needs of older women. One participant lamented, "I would not wish this place on my worst enemy."

Administrative and staff acceptance of abusive and neglectful practices included extreme forms of confinement and isolation: "prison officers confine inmates in 2 cages 15–20 minutes 25 at times 3 meals 7 days a week," "I've been locked up in a room for 23 hours a day for the past four months without an explanation from administration," "locked up in a cell 22 hours a day and not enough recreation time," "there's a lack of programs to keep the mind active," and "there are searches where property becomes destroyed or stolen." Others described stress as a result of living with "constant noise" and cells that are "constantly lit up" and feelings of despondency associated with "having to wait 2 to 4 years to participate in a prison program." One older participant noted age biases in the structure of prison: "Prisons are designed for young people. Us older folks find it hard to get a job or education here."

Internalized Negative Self-Talk

Internalized trauma and oppression also was found in the form of negative self-talk. Older adults have internal narratives that caused them psychological and emotional distress. Negative thoughts or emotions include anxiety, fear, worry, depression, insecurity, feelings of loneliness and defeat, hopelessness, apathy, grief, anger, guilt, and shame. Some older adults reported feeling anxiety about their personal health and safety, being separated from children and other family members, the physical and emotional health of their children, and the uncertainty of their future. Several older adults who were close to being released from prison described their bleak options for future employment and economic earning power: "I worry about when I get out—getting kids a place to live," "keeping a job to make ends meet," "I am scared about job opportunities upon my release, rebuilding relationships with my children," and "not being able to support them." One respondent wrote: "I believe the intent is for us to die in here."

Some older adults described feeling tormented as they grappled with the implications of their crime. One participant described fearing that "others will learn the details of my crime." Other older adults thought about how their crime affected others: "I constantly relive the decision which put me back in prison and caused me to lose everything, my wife, kids, car, all money, and possessions." "I feel guilt—my family was harmed by my actions . . . how will I face my family?"

These experiences of trauma and oppression were found at all levels among older adults in prison. The majority of older inmates had experienced adverse life experiences of maltreatment and mistreatment, and they found that the trauma and oppressive conditions of confinement presented a real challenge. Perhaps most concerning is the lack of safety and access to needed medical services, which turns their present situation into a crisis in need of an intervention. In the next section, we conduct a group analysis of older adults residing in a correctional facility similar to the culture found in this prison system.

Life Course Systems Power Analysis: Group of Older Adults in Prison

Based on the findings from the Hartford Prison Study, we have conducted a life course systems power analysis of the group of older adults in this northeastern prison system. It provides recommendations for improvement at the institutional (prison) level for older adults and the overall prison population.

Group Critical Analysis

Life experiences. A group of 677 older adults incarcerated in a northeastern prison reported an average of three traumatic or stressful life experiences in childhood, adulthood, or older adulthood. These experiences were characterized by being victims or witness to physical and sexual assault, mass disasters, family loss and separation, being diagnosed with a serious physical or mental illness, financial strain, and caregiver stress. They also commonly reported feel psychological distress at the time of the event, and the majority still felt affected by one or more of these experiences in the past year. The majority of older adults felt traumatic stress about being in prison and the neglectful and abusive conditions of confinement.

System of care interactions. The older adults reported that their experiences prior to prison took place in a variety of care systems, such as the family home, child welfare, health and mental health services, and the community neighborhood. In their current placement in prison, many reported some type of medical neglect and lack of access to needed health services. They also reported varying levels of access to mental health treatment, social services, family, and peer contact in prison.

Power dynamics. The older adults represented a diverse population based on personal characteristics such as age, race/ethnicity, gender, class, and mental and physical health status. Many reported trauma and oppression and felt particularly vulnerable and subject to abuse from younger and stronger incarcerated people and staff. Harassment, humiliation, and neglect were commonly reported. Several older adults reported significant stress related to their long prison sentences and repeated parole denials.

Suggested interventions at the institutional level. Meet with prison administration to discuss the issues facing older people in their institution and incorporate a trauma-informed approach in prison. Refer to a social worker to help address case management, physical and mental health, and social needs. Report the situation to the institutional ombudsman for further investigation. Request an organizing meeting of older adults on the unit to discuss how they would like the issues they raised to be addressed. Recommend trauma-informed care and conflict resolution models and empathy training for the entire prison community (staff and incarcerated people).

Final Reflections

Trauma is pervasive in society and is perhaps the least recognized epidemic affecting the modern world. This is a global phenomenon, and individuals, families, and communities are affected by directly experiencing, witnessing, or learning about traumatic or stressful life experiences. Unresolved trauma and stress influences the psychological, emotional, social, spiritual, and behavioral well-being of us all. It affects consciousness all the way to our collective unconscious. Research on diversity and trauma show that marginalized and oppressed groups are at the greatest risk of trauma, violence, and criminalization. Adults age 50+ in prison commonly report three or more traumatic or stressful life events in their lifetime, and the overwhelming majority report still feeling their lingering effects. This residual distress is exacerbated by the stressful prison environment; it would be difficult for any person, but is particularly difficult for aging and serious and terminally ill people, to survive and thrive in prison.

Despite adverse life experiences and the trauma of incarceration, many older adults in prison not only survive but thrive. How do they do this? In the next chapter, we explore the influence of coping and resilience as part of the psychosocial spiritual medicine that can assist in trauma recovery, aging, and overall wellness. When we were younger, most of us were taught to "listen to our wise elders." In many cases, we did not. However, these stories were not told in vain. Perhaps it is time to tune into them now.

It is not a surprise that crime and the aging prison population grew as it did. In fact, trauma is a common occurrence, and most of us are living in invisible prisons, locking our true selves away. Perhaps it is time to break the silence and listen now. Some older adults might have figured out a way to break through trauma and recover ourselves, our relationships, and the world. If so, personal and mass liberation and wellness will abound.

CHAPTER 4

"I TRY TO MAKE THE BEST OF IT"

A Look Inside the Resilient Minds of Older Adults in Prison

I try to make the best of it, I took a great big fall; I know my days are numbered, that's why I give my all. I pray for your forgiveness, Lord, my family, friends, as well. . . . I only ask one thing of you; I do not go to hell.

(prayer by an incarcerated older Latino)

D espite exposure to cumulative life experiences of trauma, stress, and oppression, a sizable number of older adults in prison are resilient and demonstrate adaptive coping. Evidence suggests that protective factors, such as coping resources, including having a positive view of yourself and the world, optimism, emotional awareness and regulation, self-reflection, physical exercise, social support, and spiritual practices (e.g., prayer and meditation), help people transcend trauma and promote health and well-being. This chapter continues to draw from the data of the Hartford Prison Study and the creative writing and photos of older adults in prison to illuminate others on how they cope with their past and current experiences, especially how some have found a way to rise above the trauma and stress of incarceration (figure 4.1). Integrating the arts and sciences, readers are guided to travel inside the resilient minds, hearts, and practices of older adults in prison. Through the lens of older people in prison, world assumptions, and coping resources theories, the chapter illustrates how trauma survivors in later life can unchain their minds. In essence, they can triumph over trauma, reclaim their innate positive

4.1

Source: ©Ron Levine/www.ronlevinephotography.com

view of self and others, and consciously reconnect to spirituality. It was found that older adults used coping practices as a form of biopsychosocial spiritual medicine to help promote health, well-being, creativity, and social and spiritual connection even under the duress of the stressful conditions of confinement.

In Their Own Words—Autobiographies of Mary and Joseph

Mary: An Incarcerated Older Woman

I am a 54-year-old woman who has spent my life sheltered. When I was 12 years old my parents separated and eventually divorced. During this time, I was a mother, wife, sister, and housekeeper. To make a long story short, my dad was a very strict Catholic with 7 children (6 girls, me being the third oldest, 1 brother who is the youngest), an abusive and mentally, emotionally, and physically alcoholic. He not only beat my mother but also us children. My dad was very deranged. He drew a gun on my mom, which warranted her to leave us children. Eventually we all left, through torture and drama, or were physically removed and reunited with my mom. To this day my mom is very depressed, ashamed, guilty, and remorseful for leaving us children. I believe she will suffer the rest of her life since she has already suffered 74 years of it. With me in here, I feel I have caused her more guilt and shame. My dad has since passed away. My relationship with him was limited, by his choice.

Since I have been in prison, I realized I chose men exactly like my father. I had been through several years of counseling prior to being locked up but was afraid to open up. At times, I am still the same and don't know why. I've lived my life, and still do, being scared, vulnerable, too trusting and just a loving, caring, compassionate, empathic hide-it-all person. To avoid this, I keep to myself and give little advice even though I have a lot to say inside but feel like I'm on display if I do. I don't like being criticized as I have always been.

I was married for almost ten years. I got married in 1995 at age 38 to a man nine years younger. I loved him so much, and no matter what he's put me through, I always will, without reason. I got pregnant and have a beautiful 15-year-old daughter who resides with my ex in Florida. Not a day goes by that my heart doesn't break because I haven't seen her really since March 2006. I also have a 29-year-old son. I raised him as a single parent. He served eight years in the military and was a challenge during his school years, and, in fact, still is today. He was married and is divorced with a son who is now 5 years old and living in Indiana with his mom. I love and adore both my children and feel I have really put them through shame.

How my experiences influence my current situation. Since I've been here in prison, I feel less worth a crap. Well, putting it bluntly, it's horrible. Some programs are helpful: Cage Your Rage/Anger Management. This is the program that really opened my eyes to see [how] my life stems back from when I was a child. My choices in men are based on what I saw when I was raised, so-called, by my dad. I am a very quiet, frightful, self-introverted adult who gets sick in the stomach. I don't know how to explain [this], but I don't want to be involved with people or this situation. I have faith that God has me here for a reason. I wanted revenge but not anymore. I was set up and am having a very difficult time getting someone to see it. I often wonder if I'm stupid or just plain naive. It's very difficult to try to find myself and explain myself where it's understandable. Shame, I deal with that every day in every part of my life. I have good days and bad ones. I just want to go home and live my life in a bubble with the ones I love. I pray recently for God to give me the acceptance. It's been since October 2006 that I've been locked up between the county and here at the prison with almost four years left. I have and still am appealing my case. It's sad that life is difficult. I've always been a person there for others and put myself last.

My experience of prison. I wouldn't recommend it to anyone of any age, color, culture, or human! In some respects, it has helped me in my faith and the strength it has given me. It has helped me realize I am important, but how do I change that? I have been exposed to several circumstances that my sheltered life prevented. I have learned to forgive but will never forget. It's just a shame I haven't had contact with my daughter. I worry about what others think of me and ask the question "Why?" all the time. Honestly, it totally sucks. I'm a 54-year-old who has lived a life for everyone, and I want to live a life for me as long as I'm well enough to do so.

A prison is a hard place. Pure Hell! I found I am more reserved, introverted, scared, and don't want to communicate at all. I am blessed to be treated with respect because I give respect. Not always is this the case, authority plays a powerful part. If you are in khaki, you are considered nonhuman. I take every day at a time and in stride. I have learned not to take things personally, don't make assumptions, let go, be impeccable with my words, and do the best I can. But I am called scary Mary. I miss my family and want to go home so bad. At first, this was a place to settle me down. Now I feel like my life has been stripped, and I don't know how I am to be accepted out in society. It's sad that people like me can't be given a chance to be out there and prove prison isn't for everyone. I don't feel there is enough mental health available on a regular basis or the comfortable feeling of just expressing yourself without the fear of being put in a cottage. Labels are so easily placed on people here.

The elders suffer the most because there isn't much for them, us. The medical here makes no sense. Until you have an ailment, you are put off and time holds you back. I have the start of osteoporosis, and I won't even complain about it because I am conditioned, yes conditioned to deal with my choice of doctors. Seeing how some people young and old are treated makes me suffer and deal with it. I look at it that I will deal with it when I get home. In the meantime, I hurt and deal with it. Prayer and God is what gets me through every day, moment, second, I am here. Overall, it's horrible and wouldn't wish this on my worst enemy. I am very unhappy. Trust and believe me on this.

Joseph: An Incarcerated Older Man

I am the second child of five with an Irish-German father and a Polish-Irish mother. They believed strongly in corporal punishment, and it was out of control. My mother was 16 when she conceived me. My parents were not neglectful, and indeed my father was a Cub Scout leader and helped build the town's little league stadium for us. He was all about helping get his sons [sports] programs. However, he hit us, and he would later explain to me that this was how he understood was the way to correct children's behavior. My mother comes from alcoholic parents and whipped us for such things as being late for curfew or not finishing dinner. I grew up afraid to speak to my parents.

My father befriended a man who became my Little League manager. This man molested me for years, sometimes in my parents' own home. I was afraid of my parents [and] couldn't tell them. As a result, when I was 13, I decided that I would never ever let anyone hurt me again and became what I saw as the toughest man on this Earth. I began doing whatever was dangerous. My schoolwork was easy, I even did my older brother's homework prior to hardening myself. I dropped programs and classes that would aim me toward college and "the sissy man life" [and] took up welding and played only football. I got a small motorcycle to ride dirt trails until I would be old enough to take to the street.

I joined the United States Marine Corps, not merely out of duty to my country but because it boasted at how tough they were. After release from the Marines, I got into a motorcycle club, moved up in the ranks, and became more hard core. One night at a bar I saw a man trying to lure young girls into the bathroom for the purpose of offering them cocaine (be it true or not in my head to sexually molest them), and I snapped a rivet. I along with a club brother got this guy out of the bar, and in a blinding rage I took his life. There is no excuse for what I did, and at the time, I had no clue what had happened. Years of self-evaluation and solitary contemplation have given me the answers to what happened and what I had to do to get ahold of the monster in control of me. There are some people I've dealt with to get an understanding and the assistance to become somewhat healed and on the road to becoming a man I'd want to be friends with should I meet him.

How my experiences influence my current situation. The more I sought to be the toughest dude on the planet, the further my humanity slipped from my grasp to the point that I blocked and locked away all caring feelings as being soft and vulnerable. They are the catalyst from which it all is rooted.

My experience of prison. This I must describe as a rollercoaster. I stayed in the hole, in ad seg, and in the security threat group management unit. And when my PTSD kicks in, I'm not a nice person. All these "isolation times" were the only times I could get perspective on certain behavior patterns that I finally started to adjust [in] the present to make a more positive tomorrow. Mandatory minimums and 85 percent NERA [no possibility of early release] do not deter crime [or] promote better behavior. I've been beaten into submission all my life, but the only thing [that] changed my behavior was an old man asking me "why [do] you always focus on the negative, why not use your leadership skills to make life better?" If all this get tough on crime worked, your prison system would not be exploding. Are we the evilest society on this third rock from the sun, or are our criminal justice policies just out of control and oppressive?

Coping in Prison

Individuals who experience traumatic events in childhood, adolescence, or adulthood may process these experiences in unique ways. For example, Mary has tended to internalize her emotions—fear, shame, anxiety, grief—and emanates a soft exterior. In contrast, Joseph has tended to bottle up his emotions—anger and rage—as well as his sensitivity. He externalized his emotions through contact sports, choosing military combat, and reacting to perceived threats with violence.

People of all ages use a variety proactive coping strategies or resources before, during, and after they are exposed to traumatic or stressful life experiences. A literature review about the aftermath of childhood trauma, health, and well-being in later life, sheds some light on the role of positive coping resources and resilience. Resilience acted as a protective factor later in life for people who have experienced childhood trauma. Resilience enabled older adults to better maintain their physical, mental, emotional, spiritual, and behavioral well-being.[1]

Protective factors tap inner and outer resources and include the physical, cognitive, emotional, social, and spiritual domains. Coping resources are characterized by feeling a sense of safety, high self-esteem, feeling satisfied with life, finding meaning in life, practicing forgiveness, engaging in physical activities, having a social support network, standing up against hatred and oppression, and promoting peace.[2] Mary and Joseph engaged in several of these coping strategies: physical exercise, cognitive coping (e.g., self-reflection and making meaning of their life), social coping (e.g., contact with mentors, family, individual or group therapy), and practicing spirituality in the form of connection to a higher self or God force.

In this chapter, we begin to unravel the secrets for transcending trauma and living a longer, healthier, and happier life—even amid environmental duress. We reveal the practices of our wise elders in prison and how some of them not only survive but thrive despite their prior accumulated disadvantages and living in a challenging prison environment. We explore their internal (e.g., thoughts, emotions, spirituality) and external (e.g., physical exercise and social contact) landscapes in prison. The coping activities in which older adults engage are a form of biopsychosocial spiritual medicine. These coping activities increase the odds of them transcending adverse trauma reactions stored in the mind and body. In addition, these activities have curative effects, promoting overall health, well-being, and productive aging even while in prison.

Older adults in prison navigate a challenging environment for daily survival. We can all better understanding how to survive and thrive by analyzing their experiences. This information can be used to improve both prison and community environments to facilitate health, well-being, and safety for people of all ages. We conclude with our research findings on how older adults in prison cope with the stressful conditions of confinement. To what extent do we have to test the human spirit through trauma, pain, suffering, and punishment in prison? How might older incarcerated adults change if we nurtured the human spirit with joy and love?

World Assumptions and Posttraumatic Stress and Growth

Individuals exposed to trauma, especially during childhood, may experience inner disruptions and cognitive and emotional distortions even later in life. Joseph sought to be the worst person on the planet due to his childhood traumas. It was his times of isolation in prison that gave him the opportunity to reflect and gain insights into his emotions and behavior. Joseph's PTSD symptoms are exhibited in the form of cognitive and emotional dysregulation, and they do not make him a "nice person." Estimates of posttraumatic stress disorder (PTSD) among incarcerated people of all ages range from 11 percent to 65 percent, which is much lower than the 65 to 95 percent of all people who report exposure to trauma.[3]

Exposure to trauma almost universally results in some psychological distress or alteration.[4] The impact of trauma on individuals may include disruptions in cognitions related to internal worldviews or world assumptions.[5] Internalizing a negative worldview may adversely influence emotions, behaviors, and judgment. Perhaps the most adverse effects of exposure to trauma are people's maladaptive psychological or behavioral coping responses. These responses may include serious mental health problems, such as depression, anxiety, or PTSD, and increase their risk of criminal behavior (e.g., illegal drug use and violence).[6]

Protective factors, such as coping resources, may help people develop a positive self-image and worldview, which in turn may influence positive health and well-being.[7] When Joseph took time to self-reflect, he was able to gain insights into "what had happened and what I had to do to get ahold of the monster in control of me." Mary also spent time in reflection and gained valuable insights, such as realizing that she "chose men just like her father." Her spirituality helped her view her experience in a positive light: "I have faith that God has me here for a reason. Prayer and God is what gets me through every day, moment, second, I am here."

Positive coping resources may account for why some individuals with difficult histories of traumatic and stressful events have a positive worldview and overall good health. Janoff-Bulman's world assumptions theory accounts for trauma, resilience, and posttraumatic growth (PTG).[8] It provides a framework that can be used to understand the inner world of incarcerated older adults (figure 4.2). When triggered by trauma, the internal worldviews of Joseph and Mary shifted from an innate positive view of self and others to a largely negative perspective, which influenced their thought processes, emotions, life choices, and behaviors before and during their current incarceration. The good news is

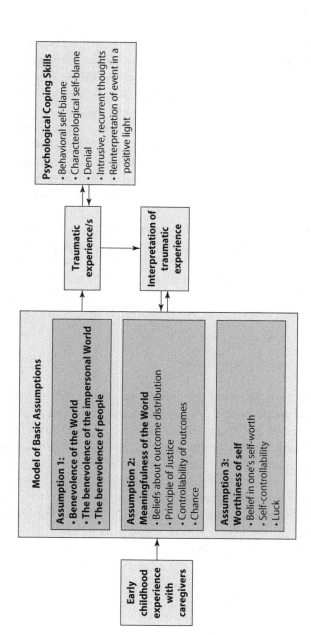

4.2 World assumptions theory

Source: Ronnie Janoff-Bulman, "Assumptive Worlds and the Stress of Traumatic Events: Applications of the Schema Construct," *Social Cognition* 7, no. 2 (1989): 113–36.

Early childhood experience with caregivers

Model of Basic Assumptions

Assumption 1:
Benevolence of the World
• **The benevolence of the impersonal World**
• **The benevolence of people**

Assumption 2:
Meaningfulness of the World
• Beliefs about outcome distribution
• Principle of Justice
• Controllability of outcomes
• Chance

Assumption 3:
Worthiness of self
• Belief in one's self-worth
• Self-controllability
• Luck

Traumatic experience/s

Interpretation of traumatic experience

Psychological Coping Skills
• Behavioral self-blame
• Characterological self-blame
• Denial
• Intrusive, recurrent thoughts
• Reinterpretation of event in a positive light

that research on people of all ages suggests that the incorporation of proactive coping resources (e.g., physical, cognitive, emotional, social, spiritual, root, and participatory coping) can help individuals better manage their lives in prison. This comprehensive biopsychosocial spiritual medicine can create momentum for a positive shift in internal world assumptions and reduce unwanted trauma reactions, including symptoms of PTSD, and promote posttraumatic growth.[9]

World assumptions theory explains how trauma and its lingering effects may influence individuals' views of themselves in the world. In some cases, traumatic experiences shatter the innate positive view of self (e.g., self-love) and the world (e.g., universal love and interconnection), and survivors may use maladaptive coping (e.g., self-blame and low self-esteem) and view their current life situation as unsafe and unjust. However, thoughts and emotions are changeable, and a negative focus can shift over time to viewing experiences in a positive light. World assumptions theory offers an inner doorway to help individuals transcend trauma and turn away from being a disempowered victim of circumstances and toward becoming an empowered creator of their experiences. For example, Joseph realized he did not have to continue defending himself from potential danger, that he could be a leader of himself and others. Mary realized that she could connect with God or a higher power to help her transcend this experience.

A Foundation for Posttraumatic Growth

World assumptions theory formed the foundation from which positive psychology theories of posttraumatic growth, such as the posttraumatic growth transformational model[10] and organismic valuing theory,[11] were built. The commonalities among these three perspectives are that they normalize (as opposed to pathologize) reactions to trauma and recognize the process and potential of trauma survivors to overcome adversity and experience profound growth and transformation.[12] For example, despite Joseph's past actions, he has the potential to honor his process toward transcending his trauma and reestablishing his positive sense of self and worldview. Similarly, Mary could honor the process of her past traumas and prison stress as her spirituality begins to reconnect with her inner self. Joseph and Mary could move from shame and fear to self-love, acceptance, and empowerment, especially if they were offered individual or group therapy or support groups.

World assumptions theory is based on the idea that we live in socially organized groups and that everyone is born with an innate propensity for positive core beliefs about the goodness of people in a caring and just world.[13] However, traumatic experiences run counter to a positive worldview and challenge the expectation of a caring and just world.[14] For example, Joseph experienced "a world locked away of all caring feelings and [he] put on a tough exterior." In contrast, Mary's experiences of parental and male partner abuse result internalizing her feelings, especially fear, anxiety, and shame.

When trauma is experienced during childhood, the consequences can be "shattered" world assumptions because the cognitive-emotional system of a child is not established in the psyche as firmly as that of an adult. Children who were abused or neglected by the very people they trusted may carry negative views of the self and the world into their adult lives. Both Mary and Joseph are in the process of shifting their views through the lens of a positive light.[15]

An early childhood environment in which children receive "good-enough" caregiving most often assures development of basic assumptions of a benevolent world and a worthy self. A positive childhood experience results in an exaggerated and optimistic outlook on the world that enables people to go through their everyday experiences with trust and security. Joseph's parents and his Little League coach were abusive, which influenced Joseph's internal construction that caregivers were not safe: "I grew up afraid of my parents" and "I was abused by my coach." When he was 13, Joseph decided to become the toughest man in the world and not let anybody hurt him anymore, which led him to "doing whatever was dangerous and avoiding the sissy man life." Since childhood Mary has identified herself as a victim of her experiences and responded by becoming invisible and not seeking the help she deserved. It is plausible that how Mary and Joseph responded to life stressors were also internal worldviews shaped by gender.

When traumatic events transpire in early childhood, alternate cognitive processing occurs that increases the risk of individuals committing a crime at some point in their lives.[16] These unresolved cognitive processes and the lack of trustworthy adults or service providers are risk factors for criminal offending. For instance, Joseph saw a group of women in a bar being lured by men and acted on his existing interpretation that they were at risk of sexual abuse. Mary seemed to be unable to defend herself in her home situation or in court: "I was set up and am having a very difficult time getting someone to see it."

Core Assumptions Affected by Trauma

Janoff-Bulman proposed three core assumptions that may be affected by trauma: benevolence of the world, the meaningfulness of the world, and worthiness of self.[17]

Benevolence of the world represents an individual's beliefs that people are trustworthy and the world, in general, is a good place.

Meaningfulness of the world represents an individual's beliefs in a world structured according to justice and fairness (good behavior is rewarded) and an individual's sense of control (human agency).

Worthiness of the self represents an individual's beliefs in his or her own
self-worth (self-esteem), internal self-control (ability to self-regulate
emotions), and personal luck (belief that one is lucky).[18]

If an individual's worldview becomes negative (the world is not a safe place;
people are untrustworthy), the person will carry those views and patterns
into interpersonal relationships. If individuals experience trauma, they may
perceive the world as unfair, feel they lack personal control over their life
circumstances, and may respond to the world through criminal offending or
revictimization. They may have low self-esteem, a low internal locus of control, and believe they are unlucky. Joseph covered his low sense of self-worth
by playing the role of being the toughest dude on the planet. Mary's low sense
of self-worthiness led her to make herself invisible. She became reserved,
introverted, and scared and didn't want to communicate at all with anyone
else in prison.

Negatively skewed world assumptions may result in maladaptive psychological coping responses in the face of traumatic experiences. For example, in
a sample of 168 college students, Janoff-Bulman found that sexual assault survivors who reported low self-esteem were more likely to attribute their assault
to a personal characterological flaw, such as "I am a bad person so bad things
happen to me" (self-blame).[19] In contrast, sexual assault victims with high
self-esteem attributed their sexual assault to a behavioral flaw that placed them
at risk, such as "I shouldn't have walked alone at night" (behavioral self-blame).
Trauma survivors who adopt behavioral self-blame feel they have a sense of
personal control, whereas those who adopt characterological self-blame remain
locked in a fixed and unchangeable world.

It is important that survivors, especially those who have also committed a
crime, come to peace with their choices. They can move beyond self-blame
to self-accountability as they reach for the positive light. In other cases, these
"shattered" world assumptions may induce adaptive psychological coping skills,
enabling them to reinterpret the event in a positive light by seeking spirituality
and social support.[20] Both Mary and Joseph are in the process of adapting positive coping resources to help them reframe their personal views of self and the
world. This positive view and meaning-making around unresolved traumatic
experiences opens the door for posttraumatic growth.

Rebuilding Assumptions

Recovering from trauma requires that individuals rebuild their positive world
assumptions. As Joseph noted, he had a breakthrough experience when an

older man in prison told him to take leadership of his own life. For individuals of all ages in the community or in prison, traumatic experiences may influence them to question their worldview, which previously was unquestionable and taken for granted. Rebuilding positive world assumptions takes time and differs from one individual to another. However, with a strong support system and a high level of introspection, it is doable. By reestablishing their shaken world assumptions, they will be able to function more effectively.[21] Shattered assumptions can be rebuilt through self-reflection, spirituality, or informal supports. The results of a latent class analysis by Maschi and Baer using the World Assumptions Scale (WAS) revealed a subgroup of older adults in prison who are resilient and have an overall positive worldview.[22]

When seeking professional help, cognitive processing therapy can act as a facilitator for individuals who are rebuilding their world assumptions. Additional interventions that may help individuals transcend the traumatic event into a new life are schema therapy, the seeking safety program, and eye movement desensitization and reprocessing (EMDR). In the next section, we review additional strategies used by older adults in prison to promote their health and well-being.

Coping Resources and Resilience

Coping resources theory can help explain why some older adults thrive in prison while others do not. Marting and Hammer define coping resources as "those resources inherent in individuals that enable them to handle stressors more effectively, to experience fewer or less intense symptoms upon exposure to a stressor, or to recover faster from exposure."[23] Similarly, Baum and Singer refer to coping resources as a "social and psychological prophylaxis" that can reduce the likelihood of stress-induced disease.[24] Individual coping resources are cognitive, emotional, spiritual/philosophical, and physical in nature, and social coping resources include social support from family, friends, and community. Coping generally refers to learning to adapt after difficult experiences.

A related concept to coping is resilience, which refers to an individual's ability to bounce back from these difficult experiences. Consistent with world assumptions and coping resource theories, the resilience literature also shows protective factors that are particularly important to overcoming adversity, such as self-introspection, emotional regulation, having control of one's life, being creative, and access to positive social support such as having a caring adult available, especially in childhood and adolescence.[25]

Coping and resilience can result in a positive shift in the perspective of oneself and one's relationship to the world. This shift is illustrated by the Words of

4.3

Source: ©Ron Levine/www.ronlevinephotography.com

Wisdom and the spiritual creative writing of Mr. J, an incarcerated older adult who refers to himself as having an Unchained Mind.

> I once was a Fool but now I am Wise!
> I once was Blind but now I See!
> I once was Deaf but now I Hear!
> I once was Ignorant but now I use Intelligence!
> YOU have your PhD,
> but I have the Knowledge and Inspiration that comes from a Higher Power,
> the one and only True GOD!
> A Mind is a terrible thing to waste, so is the Soul!

As his words suggest, Mr. J's unchained mind enables his eyes, ears, knowledge, and intelligence (inner knowing and soul wisdom) to be fully aware of his internal landscape and his relationship to the world.

Many studies have shown that incarcerated and aging people use a variety of coping strategies in their effort to manage life in prison. Coping resilience can be found in physical, cognitive, emotional, social, and spiritual domains.

Several studies suggest that social coping has an important role in positive adaptation among incarcerated people.[26] Picken found that participation in therapeutic groups and communities was beneficial for adjustment and coping for men in prison.[27] In a recent study by Sealock and Manasse, social coping had a significant effect on recidivism.[28] However, results varied by both offense and race, suggesting the need for a more intensive inquiry to help guide the allocation of resources among possible coping strategies and programs.

Spiritual coping also has been found to improve mental, emotional, and behavioral well-being among incarcerated people, especially in reducing depression, anxiety, and violence. Aday found that religion, in the form of reading scriptures and informal prayer, was the most important means of coping with prison life.[29] Religiosity/spirituality improved coping and reduced depressive symptoms and self-harm. In a review by Eytan of twelve empirical studies, religiosity/spirituality had a positive impact on inmates' behavior, reducing arguments, violence, and disciplinary sanctions.[30] Similarly, Allen and colleagues showed that incarcerated older adults who reported a greater number of daily spiritual experiences and a connection to God reported better emotional health.[31] This growing body of research supports the importance of biopsychosocial spiritual medicine in promoting coping resources and resilience, which in turn promotes trauma transcendence and overall health and well-being.

> Life Is a Privilege Prayer: Each morning before my feet hit the floor, I would say thanks for keeping me alive Dear Lord.
>
> (written by an incarcerated adult)

Neurobiology of Coping

In Their Own Words: Jamal

Now and upon my release in three months, I am interested in sharing insight that I consider valuable about the negative impact that periods of incarceration often have on prisoners. When I was sentenced, twenty years ago, the sentencing judge said to me: "I am not sentencing you to rehabilitation, this sentence is meant to be punishment." Since physical punishment is officially and constitutionally illegal, it must be assumed that the judge was talking about psychological (mental and emotional) punishment. I was sentenced to twenty-one to forty-four years of mental and emotional punishment. To cope with my stay in prison, I found it necessary to suppress and numb my emotions (which is unnatural). As a rule, I learned and disciplined myself to avoid emotional relationships because over time emotional relationships began to anger and enrage me. I am not sure what impact numbing my emotions will have on me upon my release. I have noticed this emotional detachment I have in many other prisoners, and I do not think it is a good thing. A person can easily lose a sense of their humanity by becoming emotionally numb. For one thing, it was not a deterrence from behaving contrary to the law. Now you must ask yourself what productive purpose did the punishment serve society?

Eustress, Distress, and Resilience

Individuals who experience trauma and stress commonly experience physiological and psychological responses in the body, brain, and mind. As the brain handles perceptual information regarding potential threats, it starts appropriate responses aimed at basic survival. For example, Jamal describes the trauma of incarceration and how he shut down his emotions. Jamal's response was an attempt to adapt in an extremely chaotic, violent, and overall maladaptive prison environment. As the brain and the nervous system regulate the physiological and psychological responses, the result may be either adaptive (eustress or positive stress) or damaging (distress or negative stress).[32] In the case of Jamal and many incarcerated individuals of all ages, it can be argued that it can be both.

Healthy eustress (positive stress) refers to an individual who perceives and copes with stressful challenges as if they were manageable. For example, successfully overcoming obstacles and adversity in the stressful prison environment could lead to feelings of accomplishment and transcendence. In contrast, distress (negative stress) comes with unpleasant and overwhelming feelings of being unable to cope with the stressors, anxiety, and excessive worrying about the future.[33] Jamal shut down his emotions as a survival strategy in response to the daily violence and abuse prevalent in his prison setting. For Jamal and others in similar situations, threatening life or death experiences may result in short- or long-term physiological and psychological harm. As James O noted in chapter 1, "when you treat a person like an animal, he becomes an animal."

Childhood exposure to toxic stress such as physical or emotional abuse, chronic neglect, exposure to violence, family chaos, hardship, caregiver abuse, mental illness, or substance abuse contribute to distress. This type of prolonged activation of the stress response systems can hinder not only brain development in early childhood years but also related systems, increasing the risk for stress-related disorders in adulthood.[34]

On a positive note, children who experience complex traumas may develop and refine coping resilience at any age, even later in life when in prison. Parental neglect and abuse toward children during the early weeks of life has resulted in children having fewer stress management skills, lower self-independence, and higher levels of anxiety and stress. However, unexpected biopsychosocial spiritual factors can play a key role in determining whether an early childhood traumatic experience will lead to maladaptive coping or to coping resilience. The degree of control a person has over the stress and the possibility that the person can change the situation are factors known to play an important role in the development of resilience.[35]

For individuals in prison, especially older people with frailty or disabilities, resilience becomes a challenge. However, individuals can learn resilience through experience and hardship by developing qualities that facilitate appropriate coping strategies, adaptation, and recovery from stress.[36] For example, imagine the difference that could be made if prisons were restructured to provide trauma-informed care and offer services that facilitate coping resilience among incarcerated individuals, with older adults serving as peer mentors. Imagine that prison staff were trained to manage the complexities of the prison environment in a humane way and that prisons provided self-care and wellness programming for the staff. We might then revisit Jamal's original question in this positive light: Would rehabilitation rather than punishment be more effective in assisting Jamal in turning his life around?

A Bright Sun Outside the Sally Port

The stressful social environmental conditions of prison may have an adverse physical and mental health effect on its inhabitants. Older adults are particularly vulnerable to these stressful conditions of confinement when coupled with the natural process of age-related physical and mental health decline. Yet there is a bright light of the sun outside the prison sally port. Based on existing theories and research, coping resources, especially in the physical, cognitive, emotional, spiritual, and social domains, seem to have a therapeutic effect when coping with stress and on the overall health and well-being of older people in prison as well as community-dwelling people of all ages.

Incarcerated older adults in the Hartford Prison Study described their internal worldview regarding stress and coping in prison. Based on their life experiences of cumulative trauma and stress, a pattern of "lived time" was documented while they were serving time in prison (figure 4.4). This represented a convergence of past, current, and anticipated future experiences of trauma and stress, coping, and resilience. Their internal world shifted along with their external prison environment, which was often described as monotonous, chaotic, and stressful. Unbalanced power dynamics existed (e.g., oppressor/oppressed) alongside balanced (e.g., self-empowerment, equitable relationships) dynamics.

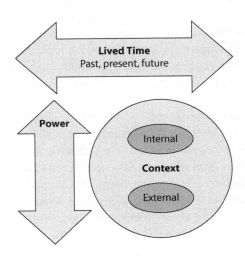

- **Lived time and meaning-making**
- Past, present, future exchange
- **Past**—Pathways to prison-differing time points of trauma and stress, coping, influencing to health and well-being in prison (early to later life)
- **Present**—Conditions of confinement
- **Future**—Community reintegration (prison reentry)
- Changing context-internal and external environment
- Examples-Family, community (i.e., homelessness), prison conditions, service system, internal and external coping
- Power dynamic—Oppressed and oppressor (prisoners/staff); dignified and/or equitable relations, self-empowerment

4.4 Prison life and meaning-making among older adults in prison

In Their Own Words: Jorge and the Prison Lifeline

My life experience as a resident of the department of corrections is not unusual. Like many, I have lost both parents, a sister, and a brother to death (figure 4.5). These unfortunate circumstances have allowed me to have unwanted emptiness, but it also strengthens me to become more responsible. As you may know, when a person is incarcerated, he has little to no dependency on help from family or friends, especially with today's economy being so out of control.

Being incarcerated does help a young person grow up fast if he chooses to apply himself to the small amount of available programs. But even if someone does not take advantage of the prison system programs, the chaplaincy department steps up in an effort to build and connect the young as well as the old with spiritual guidance by teaching men about the depravity of the creation of the human race and by sharing information about god and the connection to humanity. This is the prison system lifeline.

But like anything else in prison life, you can show a need for something worthwhile and useful, for what is best and good, but it's always left up to the individual to partake and truly submit to doing what is different in their life. Even if there is no agreement in all that . . . at least take what is good out of it and give common sense a chance. This has been my best experience of prison life. There is much, much more I would like to write.

4.5

Source: ©Ron Levine/www.ronlevinephotography.com

Biopsychosocial Spiritual Medicine of Older Adults in Prison

In the Hartford Prison Study, older adults wrote firsthand descriptions of coping in prison, and they described the sources of prison trauma and oppression as major sources of stress (see chapter 3). The other concept that emerged was coping resilience as a major source of managing their social and physical environment. Similar to prison trauma and oppression, older adults described coping as both an external and an internal experience. They engaged in one or more coping practices to facilitate their well-being. We identified seven domains of practices of well-being that older adults had described (see text box). These practice domains are root (basic needs), physical, cognitive, emotional, social, spiritual, and participatory (leadership) activities to promote well-being and reduce stress. Older adults report that their top five coping activities were exercise, reading the Bible, general reading, meditation, and participating in programs.

Practices of Well-Being of Older Adults in Prison

Domains	Description	Sample Quotes
Root	Basic needs/foundation: food, clothing, safety, grounded in love and family	"I try to be secure in myself." "I stay busy." "I avoid confrontation." "I stay away from negative influences."
Physical	Exercise (yard, run/walk, sports), medication	"I work out to relieve my stress." "I became a jogger and sprinter at 56 years old. I run five miles per day and sprint 105-yard sprints every other day."
Cognitive	Finding peace within, thinking positively, making healthy choices, puzzles, reading	"I try to think positive and try to meditate and read a great deal to take my mind off worries."
Emotional	Supportive emotional counseling, anger and stress management, music (listening), writing/ journaling, play and pleasure	"I participate every Monday in group therapy. Cage Your Rage program 10 weeks." "Write about experiences." "I have fun."
Social	Interaction with family, friends, or peers in prison, program participation	"I keep in touch with family members."
Spiritual	Church, God, pray, service to others	"Pray to God and go to church regularly here." "I attend religious services to offer my prayers and try as much as I can to be faithful to my oaths as a Muslim."

| Participatory | Leadership, taking classes or vocational training for personal advancement, teaching, leading a book club, advocacy | "I lead a bereavement group for other inmates." "I am a paralegal and seek justice for people in prison." |
| Multidimensional | Making art, music-making, yoga | "I do yoga, doctor, I do yoga." |

The majority of older adults reported participating in two activities of coping, with 23 percent indicating up to nine activities. Some individuals did not participate in any activities by choice or because there were no activities available to them. A quite interesting finding is that participants used participatory or empowerment practices to demonstrate leadership. One participant noted: "I have been facilitating a grief bereavement program once a week for twelve years and another group three times a year for the past seventeen years." Additional thick descriptions of coping resilience concern the role of family and social coping, participatory and spiritual coping, and cognitive and spiritual coping.

Family and social coping. I still have my family who keeps close contact with my children who live in Florida. My son and daughter were raised by their aunt who stepped up and took them. She's done a wonderful job raising them. My mother just sold her winder home she built in Florida in order to be near them for six months out of every year I've been incarcerated. I've followed every footstep of my children through my family because I don't have a relationship with my kids because of the obvious. And yes, I still cry myself to sleep some nights after all these years. One year ago, I became a grandfather. My baby girl gave birth to a beautiful son, and I have a picture of him. I often look into his eyes and see my daughter's eyes and even further and can see his grandmothers' eyes. Prison is tough, prison is bad, prison is everything you've heard of and more, but it's nothing to the reality of the pain I carry for my careless actions. (58-year-old incarcerated older adult)

Participatory and spiritual coping. There must be more concern for justice and fair play. The young criminal elements that I've met here just want to live a decent life, though finding a job in this economy is hard. Some of the men have shown an interest in God and His son Jesus Christ, and many are coming to the church services and attending the GED programs here. They are human beings, and many learned from gang members because they didn't have strong guidance in their homes.

4.6 "I live one day at a time not concerned if there's tomorrow, for now, the life I don't like cause I'm in prison I will borrow." (prayer written by an incarcerated adult)

Source: ©Ron Levine/www.ronlevinephotography.com

Cognitive and spiritual coping. When nobody wants you. I've changed my thoughts, and now I've changed my behavior. I realize that the right actions follow right thinking, though right thinking comes first. I have denounced and discarded all that characterizes my previous manner of life that kept me corrupt through lust and desires that spring from delusions. I now have purposely activated my mind and linked intelligence with a purpose to be lined up with God's Word. That with being constantly renewed in the spirit of my mind, having a fresh mental and spiritual attitude. I understand that I am accountable and responsible for the distorted images I once pasted upon the canvas of my imagination to get the picture painted of my life—surely I am to blame, so I live each day optimistically with renewed hope in search of tomorrow as I sit alone on the edge of night where many different complexities take shape and form in the prison life, but these are the days of our lives. . . . In the once-secret storm is an unfolding melodrama. Indeed! There's a God, and I am a dreamer and believer and that peace is found in knowing little. Dr. this was really meant to say thank you. (incarcerated older adult)

Final Reflections

Coping resources older adults in prison use have resulted in increases in positive world assumptions and posttraumatic growth. The coping narratives of older adults in prison are testaments to triumphing over adversity, even under the stressful conditions of secure confinement. Many older adults demonstrated an innate capacity to gravitate toward well-being. They engaged in inner and outer activities that promote wellness and deepen inner knowing and spiritual awareness. Several of them described their role in peer support and mentoring the younger generation in prison. One man remembered how a wise elder decades earlier, and not the judge or the prison regime, had helped him open his inner and outer eyes, learning that he could be a powerful yet sensitive man who cares about his relationship to others and the world.

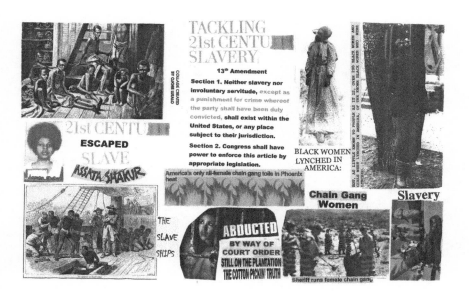

4.7 Tackling twenty-first-century slavery

Research has shown that coping deficits such as poor problem solving and negative affect heighten the risk of maladaptive behaviors such as committing a criminal offense and recidivating.[37] However, it does not take a rocket scientist or even a social science researcher to enlighten the public to the flaws in our communities and in the criminal justice system. It is just plain old common sense.

The stories of society's elders in prison speak for themselves. The collage in figure 4.7 was created by formerly incarcerated older adults, and it reveals that much more work needs to be done. We have heard their cry for help. From a new place of awareness and inner knowing, what is your perspective on what should be done, if anything at all?

CHAPTER 5

TRAUMA, MENTAL HEALTH, AND MEDICAL CONCERNS OF OLDER ADULTS IN THE PRISON SYSTEM

Decades of research, theory, and practice have established the connection between trauma experiences, psychiatric and substance use issues, and somatic complaints. However, in prisons much of the work has been focused on the younger prison population. In this chapter, we briefly review what we know thus far about older adult mental health care and then discuss how these variables manifest for an older adult prison population. It is our hope that this chapter inspires implementation of some (or all) of the training recommendations we provide in part II of this book.

Posttraumatic stress disorder (PTSD) is prevalent in the prison system.[1] However, a gap still exists in the research and practice literature regarding the lifetime/current trauma experiences and PTSD symptoms of older adults in the prison system.[2] This gap is due in part to the limited research on trauma exposure and PTSD focused on older adults in general.[3] Only a few epidemiological studies focus on traumatic exposure and PTSD lifetime prevalence in older adults. Our discussion of older adult trauma and overall mental health care in the prison system begins with a brief overview of these studies.

Older Adult Trauma Exposure and PTSD

A survey using a PTSD checklist by Frans et al. found that 73.7 percent of the Swedish older adults reported exposure to traumatic events, but the younger and middle-aged adults showed higher rates of trauma exposure.[4] However, other studies have reported higher rates of older adult trauma exposure when compared with younger or middle-aged adults.[5] Most research supports the finding that current PTSD rates decline with age even for individuals in groups with high PTSD rates, such as former prisoners of war or Holocaust survivors. For example, NCS-R data show PTSD to be less common among older adults than it is in the general population,[6] with 4.7 percent of older adults age 55 to 64 reporting PTSD in the prior year. However, only 0.6 percent of those age 65 to 74, 0.1 percent of those age 74 to 84, and 0.7 percent of persons 85 and older reported PTSD in 2010.

Several studies state that symptoms of PTSD may present in different forms in older adults and that this complicates diagnostic conclusions.[7] First, trauma may not be experienced until old age. Second, the trauma experienced much earlier in life may lead to chronic PTSD with symptom severity fluctuating over the life span. Third, PTSD may have a delayed onset in older age following years without symptoms. Some adults may have controlled their symptoms, sometimes via substance use,[8] or symptoms may not have been identified as PTSD by the individual or by professionals.

Although the data tend to show a decrease in PTSD symptoms over time, some studies report different experiences for trauma survivors who show delayed onset or for those whose symptoms gradually increased over time.[9] Even here, however, the results are somewhat mixed. Delayed-onset PTSD in older adults is a controversial concept, with some scholars arguing that this is actually the result of misdiagnosis, such as incorrectly identifying PTSD symptoms as indicative of dementia.[10]

Andrews, Brewin, Philpott, and Stewart[11] showed that delayed-onset PTSD (absent earlier symptoms) is rare; however, if delayed-onset is defined as exacerbation of earlier symptoms (or subsyndromal symptoms), then older adult delayed-onset PTSD occurs frequently.[12] Research on later-life onset PTSD focuses on the factors that contribute to the development or exacerbation of the disorder as well as the impact on the older adult.[13] For example, Solomon, Helvitz, and Zerach[14] found that veterans diagnosed with PTSD reported an older subjective age than veterans not diagnosed with PTSD. This often-reported finding underscores how trauma experiences and PTSD symptoms facilitate a substantial impact on the individual. Further evidence of this impact is seen in the recent finding that older adult veterans diagnosed with PTSD also reported poor physical health.[15]

Palgi expanded on the weathering hypothesis (i.e., emotional wear-and-tear in older age) to explain how older subjective age may result from a level of traumatic exposure endured later in life that taxes the adult's coping resources, thus impeding the successful management of PTSD symptoms.[16] Others argued the inverse, stating that subjective age may instead exacerbate already present

PTSD (or subsyndromal) symptoms.[17] These findings seem to underscore a relationship between PTSD symptoms and older age identity.[18]

In the study of traumatic exposure and PTSD, explanations of subjective age can be conceptualized within a recovery capital framework.[19] Recovery capital consists of internal and external resources that initiate and maintain psychological healing and recovery. Cloud and Granfield discuss four components of recovery capital: cultural capital, physical capital, human capital, and social capital.[20] Cultural capital consists of the beliefs associated with cultural group membership. For example, Boehnlein reported on how cultural belief systems, along with traditional family and social role expectations, influence the psychological recovery from severe trauma.[21] Physical capital includes finances, housing, and food. Acierno, Ruggierio, Kilpatrick, Resnick, Saunders, and Best compared risk factors for adults age 60 and older and adults younger than 60 affected by the 2004 Florida hurricanes; they found that low income along with a greater number of days displaced from their homes led to increased PTSD risk for the older adults but not the younger adults.[22] Human capital encompasses acquired and inherited personality traits and functioning (e.g., personal characteristics, skills, and mental health). Wrenn, Wingo, Moore, Pelletier, Gutman, Bradley, and Ressler discussed the critical impact of resiliency on the trauma experience and recovery process.[23] Social capital includes meaningful relationships (friends, family) supportive of trauma recovery efforts. The National Center for PTSD encourages family members of veterans struggling with trauma exposure and PTSD symptoms to support the healing process.[24] These four recovery capital components sound *very similar* to the coping resources and world assumptions so critical to the psychological healing process discussed in chapter 4.

PTSD and Co-Occurring Psychiatric Disorders in Older Adults

A meta-analysis highlighted seven significant risk factors for PTSD:[25]

- A history of prior trauma(s)
- Preexisting mental disorders
- Family history of behavioral health disorders
- Perceived threat to one's life during the traumatic event
- Perceived social support following the trauma
- Intense negative emotional responses immediately following the trauma
- Peritraumatic dissociation (i.e., dissociative experiences during/following the trauma)

The second risk factor, preexisting mental disorders, is critical in evaluating PTSD in older adults. Approximately 80 percent of all PTSD cases also have a co-occurring psychiatric disorder (lifetime prevalence data).[26] Consequently, a discussion of older adult PTSD must include a review of the most commonly reported co-occurring psychiatric disorders.

Mood Disorders in Older Adults

Mood disorders are common in older adults, including unipolar (depressive disorder) and bipolar subtypes. Prevalence data indicate that unipolar depression occurs in 10 to 38 percent of the older adult population.[27] Older adult depression is misdiagnosed or underdiagnosed in more than 60 percent of all cases.[28] Clinical data indicate that late-life bipolar disorder accounts for 4 to 8 percent of the inpatients in psychogeriatric units.[29] Research validates the important role of concurrent medical illness in older adults with depression.[30] In addition, adverse life events, such as losses, are a typical psychosocial risk factor for older adult suicide.[31] Furthermore, multiple stressors beyond adverse life events have been associated with suicidal behavior; these stressors sometimes precipitate a mood episode.[32]

Haigh, Bogucki, Sigmon, and Blazer reviewed older adult depression and draw a few general conclusions.[33] One, major depressive disorder is less common in late life but follows a more chronic course than for younger adults. Two, older adults with subsyndromal depressive symptoms reported impairment similar to diagnosable major depressive disorder. And three, late-life depression may be symptomatically different from depression earlier in life, but more research is needed to clarify these differences.

Bipolar disorder studies indicate that mania is a feature of 4.6 to 18.5 percent of geriatric psychiatric admissions.[34] Dols, Kupka, van Lammeren, Beekman, Sajatovic, and Stek found that late-onset mania in older adult inpatients diagnosed with bipolar disorder was 44.2 percent.[35] They further argued that late-life mania is not rare for older adult psychiatric inpatients.

Hegeman, Kok, van der Mast, and Giltay[36] noted that major depression in older adults may come with a somatic presentation (e.g., weight loss, insomnia, fatigue, pain), whereas younger adults may present with symptoms of guilt, depressed mood, or impaired sexual functioning. Valiengo, Stella, and Forlenza argue that the identification of depression in older adults is challenging due to the dissimilar array of symptoms compared to those in younger adults.[37] For instance, sadness (a common symptom associated with depressed mood) may not be a primary symptom in older adults. The following scenarios are possible:

- The older adult is depressed but does not wish to discuss emotions.
- The older adult does not recognize these symptoms as problematic and indicative of distress (i.e., they have become accustomed to feeling this way).

- The older adult presents with some less obvious symptoms of depressed mood, but because of the limited training of the diagnostician or ageism, the concept of older adult depression is not considered.[38]

Anxiety Disorders in Older Adults

Subramanyam, Kedare, Singh, and Pinto report that anxiety is one of the most common older adult mental health disorders,[39] and subsyndromal anxiety is even more prevalent than depressive and cognitive disorders. Generalized anxiety disorder (7.3 percent) is the most prevalent in older adults, followed by phobias (3.1 percent), panic disorder (1 percent), and obsessive compulsive disorder (0.6 percent). Ayers, Strickland, and Wetherell underscore several critical risk factors for anxiety disorders in older adults:

- Chronic medical conditions
- Poor health overall
- Sleep disturbances
- Stressful life events[40]

Anxiety disorders in older adults have serious consequences for a successful recovery from illness and overall quality of life.[41] Consequently, older adult anxiety disorder is of great public health importance.

Older adult anxiety is associated with a variety of health issues that include heart disease[42] and gastrointestinal disorders.[43] Older adult anxiety may also be a risk factor for the onset of late life depression,[44] and the misuse of anti-anxiety medications such as benzodiazepines may initiate a substance use disorder.[45] Similar to mood disorders, subsyndromal symptoms complicate identification and diagnosis of older adult anxiety. When using the less rigid diagnostic criteria of subsyndromal symptoms, Grenier and colleagues noted that the rate of anxiety increased from 5.5 percent to 26.2 percent for older adults,[46] which reinforces the importance of subsyndromal symptom consideration in older adult anxiety diagnosis.

Substance Use Disorders in Older Adults

The challenges of older adult substance use disorder (SUD) are documented in a rapidly growing body of research.[47] In the population 60 years old and older, 5.4 percent of adults reported illegal drug use in the past year.[48] Liu and Satterfield underscore that numerous complications exist for older adults with SUD.[49] For instance, older adults may be more sensitive to substances ingested at low levels,[50] may have interactions between substances and prescribed medications,[51] may demonstrate increased tolerance levels,[52] and may struggle with increased dementia and other cognitive impairments.[53]

In addition to alcohol and illegal drug use, older adults also struggle with prescription medications. Adults age 65 and older consume large amounts of over-the-counter medications, and many of them have a strong abuse potential:[54] benzodiazepines (for anxiety, insomnia, or seizures), opioids (for pain), and stimulants (for weight management or attention/concentration). Wu and Blazer noted that adults age 50 to 64 were more likely to misuse prescription medications than their older peers.[55] However, individuals in their fifties and early sixties will eventually grow into adults age 65 and older.

Neurocognitive Disorders in Older Adults

Neurocognitive disorder (NCD) exists on a continuum from mild to major cognitive and functional impairment. Major NCD results in significant cognitive decline relative to a previous level of functioning, whereas mild NCD involves moderate cognitive deficits that do not interfere with basic daily functioning but are associated with greater effort to maintain functioning.[56] A comprehensive review of the literature by Quereshi and colleagues concluded that individuals with PTSD demonstrated symptoms of cognitive impairment more often than those with a history of trauma exposure but no PTSD diagnosis.[57]

There seems to be a relationship between PTSD and dementia[58] as well as a relationship between PTSD and NCD. For example, recurrent major depressive episodes in earlier adulthood may increase the risk of dementia in later life.[59] In addition, late-life anxiety onset is associated with cognitive impairment and decline, thus requiring the need for neuropsychological testing to determine any cognitive domains affected by older adult anxiety.[60]

Health-Related Challenges for Older Adult Prisoners

Older inmates have a unique combination of physical and mental health problems.[61] Among state prisoners in a 2004 survey of inmates in state and federal corrections facilities age 45 and older, the majority (68.5 percent) reported some type of physical or mental health problem.[62] Prison health challenges are so numerous that the health status of prisoners in their fifties is viewed as equivalent to the health status of nonincarcerated community members in their seventies.[63] Older inmates often experience biopsychosocial problems and needs, particularly related to their exposure to unhealthy environments and habits as well as advanced physiologic age. Their health histories often include trauma and mental health issues, including serious mental illness.[64]

Most research on the impact of past traumatic experiences among older adults focuses on experiences in a community population. Traumatic past experiences appear to affect the physical health status of older adults.[65] For example, in a nationally representative sample of older adults, the young-old (age 65–74), the old-old (75–84), and the oldest-old (85 and older), Hochstetler, Murphy, and Simons found that prior traumatic exposure measured by the Traumatic Life Events Inventory was associated with declining health. Age differences among the sample had a significant impact on health in which the young-old were at greatest risk for health problems. The health and mental implications for older adult prisoners are of even more concern because they are living in a very stressful prison environment.[66]

Effects of Prison on Older Adult Offenders' Health

In the first part of the chapter, we addressed various mental health issues faced by older adults. In this section, we bridge those issues with the general stressors of the prison system as it is experienced by older adults. It is generally believed that the prison experience is a stressor that can exacerbate older adults' mental health symptoms.

Prison as a Stressor

The prison environment itself is a source of traumatic and stressful events for older adults. In a survey by Struckman-Johnson and Struckman-Johnson of 1,800 prisoners in a state prison, 20 percent had been pressured or forced to have at least one unwanted sexual contact (8 percent of the sample was age 48 or older).[67] Fifty percent reported being forced to have anal, vaginal, or oral intercourse, and 25 percent reported being gang raped.

Older adults in prison indicate that coping with death and dying, especially if it were to happen in prison, compounds the stress of prison life. Research suggests that a significant stressor among older prisoners is the fear of dying in prison.[68] From 2001 to 2006, 6,936 state prison inmates age 55 or older died in prison.[69] This includes death due to illness, AIDS, suicide, accidents, homicide, drugs/alcohol, and unknown causes. This represented 37.5 percent of all older state prisoner deaths during these years. In a sample of 102 older adult prisoners, Aday explored how family and institutional social support influenced prisoners' feelings of distress related to dying. He found that higher levels of social support had a significant inverse relationship to older prisoners' fear of death.[70]

The stress of prison was further explored in a study by Maschi, Viola, and Morgen[71] in an effort to understand the relationship between accumulated interpersonal, social-structural, and historical trauma and stressful experiences on mental well-being in later life. In a sample of 677 adults age 50 and older in prison, 70 percent reported having experienced one or more traumatic or stressful life experience. Participants also reported an average of eleven occurrences of multilevel trauma and stressful life events and lingering subjective distress related to these events. Results of a structural equation model revealed that internal and external coping resources had a significant inverse effect on the relationship between trauma or stressful life experiences and mental well-being.

Individuals who experience one or more difficult periods of chaos or change, combined with the stressful conditions of institutional confinement, are exposed to a heightened risk of adverse mental well-being. Among older adults in prison, these experiences may include being exposed to childhood physical and sexual victimization, the unexpected death of a loved one, being diagnosed with a serious illness, participating in combat, natural or manmade disasters, and financial stress or poverty.[72] Further work by Maschi, Viola, and Koskinen analyzed the experiences of 677 incarcerated adults age 50 and older who reported trauma, stress, and coping in prison. The lack of contact with and concerns about family were the primary cause of trauma and stress (45 percent), followed by interpersonal issues (31 percent), institutional problems (29 percent), and cultural differences (15 percent).[73]

Incarcerated youth and adults enter the prison system with complex trauma and stress histories that place them at heightened risk for strain across their life course.[74] In a study of 373 male juvenile offenders incarcerated in the California Department of Juvenile Justice facility, participants reported trauma and stress from a variety of living conditions, including residing in a dangerous neighborhood, living with a divorced parent, and experiencing the death of a loved one or close friend. Many individuals had a history of childhood physical and emotional abuse and had lived with one or more parents who used or abused alcohol or drugs.[75] In another study of 224 incarcerated adult women, more than half (64 percent) reported a history of childhood sexual abuse.[76] In a sample of fifty-nine incarcerated and fifty-five wait-listed women, participants reported abuse histories before prison as a child or as an adult that included forced sexual intercourse (72 percent), physical assault (86 percent), and being attacked with a weapon (56 percent).[77] In a sample of 677 older adults in prison, 70 percent reported a history of some type of life course trauma that causes them a high level of subjective stress. These traumas included childhood physical or sexual abuse, combat and war experiences, living in a violent neighborhood, the death of someone close, caregiving stress, having another incarcerated family member, or being diagnosed with a serious illness.[78]

A great deal of information is available on trauma prior to incarceration, but little research has been done on the sources and consequences of trauma and stress related to incarceration among older adults in prison. For many incarcerated older adults, the prospect of living out the remainder of their lives in prison is highly stressful.[79] Isolation, boredom, bullying, and fear of potential victimization from physical and sexual assault have adverse physical or psychological consequences.[80] In Aday's study of twenty-five first-time older adult offenders housed in a maximum security facility in the southeastern United States, many reported feelings of fear, depression, and anxiety as a result of the vulnerability of living in a hostile environment and feelings of shame related to the social stigma of crime. They expressed worries about declining health and uncertainty due to continual changes in the quality of health care delivered.[81] Other studies have found that older adults in prison report feeling lonely due to separation from their families and are depressed or anxious because they lack choices regarding their living conditions.[82]

These issues regarding trauma and stress related to incarceration, either alone or in combination, can exacerbate current psychiatric distress or facilitate the development of new mental health disorders. Mental health experiences for older adults in prison can be conceptualized as an adverse reaction to the extreme stress of prison. According to Selye, a response pattern to chronic stress occurs in three stages.[83] First, the individual has an alarm reaction, which is an adrenaline discharge response to the shock of one or more events. For older adults in prison, this can be the initial shock of first being incarcerated or being a victim of, or witness to, prison violence by guards or other inmates. A subsequent countershock is characterized by increased adrenocortical activity. If the intolerable stimulus continues, such as serving a long prison sentence or being subject to daily prison violence, the individual enters the second stage of resistance wherein the alarm reaction disappears. Although resistance to the original stressor appears to increase, the capacity to tolerate other stressors, such as separation from family, decreases. If the stimulus continues, resistance gives way to exhaustion. This theory suggests that the stress of incarceration may have an adverse influence on health and well-being or exacerbate chronic or serious illnesses among incarcerated people.

Older Adult Prisoners and Mental Health

Offenders have documented mental health disorders, including PTSD, anxiety, depression, and impulse control disorders, that could be a consequence of previous life course traumas. The findings that earlier traumatic experiences may have ongoing and cumulative mental health consequences into older adulthood, including psychiatric disorders, maladaptive stress responses, and revictimization, suggest that older adults in prison may be at increased risk.[84]

However, there is limited research on how older prisoners process trauma and stressful life events. Studies using community samples of older adults suggest that the accumulation of life course trauma and stressful life events can increase the risk of adverse emotional, psychological, and behavioral responses, including posttraumatic stress symptoms. Little research has examined older adult prisoners' life course accumulation of trauma and stressful life events and their current subjective impressions and associated psychiatric symptoms. The lack of research on trauma and stressful life events among older prisoners is a significant oversight that needs to be rectified. Older prisoners are at a higher risk than their younger counterparts for injury, victimization, declining health, and dying in prison.[85] If exposure to cumulative trauma and stressful life events continues to be unidentified and unaddressed, unresolved subjective distress about these events may increase the persistence of or resurface symptoms of posttraumatic stress.[86]

The life course perspective emphasizes how personal and historically significant life events, social relationships, and age act as critical factors that influence individual development and later life outcomes, including mental health.[87] Age also may act as a protective factor because subjective experiences of past trauma and stressful life events often change over the life course. Over time individuals may develop more resilient responses, such as cognitive and emotional coping resources, including intellectual and emotional maturity. Similarly, cumulative advantage/disadvantage theory examines the cumulative impact of trauma and stressful life events, such as violent victimization, poverty, financial strain, and poor health, and asserts that these events may have a cumulative life course effect on individuals' overall well-being.[88] Adaptive emotional and cognitive coping resources may act as protective factors. For some older prisoners, it is plausible that the accumulation of adverse traumatic and stressful experiences contributed to their disadvantaged position, especially if they continued to feel unresolved subjective distress about these events.[89]

Sexual victimization should garner individualized attention because of the disproportionately high rates of previous sexual victimization within this population. Sexual victimization among offenders occurs at much higher rates than in the general population,[90] and individuals with traumatic victimization experiences prior to incarceration are at increased risk for revictimization in prison. If traumatic histories are left unrecognized and unaddressed, a cycle of retraumatization and risk of sexual victimization will continue to fill prisons with victims in need of specialized care.[91]

Research indicates that childhood or adult sexual victimization (or direct exposure to such victimization) may have persistent or intermittent mental or physical effects, such as continued revictimization, psychiatric disorders, maladaptive stress responses, physical disabilities, and even premature death.[92] The type, timing, and duration of symptoms may vary. For example, subjective traumatic experiences that first occur in childhood may be accompanied by feelings of intense fear, helplessness, or horror.[93] These feelings may occur immediately following the childhood traumatic event or remain dormant and then resurface in later life.[94] When a traumatic experience is marked by intensity, duration, and chronicity, such as prolonged exposure to sexual victimization, the likelihood of posttraumatic stress symptoms is also prolonged and may extend later into the life course.[95] Maladaptive coping strategies (such as substance use) may develop throughout the life course.

Many prisoners enter the prison system with a substance use disorder or problematic substance use behaviors. The National Center on Addiction states that substance use disorder (SUD) is a pervasive problem in the U.S. prison system, suggesting that one-half to two-thirds of those incarcerated meet the criteria for substance abuse or dependence disorders.[96] Fazel, Yoon, and Hayes found that alcohol use disorder was highly prevalent in prisoners, with a pooled estimate of 24 percent.[97] They also found that drug use disorder was as high as the alcohol estimates, and possibly higher for female prisoners, with a pooled estimate of 51 percent. Although there is ample research on prisoners and substance use (see CSAT for review[98]), most of this work has focused on younger offenders, and very little research addresses older offenders' SUD issues. In an attempt to fill that gap, Maschi, Gibson, Zgoba, and Morgen examined older and younger offenders with substance use disorder.[99] Older offenders possessed significantly more traumatic experiences, negative reactions to these traumas, heightened stress, and more mentally unhealthy days per month than younger offenders, and this was coupled with significantly weaker cognitive coping resources to handle these psychological stressors. Despite the self-reported psychological distress, the majority of older offenders with SUD did not receive in-prison mental health or SUD treatment services. Only one-quarter to one-third had a visit with a psychologist, social worker, or psychiatrist in the past three months, and only one-third had received any form of in-prison SUD treatment or AA/NA meeting services in the past three months.

Older Adult Trauma, Mental Health, and Addiction Experiences in Prison

We reviewed some recent basic prison demographic data in the introduction to this book. Those data tell an important story about criminal offense histories,

including racial/ethnic, gender, and sentencing experiences for those in the
U.S. prison system. We make a few additional points here:

- Older adult mental health/addiction diagnostic issues are a developing field,
  and many areas lacking consensus.
- Myriad variables can play a role in how an older adult experiences and
  presents mental health issues.
- Older adult mental health/addiction issues for those incarcerated are in great
  need of theory building and research inquiry.

To emphasize the need for additional research, we provide a brief and incomplete review of data from a publicly available version of the 2004 "Survey
of Inmates in State and Federal Correctional Facilities" conducted for the
Bureau of Justice Statistics by the Bureau of the Census. The survey provides nationally representative data on inmates held in state and federally
owned and operated prisons. Data were collected via personal interviews
conducted from October 2003 through May 2004, with inmates providing
information such as current offense and sentence, criminal history, family
background and personal characteristics, prior substance use and treatment
programs, and prison activities, programs, and services.[100] We have included
data only for those 50 years old and older (14.8 percent of the total sample),
providing a basic—but telling—picture of the experiences faced by older
adults in prison. However, more research both on the older adult in prison
and a comparative analysis between older and younger adults in prison needs
to be pursued.

Physical and Sexual Abuse

Of older adults with an abuse history, 52.4 percent reported that the abuse
occurred before they were 18 years old (i.e., an adverse childhood experience). The relationship between physical or sexual abuse and trauma, PTSD,
and other mental health issues is well established, and table 5.1 illustrates
that older adult offenders are at significant risk for the development or
exacerbation of mental health issues. For example, an older adult with
a physical or sexual abuse history who witnesses or is a victim of physical
or sexual abuse in prison (which is quite common[101]) is at high risk for retraumatization. If retraumatized, the need for mental health services is critical.
However, in-prison comprehensive mental health and addiction services
are quite limited,[102] leaving many older adult prisoners to suffer and worsen
in silence.

TABLE 5.1 Lifetime prevalence of physical and sexual abuse

Abuse Type	Number in Sample	Percent
Physical abuse only	42	7.7
Sexual abuse only	14	2.6
Both physical and sexual abuse	28	5.1
Not abused	447	81.7
Missing data	16	2.9

Substance Use

Older adults reported illegal substance use, and a little over one-quarter indicated illegal substance use in the month before their most recent offense (table 5.2). This speaks to the pressing need for effective substance use screening at prison entry that identifies the unique history and presentation of potential problematic substance use in the older adult offender.[103] How many of these older adults were using illegal substances to cope with mental health symptoms related to trauma experiences and other psychiatric disorders?

These data are important for two reasons. First, of the 547 older adults studied, 23.8 percent met *DSM-IV* criteria for substance abuse, and 18.5 percent met *DSM-IV* criteria for substance dependence.[104] Consequently, a good number of the older adult offenders reporting treatment history data were in

TABLE 5.2 Illegal substance use in month before the offense (minimum 5% reported)

Substance Used	Number in Sample	Percent
Any illegal substance	149	27.2
Marijuana	80	14.6
Cocaine/crack	76	13.9
Stimulant medication without prescription	36	6.6
Methamphetamine	31	5.7
Heroin/other opiates	28	5.1

TABLE 5.3 Substance use treatment history

History	Number in Sample	Percent
Any treatment ever	90	16.5
Any treatment ever while incarcerated	56	10.2
Any treatment ever while on probation/parole	24	4.4
Any treatment ever while under correctional supervision	69	12.6
Any treatment since admission to prison	41	7.5

prison with a current or previous substance use issue. From that perspective, these numbers seem lower than expected.

Two, as discussed by Sartre, Morgen, and myriad others, older adult substance use treatment is unique because of presentation, problematic symptoms, and co-occurring disorder prevalence.[105] Consequently, consistent age-appropriate treatment is critical. The data in table 5.3 include "any treatment ever," which can easily capture those who went to treatment for only a few sessions or sporadically. Recall that many older adult offenders, despite having a substance use issue (as well as reporting significantly more traumatic experiences, negative reactions to these traumas, heightened stress, and more mentally unhealthy days per past month), failed to receive adequate in-prison substance use care.[106] Only one-third of older offenders received any form of in-prison treatment or AA/NA meeting services in the past three months. A much more thorough examination of substance use treatment services is needed to adequately evaluate the quality and consistency of in-prison substance use prevention and treatment care.

Mental and Physical Health

The quality and consistency of mental health services (table 5.4) and physical health services (table 5.5) vary throughout the correctional system. The problems with prison mental health and medical care are well documented,[107] as is the $8.1 billion spent on prison health care services for incarcerated individuals in fiscal year 2015. However, more research is needed to understand the effectiveness of medical and mental health care in prison, although reporting limitations may impede the ability to fully capture the scope of medical and mental health care needed.

A legitimate question in need of further inquiry is how many older adults failed to receive mental health services due to self or professional screening

TABLE 5.4 **Mental health history**

History	Number in Sample	Percent
Mental health treatment one year before arrest	74	13.5
Mental health treatment since admission	106	19.6
Taking prescription medication for mental health at arrest	55	10.1
Taking prescription medication for mental health since prison admission	93	17.0
Diagnosed with at least one mental health disorder	127	23.2
Never admitted overnight at mental health hospital	494	90.3
Diagnosed as seriously mentally ill or admitted to mental health hospital in year before arrest or since admission	51	9.3

TABLE 5.5 **Physical health history**

History	Number in Sample	Percent
HIV+	5	0.9
Any medical problem	394	72.0
Currently diagnosed with cancer	13	2.4
Currently diagnosed with diabetes	98	17.9
Ever diagnosed with TB	39	7.1
Seen a doctor since prison admission for current medical problem	357	65.3
Surgery since admission	117	21.4

that did not meet the *DSM-IV* criteria for a diagnosable mental health disorder. How many older adults came to prison with subsyndromal mental health issues (e.g., anxiety, mood, or trauma-related issues) that caused them distress and impairment but went unrecognized, only to slowly exacerbate during the long course of exposure to various prison stressors?

Recidivism

In a cross-section correlational study of 607 adult males age 50 and older in a northeastern state correctional system, a series of analyses revealed that drug offense history had a significant moderating effect on the relationship between trauma and recidivism. However, minority status or violent offense history was not found to be a significant moderator of the trauma and recidivism relationship. These findings suggest prevention and intervention efforts, including reentry planning, would benefit from incorporating trauma-informed approaches and principles of restorative justice that facilitate individual, family, and community healing.[108] Few other studies have examined the relationship of trauma and criminal offending in later life.

Research has examined the relationship of age and recidivism, showing an age-related decline in criminal offending and recidivism among adults age 50 and older, and a recidivism rate between 1 percent and 5 percent. These findings suggest that releasing someone age 50 or older poses a low risk to public safety.[109] Research also has shown that the risk of recidivism is lower among older people than among younger people, including those with sex and violent offense histories.[110] In addition, individuals age 50 and older who committed a sexual offense (12 percent) are 50 percent less likely to recidivate than individuals who are younger (26 percent) and committed other types of offenses at release (35 percent).[111] Moreover, after five years in the community without reoffending, recidivism risk declines by half, and after ten years by half again. Increased age, it appears, is a protective factor against future offending regardless of the age at which the offense occurred, age at sentencing, or age at release from incarceration.[112]

Recidivism can best be understood as both the process and the outcome of the interaction between mental health, addiction, trauma, and overall health for older adult offenders. Using the sample of older adult offenders age 55 and older (*n*=344) from the Hartford prison study, we can see the role of recidivism in this population:

- Those who had a previous prison sentence (*n*=212) reported a significantly greater mean number of trauma episodes in a lifetime (M=12.00, SD=5.41) compared to older adults (*n*=126; M=8.21, SD=5.06) without a previous prison sentence, t (336) = 1.16, p<.001.

- Those who had a prior prison sentence (n=212) reported a significantly greater mean subjective reaction score to these lifetime trauma episodes (M=34.13, SD=24.71) compared to older adults (n=122; M=23.31, SD=19.17) without a previous prison sentence, t (332) = 8.33, p<.001.
- When examining substance use disorder or mental health disorder diagnosis as a predictor of recidivism history in current prison admissions, only a substance use disorder diagnosis significantly predicted (p<.001) recidivism history (B=1.56, SEB=0.31, OR=4.75); older adults diagnosed with substance use disorder were 4.75 times more likely to have a previous prison sentence.
- When comparing those with and without a previous prison sentence, a history of recidivism did not result in significantly greater levels of reported trauma symptoms, prison stress, or number of days in the past month individuals experienced physical or mental health problems.

Final Reflections

All the concepts we have discussed seem to converge either directly or indirectly in this chapter. Older adults are a consistently growing population in prison. Unfortunately, these same older adults do not benefit from a robust and consistent body of literature regarding their mental health experiences and symptoms. What we do know points to an older adult in prison who probably has a history of one or more traumatic experiences, co-occurring psychiatric and substance use symptoms (diagnostic or subsyndromal), and a long-standing history of little or no care for these substantial challenges.

CHAPTER 6

HOW DO WE CO-CONSTRUCT COMMUNITY?

A Conceptual Map for Reuniting Older Adults in Prison with Their Families and Communities

In the middle of difficulty lies opportunity.

—Albert Einstein

In this chapter, we explore what happens when older adults are released from prison. We provide an overview of the barriers and the facilitators that support smooth care transitions and community reintegration of older adults released from prison. Using data from the authors' Co-Constructing Community Project (see appendix 1), we integrate the perspectives of key stakeholders, community service providers, and formerly incarcerated older adults to illustrate the level of community preparedness required to reunite older adults with their families and communities. In phase two, thirty-one formerly incarcerated older men and women participated in one ninety-minute in-depth one-on-one semistructured interview. Both staff and formerly incarcerated adults most commonly reported that structural barriers (i.e., employment and homelessness) posed a challenge to successful reintegration. They also reported personal and social barriers that included a history of substance abuse, lack of family, and no other social supports. Formerly incarcerated older adults also shared their experiences before, during, and after prison, especially related to informal and formal caregiving. They explained that these caregiving experiences had a powerful influence

6.1

Source: ©Ron Levine/www.ronlevinephotography.com

on their notion of family and community and how they navigated their most recent community reintegration experience. We conclude with a conceptual map for co-constructing community, which provides a formula for successful reunification of older adults with their families and social environments and inspires creation of safer and healthier communities.

The number of aging people behind bars has increased by more than 1,300 percent since the early 1980s, and this had led us to seize this opportunity to provide creative solutions to massive incarceration of the elderly, which is projected to increase fourfold by 2030.[1] Administrators and staff at correctional systems are struggling to manage the subgroup of older and chronically ill inmates who have significant long-term health, mental health, and social care needs.[2] Today society is at a crossroads. We can continue to ignore the crisis, or we can redefine the crisis as an opportunity to identify not only the root of the problem but also solutions to mitigate the continued growth of aging people in prison. There are golden opportunities for communities to come together to deliberate on the costs, risks, and benefits of dismantling the stricter sentencing and parole release policies adopted in the 1970s and 1980s.[3] Many individuals, families, and communities affected by crime have been robbed of the opportunity to process their individual and collective grief as we continue to tuck the problem away behind the walls of prison. We have lost the voices of elders behind bars who may have wisdom to offer. Their years of self-contemplation have led them to figure out a way to heal deep wounds inflicted by harm, and they provide tender care, using gentle hand strokes with a soft cloth of compassion on the faces and ailing bodies of the seriously ill and dying in prison.

We have the opportunity to look at this age-old problem in a new way. If we fail to reform our current punitive practices and policies, the economic and human costs of sustaining our strict criminal justice policies will become even more dramatic. For example, in the United States, it seems we fear aging, diversity and difference, dying, crime, and victimization more than going bankrupt. Federal and state governments spend a combined $77 billion annually to operate correctional facilities and keep danger out of sight and mind.[4] About 20 percent, or $16 billion, is spent on health care for older adults in prison.[5] Keeping older people in prison is costly. It costs twice as much ($68,000) per year to incarcerate people 50 years old and older than younger persons ($34,000).[6] The human and moral costs are also high. For more than three decades, local and global media have shown haunting images of seriously ill, frail, elderly people in prison, some chained to their bed within hours of their death. These images compel us to reevaluate our assumptions concerning crime and punishment.[7] The media has also shared stories and images of "peer specialists"—inmate volunteers who provide compassionate end-of-life care.[8] Their altruistic behavior is in stark contrast to that of many community service providers, some of whom deny services to this vulnerable population, often based on their criminal conviction histories alone, such as a history of violent or sex offenses.

The economic and human costs challenge communities to revisit a universal commitment to basic human rights for older persons, prisoners, and disenfranchised populations.[9] Older adults and those with mental or physical disabilities represent a large part of the prison population.[10] Discussing ethically appropriate sentencing policies and intervention practices that foster compassion and care, as opposed to punishment and incapacitation, are important areas for public debate and deliberation.

After more than thirty years of punitive criminal justice policies, we urge our fellow community members to reflect on the aging in prison crisis. Is this the kind of common humanity we want our children to inherit or how we want to be treated as grandparents? Can we envision alternative strategies that reinforce personal accountability alongside compassionate care for those victimized as well for those who committed offenses? Can we engage our wise elders in conversation with younger generations to find a better way to resolve strong emotions such as betrayal, grief, anger, and rage? Are there creative ways to work together to forge new solutions that foster intergenerational family and community justice for all?

6.2

Source: ©Ron Levine/www.ronlevinephotography.com

Disrupting the Cycle of Aging, Trauma, and Criminal Justice Involvement

Many older adults in prison have experienced earlier or later life trauma. We wish we could tell you that it stops there. However, based on our data, release from prison is also stressful and can initiate a new trauma for older adults. As reviewed earlier, accumulative traumatic experiences include childhood abuse, neglect, exploitation, natural or human-caused disasters, war, the death of a loved one, widowhood, and receiving a serious physical or mental health diagnosis.[11]

Most would think that older adults' lives would get better once they are liberated from prison, but that is not always the case. If cumulative traumatic experiences are not addressed before or during imprisonment, the trail of unresolved trauma will follow older adults into later life. For example, biopsychosocial consequences of trauma among older adults may include revictimization; physical, cognitive, or emotional impairment; dementia; serious mental illness; posttraumatic stress disorder, depression, or psychological distress; substance abuse; social isolation, and early mortality.[12] Older adults released from prison are particularly vulnerable to age discrimination and other barriers that limit their access to quality services and justice, especially if they reside in a poverty-stricken or violent neighborhood. Older adults released from prison may be subject to elder abuse and neglect in public housing, community medical centers, social service agencies, or residential facilities such as skilled nursing homes or assisted living and acute care facilities. The caring justice movement has awakened, and individuals and communities are beginning to seek innovative solutions that enhance public safety and promote health and well-being for people of all ages. Interdisciplinary scholars, practitioners, and concerned citizens continue to seek solutions to break the cycle of poverty, trauma, and criminal justice involvement. However, we can do much more inspiring things as a community.

In the United States, roughly 700,000 people of all ages are released from prison each year to return to their communities, often under community supervision or parole.[13] Within three years, two out of five will recidivate and return to prison for parole violations or new convictions. Age is an important factor influencing who will return to prison and who will not. Adults age 55 and older are less likely to recidivate (0 to 2 percent) than their younger counterparts (43 percent). Official statistics consistently show that the public safety risk for crimes committed by released inmates is much lower for those 55 and older than for those under age 55.[14] Policy makers and key stakeholders interested in tackling mass incarceration of older adults can look to *Unger v. Maryland* for one possible solution. More than 130 older adult prisoners serving life sentences were freed on probation following this landmark ruling by Maryland's highest court. Besides saving taxpayers $120 million in the first year after release of these older adults (age 55+) in 2013, there has been an 80 percent reentry success rate.[15] Yet elders released from prison often encounter negative societal attitudes, stigma, and discrimination that is confounded by their age and criminal conviction histories. These socially induced barriers may impede their efforts to gain access to services, housing, and employment and create unnecessary hurdles for them to surmount.[16]

Sadly, the challenges many older adults experienced in prison do not end when they return to the community. In fact, formerly incarcerated older adults continue to be exposed to challenges that often began with limited access to health, education, and employment opportunities before they went to prison.[17] These same challenges remain upon their release, and they are now compounded by age and other forms of discrimination. Community service providers are often reluctant to provide services to formerly incarcerated older adults, including terminally ill individuals. To promote successful aging and dignified dying for incarcerated adults, we must be prepared to offer integrated services in the health, social, and legal care domains, and we must accept seriously ill and dying people in community care settings. A culturally responsive, holistic approach with coordination of care requires community preparedness and interdisciplinary cooperation, communication, and collaboration among professionals, paraprofessionals, and other key stakeholders that balance the need for autonomy and support.[18]

We challenge readers to think outside the social structures of the prison box and visualize communities of care that do care. Release from prison requires reunification of older adults with their families and communities. Definitions of community vary across disciplines and are conceptualized as a geographic location (e.g., group of people living in the same location), an emotional connection (e.g., a feeling of fellowship with others as a result of sharing common attitudes, interests, and goals[19]), or a cultural group (i.e., a unified body of individuals or a spiritual connection). These collective definitions suggest that community can be a physical, psychological, emotional, social, or spiritual experience. A formerly incarcerated older person described his internal and external experience of connecting with community as beginning with connecting to himself:

> I mean, at the end of the day it's about doing what I can do to help myself. It's a process, it really is. To me it is a system within itself. Doing what I can do for myself, then my family, then that immediate community.

It is important for communities to start visualizing correctional institutions as part of the community and subject to the same common humanity. Together we can craft a coordinated response in which agencies work in partnership to provide high-quality health care for all older adults, including the formerly incarcerated, thus saving the millions and billions of dollars currently spent on geriatric incarceration.[20]

Ecological systems theory, the person-in-environment perspective, and social support theory help to illuminate the complex relationships among older adults, their families, and communities with prisons. Ecological systems theory posits reciprocal interactions among different subsystems (e.g., macro, mezzo, micro), such as older adults with histories of incarceration, their families, local communities, and society at large. Similarly, the person-in-environment perspective conceptualizes a person's living energy unfolding across the life course in dynamic and reciprocal interaction with his or her social environment (e.g., community, neighborhood, and society). Finally, social support theory explains the factors that influence successful community reintegration, such as care providers' formal and informal support networks. (See chapter 2 for a more detailed description of these theories.)

In the best of societal conditions, individuals of all ages have access to rights and needs, self-mastery or control, and are highly adaptable to changing circumstances. The physical and mental health of older adults released from prison may be significantly compromised by a poor health history that is compounded by the trauma of incarceration. Thus older people released from prison often face new challenges navigating the social-environmental context and balancing capabilities for maximum health and well-being, especially after serving a long prison sentence. Instrumental support to formerly incarcerated older adults consists of concrete services that may include food, clothing, or access to housing. Another important and often overlooked factor that influences older adults' successful reintegration is emotional support, which not only represents what family and care providers can do to make these adults feel loved and cared for but also helps foster a sense of dignity and self-worth in their lives.[21]

The next sections explore the perspectives of community care providers and formerly incarcerated older adults and the factors that influence successful community reunification of older people released from prison. The narratives presented in these sections are from our Co-Constructing Community Research Project (see appendix 1).

Service Provider Perspectives

Service providers commonly reported structural barriers, including employment and housing (i.e., homelessness) as posing challenges to success in their work with older adults. They also reported personal and social barriers that include histories of substance abuse and a lack of family and other social supports: "When the family is not supportive, it makes it a little harder for a person who honestly has a desire to get on the right path." Staff reported other factors they perceived as facilitating successful reintegration. These included access to employment, social security, and transportation services. Social facilitators included family support ("family being part of their life") and having a relationship with staff to provide guidance, structure, motivation, and understanding. Staff also described the beneficial effects for older adults who had developed higher levels of "mental/emotional maturity" and used interpersonal skills that reflected "positive communication." The older adults had the potential to become mentors. For formerly incarcerated older adults, especially those who have served long sentences, a staff member stated that it is important to "provide them with opportunities to be healthy role models." Overall, the staff perceived internal and external supports or resources as helpful in facilitating the successful reunification of older adults with their families and communities. Balancing autonomy and empowerment with support, including leadership and mentorship opportunities, was described as essential.

Formerly Incarcerated Older Adult Perspectives

Thirty-one older formerly incarcerated men and women shared their personal experiences pertaining to the community reunification process. The results of the qualitative data analysis revealed two major categories: (1) the person in the community care environment and (2) the reunification journey. These themes are reviewed in that order.

Person in the Community Care Environment

We describe *community* as an interactive process between the person's internal experiences and the external environment. Community is a physical location, but it is also a psychological, social, and spiritual experience. Two formerly incarcerated African American older adults shared their wisdom about how we are all interconnected:

> It starts in the community. It starts at home, then the community, and if all else fails the criminal justice system.
>
> I mean, at the end of the day it's about doing what I can do to help myself. It's a process, it really is. To me it is a system within itself. Doing what I can do for myself, then my family, then that immediate community that I may be in, and then subsequently, ultimately the greater community.

Older adults also shared their experience and meaning-making regarding informal care (families and friends) and formal care (professionals and service

6.3

Source: ©Ron Levine/www.ronlevinephotography.com

providers). Older adults described the qualities of caregiving that were helpful to them as well as those less helpful and in some cases neglectful and abusive. One 59-year-old Latina participant shared her positive interaction with a police officer when she was a teenager:

> My experiences with professionals have varied. As a teenager when I first got into the system, I met some very nice officers. We don't even want to arrest you, you're soliciting. Call your parents. You know, give me your number, let me call your mom and dad. If they come get you, we're not even going to fingerprint you. Ma's response was, I could care less, keep her. There's good and bad in all. There was one particular officer from my community that literally sat down and talked to me and listened to my problems. He's like, you know, here's what you can do. He was one of the first people I think within the system that reached out and said, you know, we can find a solution to this.

In contrast, this 51-year-old described a negative care experience with correctional staff during his most recent prison term:

> The staff would be sending everybody a paper for [your] birthday, to fill out to get a new birth certificate or social security card if you need it. However, they

take these papers and they just sit in whoever's desk. Because they only send it out after a while, and once the stuff come back, like your birth certificate your, um, social security card, they keep it. They don't let you have that stuff in prison, so they got to hold onto it. By the time you get released, guessed what? It's lost. So, you know, it's like they don't take care of nothing in there. So, once you got out, though, you are expected to navigate your way around the city with no problems and get your documents, food stamps, medication, and see a doctor?

These older adults shared their positive care experiences with community reintegration, staff, family, and peer support networks after their release:

I've been to Fortune Society reentry program, staff over there just they love me. The respect I got from people, genuine love and caring. They go out of their way to help me.

Well, I happened to meet a good woman at my church, and that's the woman I married, and she has these friends, and that's how I got hooked up with some of the stuff.

The qualities of helpful caregivers include valuing human potential and transmitting unconditional love, dignity, worth, and respect. Older adults said it was most helpful when caregivers were authentic, empathic, compassionate, solution-focused, responsible, resourceful, used positive communication (e.g., active listening), and provided guidance and care linkages (when needed). When these qualities were present, some older adults described feeling loved and cared for. Such qualities tended to have a focusing and positive effect on them.

The Reunification Journey

The reunification journey was the second theme identified. It was described as a temporal process with physical, psychological, emotional, social, and spiritual components that began in prison. Factors that influenced their reunification were older adults' perceptions of personal safety and their level of access to internal and external resources or supports. Higher levels of perceived personal safety and access to internal and external resources helped them to prepare, survive, and thrive during their reunification journey from prison to the community. In their absence, older adults had more challenges to confront when navigating the reunification journey.

I prepared myself for my release date. So I wasn't worried about anything because I had [an] idea already. My friend, my best friend, held all my clothes

6.4

Source: ©Ron Levine/www.ronlevinephotography.com

and property for me, so I really wasn't worried about that. And even when I got home, like about a couple of days after I got home, I was worried about a place to stay. But then I didn't because my same best friend let me live at his apartment while he lived with his house.

I wasn't prepared at all. They didn't have anything, no prerelease situations hooked up for me. There was nothing there, except when you go to the parole board they said, well, you're going to go home. And only then—before you go to the parole board they like try to prepare you that you're going to see the parole people, and then once they say you're going home on parole that's all that they tell you is that you're going home. Then they send you back to your cell and you get a release date. And maybe a week or two they'll say you're going to live here or you're going to go with a family member or another relative. But that's about it.

Once released from prison, older adults continued to access internal and external resources/supports to navigate their journey. Those who felt they were "thriving" described internal resources that fostered their resilience despite the adverse conditions in their environment. These included positive thinking, self-awareness, self-compassion, self-forgiveness, and self-discipline. Other important internal resources were altruism, autonomy/independence, human agency, self-determination and regulation, adaptability, and resourcefulness. Many older adults had an intention to succeed with a plan and used problem-solving strategies, particularly when faced with challenges.

The only thing I'd say about prison is it can be a learning experience if you use it for that. It's negative, but it doesn't have to stay negative, because a lot of good, there's a lot of positive that can come out to it.

I am a 51-year-old African American man. I did sixteen years in prison for manslaughter, and I learned a lot in prison. It took me time to learn about myself. I was a closet gay person, and I am HIV positive. I didn't want nobody to know who I was, and now I'm learning how to live life. I'm in a relationship for six years, and I love myself today. Now I am a peer support worker at a local agency.

Some older adults identified a critical point in time after being released from prison that challenged their commitment to success:

The difficulty for me at first was changing my mind-set. With me, when I get stressed, it's so much easier just to think and jump and go back to the old behaviors. So, I think to stay out you really got to change how you deal with your issues, how you deal with the stress.

When some people first get out, they do the first dumb thing they stop on. That's what we do, because nine times out of ten, the first thing we stop on is dumb. So, you know, that's what we go back to, the dumb things we used to do.

External resources and social supports are an important component that helped them navigate the reunification process. These supports included family, mental and physical health services, education, and training in basic living skills.

My family, right now my family's my biggest supporter because I can say that and I can say that freely because there was a time when I couldn't even go, the furthest I could go was on the stoop, you know, because of, you know, my behavior, you know, my behavior with the drugs and stuff like that you know. So, like my family and now I have my program. You know, the system is screwed up, but one thing I have to give them credit for, they take care of their people who are HIV positive.

The most important thing for me was getting in contact with people who have the resources for me to survive. Trainings, mental health care—I learned computer skills. I went back to college. I did the footwork and found people who can help me navigate living in my community. Basic living skills that I didn't have prior to my incarceration. And it took a long time, about a year, to put all this in place.

Getting employment was my biggest challenge. Finding a job that not only could help me pay my bills but pay my way through life. But also have room for me to grown in. I've had—worked as a dishwasher, those jobs were nowhere jobs, because I had to learn some skills to make myself more employable.

Challenges to reunification included living in unsafe housing and communities and lacking access to social services to help them obtain basic identification, social welfare benefits, clothing, housing, and employment. Many older adults were able to overcome these hurdles, but others described the community's inability to recognize and provide basic needs to formerly incarcerated senior citizens:

My community? Where I reside now is drug infested, dangerous, low income.

When I did get out at that time I ended up in the shelter, because I had no living relatives to stay with or no friends that I could live with, so they placed me in a shelter. It was very rough. All they provided me was a roof over my head, and I was left to fend for myself.

Well, I did have a lot of problems, as far as getting food, shelter, medications, and all that. I did have problems. We had started the food stamp process while I was in prison. But even this is months before, and by the time I got out, I still had problems getting it because of information that I didn't have, like ID. And at that time I didn't have my birth certificate, social security card, driver's license, and passport, or nothing. Nothing, I had. So, I had a lot of problems. So, I had to go start from the beginning. I had to go get ID. And that's sad because these people need these IDs as soon as they step out of prison. Without ID you don't exist. It is like you're not living, so it's important to have the ID.

Final Reflections

Service providers and formerly incarcerated older adults identified internal and external resources and supports that influenced the likelihood of success or failure in the reunification process. Engaging the bond between the individual and care systems is a major factor in transcending problems as well as in reunification of older adults with their families and communities. Older adults referenced external resources to help navigate the reunification process that are consistent with informational, instrumental, and emotional social supports.[22] Informational support from care providers included how to complete an application or where to find a service provider. Instrumental support consisted of providing concrete services such as transportation. Emotional support from family and care providers was commonly identified. Older adults reported feeling loved or cared for by family members or formal care providers who offered encouragement and positive feedback. Overall, these findings suggest that the responsibility for successful integration of formerly incarcerated older adults to the community rests on the individual, the community, and the interactions between them. It is of significant interest to society to provide adequate support services to ensure safer and healthier communities for people of all ages.

A Road Map for Success

How can communities work together to create a road map for success for healthy, safe communities and successful integration of older adults when they are released from prison? What would it look like? The True Grit program is a senior structured living program for adults age 50 and older in the Nevada Department of Corrections, and members offer a road map from prison into the community that facilitates personal accountability and mutual support for individuals who committed crimes.[23] The True Grit program combines humanistic and rehabilitative principles with human development activities that foster holistic well-being in the physical, psychological, emotional, social, spiritual, and empowerment domains. As part of the recovery process, participants in True Grit draw a map of two roadways; one path leads to rehabilitation, recovery, and reintegration (right side) and the other leads to recidivism (left side). The metaphor is clear; a left turn leads to Risky Lane and to more time in prison, and a right turn leads to Responsibility Way and a holistic senior structured living program. Risky Lane leads to Destructive Drive, which is fraught with roadside distractions, such as gambling, drugs, reinforcement of criminogenic thinking, affiliations with gangs, and social segregation. This might then lead to Expiration Avenue, the parole board, and a maximum prison sentence. Recidivism Road has more roadside distractions, such as criminal thinking, relapse, emotional problems, abusive relationships, addictions, isolation, and a parole violation, and it leads to the Way Back Highway.

If participants of the True Grit program choose Responsibility Way, they are headed to a holistic structured senior living program. The beneficial effects of choosing Accountability Way are clear; they can participate in structured human, social, and spiritual development activities while in prison. On this path, incarcerated older adults will enjoy "attractions" such as human and social development programming, vocational and educational training, including health literacy and practices and self-help programs. In addition, there will be cognitive enrichment and specialized programs such as reintegration preparedness. Accountability Way leads to Hope Avenue and Release Road via the parole board. Finally, Release Road leads to Success Road, which has more beneficial "roadside attractions," such as employment, housing, therapeutic support, physical and spiritual wellness, healthy aging and relationships, charitable giving, restitution, and integrity (life review to attain personal wisdom). The handshake at the end of Success Road represents a social contract with their communities to be productive senior citizens.

Although this road map metaphor was created for the personal development and accountability of incarcerated older adults, it is also a metaphor for community development and accountability to its members. The road map represents a two-way street of social responsibility: prisons are part of the community regardless of their proximal or distal physical location. There is no guarantee that all of the perceived resources on Success Street are available or accessible to older people with criminal conviction histories. For example, in New York most of the people at the highest risk for receiving long prison sentences live in poverty and reside in crime-infested urban minority neighborhoods, such as Manhattan and the surrounding boroughs. They left these neighborhoods for prison, and they are likely to return to them as senior citizens. There is no guarantee that incarcerated older adults will have opportunities to become involved in the kinds of programs that research has shown to be beneficial. Furthermore, there is no guarantee that they will be treated justly by their parole boards. The individual may uphold his or her half of the social contract if given services and opportunities, but there is no guarantee that service providers will help connect them with housing, employment, or short- or long-term residential care. From a community development perspective, it is the obligation of the community to create a system of care that is collaborative and that promotes a healthy and safe environment for everyone.[24]

Conceptual Map for Co-Constructing Communities

How do we co-construct our own road maps that foster holistic well-being and justice across the life course? Both problems and solutions reside within the individual and community context, and corrections and the criminal justice system are a part of this system. The primary community roadway is Unity Circle, and its secondary roadway is Care Way (see figure 0.1). Unity Circle is populated with informal care networks (e.g., family, peers, and other social networks) and foundational supports (e.g., food, housing, and transportation), and all individuals are entitled to two primary sectors of care: universal access to education and health care.[25] The Unity Circle of community is the source of self-care and informal caregiving; it is where individuals learn socially responsible behavior and accountability. Access to education is a key factor in opening possibilities for future employment and obtaining a meaningful vocation. Access to health care is critical for prevention, clinical intervention, and treatment of individuals. People enter Care Way when they need professional assistance, physical or mental health services, or substance abuse treatment. The criminal justice system is a system of last resort. The model encourages planning for more effective prevention and intervention strategies to keep communities safe and healthy.

Recommendations

Formerly incarcerated older adults have contributed their ideas on how we can co-construct community together. Newly released prisoners and those released on probation need help to join the communities to which they return. Here are their thoughts in their own words.

Foundational Supports

- As far as food, you need your social service referrals unless you have a way to support yourself.
- Clothing I think they could help you better. I think we mentioned one time if you get picked up and it's winter and you're coming home and you're released in the spring and summer at least give you, nothing major, three changes of clothes that are I think weather appropriate.
- Housing I think coming out, unless you already have something that's been established, and you've been there short term or long term you definitely need housing help. It's difficult out there for housing and employment. And everybody's doing the background checks now. So it's difficult to get decent housing and a job. You need the referrals.

Specialized Health and Mental Health Supports

- Home care if they need it depending on both their physical and mental health. Those are the things that need to be set up before you release the person.
- In old age you need more mental—definitely more outreach for the mental health.

- You've got to look at their health history, their past mental health history, and they're going to need—there's Alzheimer's on the rise with prisoners in there. You have to work on that. You can't just send them back out cold. They especially need the support services.

Family Engagement and Support

- You got to reach out to their family members, help the family members understand.

Other Sources of Social Support, Guidance, and Representation

- The connections are what we need, positive connections out there.
- We need guidance. I think a lack of guidance is what's gotten us into this mess in the first place. And to stay out, the attitude, society needs to change the attitude. The workers need to change the attitude.
- We definitely need more senior reps. It's hard enough to deal with things. And with senior issues it's so much more complicated.

Community Support and Transformational Justice

- Look at the environment they're going back to. Try to make changes. Let them spend their time knowing they are not going to just [be] sent back to the same situation.
- The way our country goes about its corrections, its crime and punishment, is different than let's say Norway. First of all, you would never do the kind of time that we do in this country. You're only going to be able to do only to a certain point, and they consider that to me a lifetime, for example. The access to the computers, your living circumstance in there, and the professionalism of those folks who work there is like night and day.

Older adults who have experienced life in prison are key stakeholders. Their voices must be heard and considered in ongoing deliberations on community justice, practice, and policy reform for all ages. Co-constructing community at the local level is best facilitated by open communication, cooperation, and collaboration among community members, including service providers. As the narratives of older adults suggest, whether care transitions from prison to the community are smooth and short, or uneven, uncomfortable, lengthy, and costly, involves the cooperation of multiple actors and service systems.

Based on our prison and community reintegration study findings, eight factors can either create barriers or facilitate successful care transitions for aging and seriously ill individuals released from prison.

1. Value conflicts about health versus crime and punishment
2. Early detection and identification of health concerns
3. Timely response to distress
4. A discharge planning mechanism
5. A discharge planning and a care transitions plan
6. Family involvement and preparedness
7. Collaboration between corrections and community service providers
8. Adherence by service providers to nondiscrimination laws and policies

We hope communities and service providers will evaluate their level of competence in addressing these needs for formerly incarcerated seriously ill and older adults.

6.5

Source: ©Ron Levine/www.ronlevinephotography.com

Successfully transitioning the aging and seriously ill, including those with dementia, from prison to the community is an important aspect of facilitating the right to health for this often overlooked and underserved population. However, many correctional systems report that it is difficult to get community service providers to accept formerly incarcerated clients, regardless of their age, health status, and low public safety risk.[26] With the recent wave of health-care reform and a concerted effort to improve care for patients transitioning within and across care settings,[27] we have an opportunity to reconnect the fragmented linkages between corrections and community service providers through transitional care planning.

Transitional care planning provides coordination and continuity of health care when individuals or patients are transferred between different levels of care in the same service setting or across different service settings.[28] In the case of the seriously and terminally ill, one pathway is from prison into community home-based or institutional settings, such as skilled nursing homes. Effective care transitions reduce readmission rates and their associated high costs.[29] In the ideal situation, transitional care or discharge planning is the result of the cooperative effort of the patient, the family, and service providers.

Care transition assessment and planning (also referred to as discharge planning) often include identifying linkages to housing, health, and social services, including Medicare and Medicaid benefits.[30] As noted earlier, community service providers may deny placement to formerly incarcerated individuals because of their offense history, such as violence, sex, arson, or even drug offenses. Denial of services often leaves aging or seriously ill individuals to linger in prison while awaiting community support.[31]

CHAPTER 7

"COMING OUT" OF PRISON

LGBTQ+ Older Adults' Experiences Navigating the Criminal
Justice System

L GBTQ+ older adults involved in the criminal justice system is a
largely overlooked group. In this chapter, we reveal their untold
stories of negotiating their intersectional identities before, during,
and after incarceration. Our Coming Out of Prison Study (see appendix 2)
sheds light on the ongoing coming out process for LGBTQ+ older adults as
their multiple intersectional and stigmatized identities are recognized, such as
being a racial/ethnic minority, LGBTQ+, elderly, HIV-positive, nonconforming
gender identify, serious physical and mental health issues, trauma, addictions,
and criminal justice histories, including previous incarcerations. We conclude
the chapter with recommendations for services and policy reform suggested by
formerly incarcerated LGBTQ+ elders.

Trauma and oppression can affect diverse groups in a variety of ways, and
LGBTQ+ individuals may experience criminalization and incarceration in
unique ways. However, little information is available on LGBTQ+ people's
experiences in prison. In a report on sexual victimization in jails and prisons,
12.2 percent of incarcerated adults identified their sexual orientation as gay,
lesbian, or bisexual; 8.5 percent of jail incarcerated individuals reported sexual
victimization from peers; and 5.4 percent of incarcerated individuals in prison
and 4.3 percent of individuals in jail reported victimization by staff.[1] Incarcerated
adults with mental health needs who identified as not heterosexual reported
the highest rates of inmate-on-inmate sexual victimization (14.7 percent of jail
inmates and 21 percent of prison inmates). In California, a study of violence in
prisons showed that transgender women in men's prisons were thirteen times
more likely to experience sexual violence than other incarcerated persons.[2]

7.1

Source: ©Ron Levine/www.ronlevinephotography.com

LGBTQ+ people are at high risk of having health-care concerns while incarcerated that include sexually transmitted infections (STIs), including HIV/AIDS, and mental health and substance use disorders. Institutional policies prevent hormone or transition-related care, so the health care of transgender incarcerated individuals is often an administrative issue rather than a health-care issue.[3] Other risk factors that involve the LGBTQ+ population are family rejection, homelessness, and unemployment brought about through bias and discrimination against them. When in prison, LGBTQ+ individuals may reject (lack) prison-based rehabilitative services for fear of being assaulted by other incarcerated individuals or correctional staff. LGBTQ+ elders released from prison, especially those with complex comorbid health and mental health issues, may experience the collateral consequences of incarceration, ageism, and homophobia.[4]

The pathways to prison for LGBTQ+ elders may include one or more cumulative inequalities, such as social disadvantage based on age, race, education, socioeconomic status, gender, disability, legal or immigration status, and sexual minority status.[5] These accumulated inequalities can influence their access to health and social services, economic resources, and justice across the life course.

We draw from our Coming Out of Prison Study to explore the experiences of formerly incarcerated LGBTQ+ elders before, during, and after their release from prison (see appendix 2 for study details). We conclude with a discussion of LGBTQ+ affirming and sensitive interprofessional and interdisciplinary policies and practices, and we incorporate service system and community reforms suggested by formerly incarcerated older LGBTQ+ adults.

Narratives of Older LGBTQ+ Adults Released from Prison

An overarching theme of self and the social mirror emerged from life course history narratives of LGBTQ+ elders released from prison (figure 7.2). All of the older LGBTQ+ adults described a lifelong process of negotiating and managing

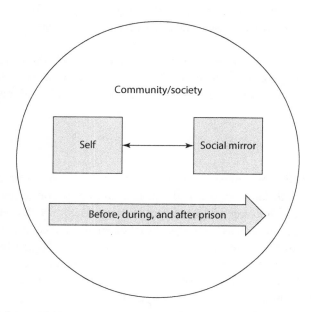

7.2 Self and the social mirror is an overarching theme of LGBTQ+ elders' experiences of personal and social integration before, during, and after prison

the visible and invisible prisons of multiple oppressions and social stigmas, which were confounded by their criminal justice involvement. Older LGBTQ+ adults perceived themselves in relationship to the social mirror of family, peers, and society in an ongoing, dynamic, personal, interpersonal, and historical process. Older LGBTQ+ adults reflect or deflect positive or negative social messaging they experience from family members, peers, service providers, and society. When asked, "Can you please tell me about yourself?", older LGBTQ+ adults most often include the whole of their multiple parts in their narrative:

I am an African American female, 55-year-old lesbian. I'm presently unemployed. I was incarcerated for like six years on a drug charge. It wasn't easy but I'm okay now.

I'm a lesbian. Presently I'm not in any committed relationship or anything like that. I'm focusing on my recovery and just trying to stay in the community.

I am Latino and LGBTQ. I did sixteen year in prison for manslaughter. I learned a lot in prison. It took me time to learn about myself. I was a closet gay man. Didn't want anybody to know who I was. I'm learning how to live life and I'm in a relationship for six years and I love myself today.

I am a gay male. I did ten years, six months in prison. I'm in a committed relationship for the last six years. I'm presently working in the mental health field in a psychosocial club and advocacy program for LGBTQ+ members. I am a liaison between their therapist and the supports services they receive. One of the things that I'm trying to do after coming out of prison for so long is to establish a working relationship and being a productive person.

Most older LGBTQ+ adults identify themselves through their racial/ethnic minority status, age, HIV-positive, LGBTQ+, formerly incarcerated with a mental health or substance diagnosis, and occupational and relationship status.

Social Stigma and the Mirror

Many older LGBTQ+ adults shared their early social mirroring experiences in relationships with families, peers, the local community, and society at large. Some described choosing which aspects of themselves they shared based on the social situation, such as their age, sexual orientation, race, disabilities, and incarceration history. Their lifetime experiences of social stigma from family and other social circles was related to one or more stigmatizing identities, and older LGBTQ+ adults often chose to express or hide certain aspects of their social identity while in prison or in the community.

HIV status and family: My immediate family all know my HIV status but not my father. Even though I know he would love me because I'm his son, he wouldn't have a choice. I just don't feel comfortable coming out telling him that I'm HIV positive. I brought it to my mother's attention, and she said don't tell him. I don't know why; we're just keeping that a secret. But everybody else knows.

Mental health status and family: Growing up, my family wasn't really cool with being mentally ill so I couldn't be mentally ill. I was not able to go to a psychiatrist. I was not able to take medication, and I was damn sure not able to talk about how I felt or what was going on. So I self-medicated with drugs. The voices were getting loud: drink a little bit more, smoke a little bit more. I had voluntary hospitalizations, but a lot of the times involuntary because my mother had to put me there. I can't even count. Let's say thirty times from the age of 26 to 35. I think I went to the psych hospital about two or three times a year for like ten to twelve years.

Sexual orientation, violence, and corrections: In jail and prison, they all knew my name, "R." One guard said, "yo, R's back." I used to stay in the lockup a lot for my violent behavior, and she would ask, "like are you sure you are a homo?" The officers used to tease me like how could a homo be doing all this violence. "Homos don't do that," they would say.

All ten older LGBTQ+ adults described facing challenges incorporating their multiple social identities or locations and reported that negative social stigma has been an ongoing challenge in developing and maintaining a positive self-identity. They described developing an immunity to societal stigma to foster a more compassionate sense of self. In fact, many older LGBTQ+ adults described a "coming out" as a self-love and acceptance process that integrated their multiple identities or social locations. One Latino elder said it quite simply: "And today I love and accept myself."

Older adults described using selective disclosure with people or circumstances as a coping strategy. They made choices about where and when to share or not share one or more aspects of themselves and described how they prepared themselves psychologically and emotionally to deflect or reject social stigma. One 55-year-old formerly incarcerated African American woman shared her attitude toward others:

I personally don't care how a person feels about me. My attitude is that if you don't like what I represent, don't say nothing to me. As far as me being LGBTQ+ and being incarcerated, it has not been a problem for me.

A 50-year-old Haitian man discussed why he needs to protect and vocalize his rights to deflect and reject society's views toward him:

I put my guard up in every way possible because I am gay, HIV positive, black. So I had to defend myself along the way, so I don't get swallowed up. I'm capable of advocating for myself, especially when I need affirming program services. If you can't advocate, that becomes a stumbling block for people like me.

Coping with the Trauma of Incarceration

All of the older LGBTQ+ adults acknowledged the cruelty of prison, especially for older LGBTQ+ adults. The culture of prison was full of systemic bias and discrimination that limited their access to rehabilitative services and basic safety and protection. Yet despite the cruel conditions of confinement, inmates acknowledged that they were able to use their prison time to gain greater insight and clarity about themselves and to take accountability for their crimes. Three older LGBTQ+ adult men described their experience in prison:

> It was like this in jail and prison, if you are male and gay so you should like it, you know. It was really hard to go through that and try to deal with the day you know, and days were long you know. You were up at 7 a.m., and even your time locked in your cell wasn't a safe time because, if they wanted you, they could tell a correctional officer to crack your cell and they would run in on you. You know it was really frightening. It was hard to get yourself mentally ready for the morning because you never knew what was going to happen that day, and that's a real terrible feeling like, what's going to happen to me today. Every day was like I got to keep up. I got to keep up. I got to look left and then right.
>
> People were just being abused all throughout my stay, and the LGBTQ+ people were just assaulted so many times on a regular basis. Everyone got it, but the LGBTQ+ men, they were washing other inmates' underwear. And anything their parents or friends sent them, inmates would take them. They would make them cook for them and wash their pots. It was just frightening.
>
> The correctional officers (CO) didn't care about anything. They watched gay people get raped. They would walk the tier and see a gay person being raped or beaten up in his cell, and they would keep on walking. They would see gay people get beat and raped in the shower room, and they wouldn't say anything. And when you needed help to cry out to the CO, it was like crying out to air because they weren't going to do anything.

Older LGBTQ+ adults described choosing among three gay identity coping strategies: fight, flight, or keeping it out of sight. *Fight* entailed defending their right to be openly gay. In contrast, *flight* was described as distancing from one's LGBTQ+ identity in prison (often based on fearing for their safety). *Keeping it out of sight* meant selectively disclosing one's LGBTQ+ identity to some others in prison.

> *Fight*: How did I cope with being gay in prison? I did when in Rome, you do as the Romans. I was in prison, I did what prison people do. So I hung out with a crew that were crazy. I was hearing voices, I was crazy, so we did

the same thing, and the only reason they accepted me is because I was just as dangerous as they were. I was always gay all my life, so when I got in jail, I never went into secure segregation or into the gay quarters. I always went into general population. I made myself deal with what was going on. I became one of the people that were there. I don't know if the fighting was more because I was LGBTQ+ or because it's just what you do in prison. But I went through a lot being an openly gay person in prison because the attacks and things that I had observed happen to gay people were really frightening. I just made it a way of my dealing in prison that it wouldn't happen to me, so I became a really, really wild person. They have a name for gays like me in jail, and it's homo thug. I became like one of the fearless gay people in jail. I just didn't want to be raped.

Flight: Well, nobody knew I was gay. Only a few guys I let know, but other people, I just say no, I'm not gay. I am an old man. You know having sex in prison is not acceptable. If you get caught, they send a letter to your house, or they tell your family over the phone. You go to the box [solitary confinement]. Some correctional officers, they'll let you be with their cell. Some inmates paid the officer off with cigarette or with drug to do so.

Out of sight: It was a hard life in prison because you had to walk around like on pins on needles, especially if you were gay or bisexual. I wasn't the type of person to walk around [and] advertise, and only a few people knew. I wasn't the type of person that wanted to be taken advantage of and being raped. So I had to learn how to defend myself in prison. I went through a lot of tough times. It wasn't that easy for me. But I'm easy to get along, with so I guess word of mouth got me by. I was able to get along with everybody. I wasn't selfish. I stuck with who I needed to stick with to get by in prison.

Older LGBTQ+ adults used diverse coping strategies to manage their identity in prison for their safety, protection, and daily survival.

Coming Out of Prison

The self-perceptions of older LGBTQ+ adults continued to evolve after they "came out" of prison. Those with long prison sentences described feeling fearful about being released from prison, especially if the prison staff did not provide prerelease services. They faced the challenges of returning to the community with the stigma of having served time, and they emphasized their need for resources and life skills before being released into the community. This included knowing how to make a budget, how to cook, how to find employment and housing, and how to access physical and mental health care and other social services.

Some had been in the prison system for so long that they felt institutionalized, and they were not sure how they were going to survive in the community. As one participant said, "In prison you are told when to get up, meals were prepared, and the day was planned; thinking about reentering the community with no supports in place was a challenge." One 50-year-old formerly incarcerated Latina lesbian described her adjustment to coming out:

I've been out almost four years. I came out at 46 years old. There was nothing for me out there, which made coming home a little more frightening, and for the LGBTQ+ it's like that. Why leave prison? I'm getting three hots and a cot. And I don't have to fight for the food. Some of us don't want to come out. I thought, what am I going to do at this late age? I didn't know what I was going to do, where I was going. I knew I didn't want to go to a program and stay at a program and then get pushed out to the street.

A 50-year-old gay male participant described how he prepares himself psychologically, emotionally, and spiritually to triumph over the challenges of community reintegration:

Everything's been beautiful. I just don't allow it to be any other way. Every day I wake up, I'm so appreciative to not be behind bars. Nothing that comes up, no weather conditions or anything, and my partner says, baby, you are up at 6 o'clock no matter what goes on. I praise God in the morning. I think I was given a second chance at life, and I just don't want to mess it up. I can't say there has been any difficulties. There's been situations, and I just take them in stride. I went into [the] mainstream community, not a program. I didn't wait for the housing because I was in a relationship. They informed me that any of the housing that I got would not allow me and my partner to live together. And as I said I'm 50, I'm not going to be living alone and going to see my partner who lives in the Bronx and I'm over here, you know. They are not recognizing LGBTQ+ relationships. That's an issue.

Some older LGBTQ+ adults talked about the advantages of being HIV-positive, or having a serious mental illness, because some benefits were available to them:

Being LGBTQ+ and be labeled HIV, you get a lot of stigma, but you get a lot of support on your transition out of prison. Otherwise, we don't get any services at release. We don't even get the assistance to try to get housing. You have to find a social worker, who might or might not help you.

Most older LGBTQ+ adults shared how reentry or housing supports and services were not LGBTQ+ and aging friendly. This social situation made most LGBTQ+ older adults choose to selectively disclose their sexual orientation:

> The housing that I was in was lovely, but I was with people that weren't LG affirming and weren't as mentally equipped. This environment wasn't safe or healthy for me because I was a gay man living with straight men, like prison.
>
> Well, when I came out, there was a reentry program. I worked with them very well. They helped me out in a lot of ways. I went to school and a training program with them. I even got jobs through them. So the reentry program helped me out a long way until I was able to get on my feet again. But they did not have LGBTQ+ and aging services. So I kept in the closet. I didn't see too many openly gay people, just straight thugs on the streets after prison.

Older LGBTQ+ adults experienced discrimination based on their offense histories, especially for violent or sexual offenses. These restrictions included where they can live, such as living a certain distance from a school, park, or public housing. They also described having to live in an unfamiliar or unsafe community, and curfews or required parole appointments made finding employment or attending a program difficult. Two older LGBTQ+ adults described the drawbacks to not having services that integrate LGBTQ+, aging, and criminal justice services:

> When you get out of prison, if you are LGBTQ+, they have a few things. But for our age, 40 and 50, there are no specific services. They don't even have housing where they can sufficiently put you. Yeah, they got one LGBTQ+ elder program now, but I don't see them helping people coming out of jail. That's support for LGBTQ+ people on the street. For LGBTQ+ coming out as senior citizens and you are LGBTQ+, and they are going to push you into the LGBTQ+ youth center. But for anybody over that age, there's nothing.
>
> And then when you get 50, it's like you're on your own, we're letting you go but where you go is on you. They don't have any kind of referrals. They have no kind of support, so everything is really on you to be strong and look for, but people get discouraged really quickly because it's like next to no that you are going to find services. And the services that they have, they may not be able to accept you because they are at their quota with LGBTQ+ but 40–50+. We have to depend on our family, and most of us don't have that because we are gay or old.

Several The LGBTQ+ older adults found help at the Rainbow Heights Club, a social support and advocacy program that is affirming for LGBTQ+ elders released from prison. It is located in Brooklyn, New York.

> There is not a lot of services for LGBTQ+ people in the community that are older and released from prison. I thank God for Rainbow Heights and being a person that can provide service for people that have nowhere to go to be themselves, to be safe, to eat a meal. To get support and referral to a lot of things that they may need in their life but Rainbow Heights is one.

These findings illustrate that LGBTQ+ elders released from prison do not have LGBTQ+ and aging affirming services readily available to them. Despite the lack of community services, many formerly incarcerated elders were resourceful in getting their physical health, mental health, housing, and social service needs met.

Final Reflections

Many factors account for the lack of culturally responsive treatment of LGBTQ+ elders with criminal justice histories. These include the fragmentation of services, a lack of communication between service providers, and a lack of training to work with LGBTQ+ elders who have multiple intersectional identities. These incarcerated older adults would benefit from increased attention and community services during the reintegration process.

When LGBTQ+ people of all ages feel that they cannot reveal their true identity to access services they need in prison or in the community, they remain invisible, marginalized, and misunderstood by heterosexual social service providers.[6] Fear of discrimination and exclusion lead to avoidance of disclosure, and perhaps the most stigmatized of all LGBTQ+ populations are the older people involved in the criminal justice system. Many would argue that this population has even been marginalized by the LGBTQ+ rights movement. A growing body of evidence indicates that the LGBTQ+ community is beginning to recognize, accept, and respond to the criminalization of LGBTQ+ people and their less than fair treatment in the criminal justice system.[7] Offering an affirmative and welcoming response to LGBTQ+ people of all ages returning to their communities from prison is a good place to begin because the communities they return to also includes LGBTQ+ people.

There is a lot for us to learn from LGBTQ+ elders released from prison about coming out to our true selves. The central theme of self and the social mirror suggests that they were able to see who they truly are despite the distorted images projected on them by their families and society. Older LGBTQ+ adults described a process of reclaiming their true selves in the form of a deep uncon-ditional self-love, self-forgiveness, and self-acceptance. Their awakening to their true selves was a true triumph over a lifetime of experiences of family and community bias, prejudice, discrimination, and violence based a single aspect of themselves.

Most of the older LGBTQ+ adults in prison used adaptive coping strategies to navigate societal oppression in community and institutional settings. As they looked into society's mirror, they were able to hold onto the unconditional self-love, self-forgiveness, and self-acceptance they had worked to create. If this population can find their way to self-acceptance, surely anyone can do it, including you. It is just a matter of coming out of your invisible prison where you hide aspects of yourself that others in society may perceive as unacceptable. Many of the older adults expressed remorse for their criminal actions. They understand that they cannot change their past, but they now have full control of their present and future actions and reactions.

In a review of the literature on the needs of older LGBTQ+ people, Addis and colleagues found that discrimination based on sexual orientation influ-enced the extent to which LGBTQ+ adults are able to meet their needs in health and social services.[8] Similarly, the narratives of older adults who came out of prison underscore their struggle to be recognized for their true selves. By embracing their intersectional identity, they were able to overcome soci-etal barriers and achieve personal liberation and empowerment. Many older LGBTQ+ adults expressed a strong desire to engage in a dialogue about the problems and to suggest solutions for LGBTQ+ minority elders with histories of criminal justice involvement. These recommendations included adoption of more gay and aging affirming services and policies, special population consid-erations, wraparound services, and liberation and empowerment-based inter-ventions, creating a holistic response for LGBTQ+ persons of all ages who are at risk of criminalization or ongoing criminal justice involvement.

Consistent with previous work, our study found access to educational resources to be very important. Older LGBTQ+ adults in prison and in the community experience discrimination in access to education. While incar-cerated, many LGBTQ+ people did not attend or were not allowed to attend educational classes because of personal safety and prison management issues. Upon release they also faced discrimination from medical professionals, ther-apists, and social service providers, especially with regard to housing. One participant described how discrimination on the basis of LGBTQ+ identities creates a prison in the community and commented, "What's the difference from being in jail?"

An affirming-based recovery approach is recommended to assist LGBTQ+ elders being released from the criminal justice system so they will feel com-fortable accessing services and other important supports. Engagement without exacerbating the dual stigmas of their LGBTQ+ identity and criminal history is essential to begin establishing a helping relationship. It is estimated that 12 percent of justice-involved men and 24 percent of women have a mental health or substance use disorder.[9] Many researchers indicate that this may be even higher in the LGBTQ+ population.[10] For any treatment to have efficacy, it should target the whole individual and not just the presenting disorder. Best practice models may include supported employment, family education, peer support, case management, and advocacy services. Community agencies that allow for socialization and acceptance are crucial as LGBTQ+ elders reenter the community from prison. Isolation, discrimination, and lack of positive supports can only produce a negative outcome.

Organizations like the Rainbow Heights Club, a self-help and advocacy program specifically designed to provide services to LGBTQ+ individuals, may be a key component in community reintegration.[11] Located in Brooklyn, New York, Rainbow Heights describes itself as an advocacy program for LGBTQ+ adults who are mental health consumers. Their mission is "to bring innovative, affirming, and effective treatment advocacy and support services for LGBTQ+ people living with mental illness in an atmosphere of hope, recovery, and partnership."[12] The services they provide include socialization, support, peer advocacy, and psychoeducation for emotional wellness and recovery.[13]

A final recommendation is the infusion of trauma-informed care for LGBTQ+ and older people reentering the community from the criminal justice system. Similar to Ka'Opua and colleagues,[14] we recommend that returning prisoners have timely access to social service programs and to trauma-informed care to help them cope with past trauma histories, including the trauma of incarceration.[15] We must respond with services and policies that provide an affirmative model for recovery and social reintegration.

PART II

REALIZING A CARING JUSTICE WORLD

CHAPTER 8

A CARING JUSTICE PARTNERSHIP PARADIGM

Transforming the World from the Inside Out

In matters of truth and justice, there is no difference between large and small problems, for issues concerning the treatment of people are all the same.

—Albert Einstein

In this chapter, we build the case for a new collective vision of caring justice to address contemporary social and environmental problems such as the aging in prison crisis. We argue that the aging in prison crisis is one more piece of evidence that our old ways of thinking about social problems and the solutions generated have fallen short. We present a new way of thinking, referred to as a *caring justice partnership paradigm*, which is a daily philosophy and way of life that promotes personal and relational evolution. We draw from innovative interdisciplinary perspectives in physics, philosophy, and humanistic and transcendental psychology. We describe how a caring justice partnership paradigm implemented at the personal and collective levels can transform the world from the inside out, becoming a safer and healthier place for people of all ages. Not only will we create a better world for older people in prison but also a better world for all of us.

Professor Lewis B. Smedes once said, "To forgive is to set a prisoner free and realize that prisoner was you." Take a moment to reflect on this statement. How do we make sense of it in our lives and in the lives of aging people in prison?

We have had the unique opportunity to look inside the hidden world of the shadow box called prison and have vicariously experienced being an incarcerated older adult in khaki pants and unlaced boots. Older adults shared their experiences before, during, and after prison. They spoke of social structural trauma/oppression, growing up in poverty, lacking access to quality education and health care, and experiencing discrimination based on racial/ethnic and other minority identities, which put them at risk of criminalization and criminal justice involvement. Their memories and feelings of guilt, fear, anger, and shame were locked away in their minds and buried in their bodies.

Some of you may have faced a challenging environment in which you turned inward, discovering inner resources that helped you cope with the situation. Being exposed to an oppressive, uncaring, and violent world at home and in neighborhoods and school may resonate with your own experiences. Perhaps the only significant difference between us and older incarcerated adults is that we have never been in a physical prison.

Many of the older adults in prison openly shared their insights into the causes and effects of their experiences and actions on themselves and on others. Some released their pain and reclaimed an inner world of self-love and rebuilt a relationship to a higher power and to humankind. From inside prison, they released negative family and societal judgments about who they were and what they deserved. Some understood and forgave their transgressors and found self-forgiveness. This enabled them to give and receive love and compassionate care, ending a multigenerational cycle of hatred and harm.

As the one prisoner shared with us, once we change from the inside, the prison exit door opens to a world of pure and unabashed freedom. It behooves us to release the fear of difference that separates us from others and to embrace unity consciousness. If we forgive ourselves and others for their transgressions, our collective moral panic may subside. Once we open our hearts to our fears, guilt, betrayals, and other uncomfortable emotions, do we need to continue to punish those who no longer pose a danger or threat to us or society?

Older adult prisoners showed strength and wisdom through their strategies of coping and resilience. Many discovered self-love, forgiveness, and acceptance during times of contemplative solitude. Older adults also guided and nurtured younger people in prison, and mentoring others had positive effects on their physical, mental, emotional, social, spiritual, and behavioral well-being. We can all access self-healing capacities that complement traditional health services. When we genuinely love, forgive, and accept ourselves and each other, we set ourselves free from inner conflict and reach the heart where caring justice lives.

Older adults in prison shared their experiences of care before and during imprisonment, as well as their anticipation of being released. They described experiences of care from families, communities, and prisons that were devoid of dignity and respect. Displays of power often resulted in abuse and punishment, excessive use of force, intentional and unintentional neglect, dishonesty, manipulation, bullying tactics, narcissistic self-centeredness, greed, and recklessness. At times they felt degraded, oppressed, guilty, powerless, fearful, worthless, and shamed by family members or professional caregivers, including health and social care providers and corrections officers.

Witnessing or learning about trauma through media stories can have a negative effect on all of us. We become secondary witnesses to traumatic experiences such as domestic violence, community crime, and terrorism. A combination of adverse experiences in different social contexts may trigger criminal behaviors fueled by strong emotions, such as hatred, revenge, betrayal, dogmatic beliefs, cognitive distortions, or delusions of grandeur. Perhaps the underlying root of multisystemic oppression and bondage is the unnamed "dis-ease" of love sickness, and as the LGBTQ+ elders in prison taught us, the antidote is unconditional love and compassion from a caring person or people.

The old way of understanding our contemporary social and environmental problems has run its course. Replacing the abusive and punishing environment of prison with a caring environment may assist in the rehabilitation of incarcerated older adults eligible for prison release. Many older adults are denied parole based on their violent criminal offense history and are destined to spend their lives in prison, but we can create a fairer playing field by balancing care and justice for everyone involved. One older adult stated that the reentry staff "gave me genuine love and caring and respect. I walked out of there feeling at home and loved and worthy."

We offer a new way of looking at the same old problem and propose a caring justice partnership paradigm to address issues of care and justice. We draw from leading-edge thought in physics, philosophy, humanistic and existential psychology, and social work. We argue that we can resolve the aging in prison crisis by shifting from a problem-based focus to a solution-based focus. We describe how caring justice can be used at the personal and collective levels to transform the world from the inside out.

The truthfulness and sincerity older adults sensed from these compassionate caregivers formed the basis for trust and a relational/therapeutic partnership. Older adults perceived these helpful caregivers as empathic, compassionate, and nonjudgmental. One older adult with serious mental illness shared that it was not until he had "a compassionate psychiatrist who did not judge me and made me feel loved and safe even in prison" that he began to take his psychotropic medication again. These caregivers were adept communicators, using verbal language and nonverbal behaviors (e.g., speaking to them with dignity and respect; using active listening) to build the relationship.

Some older adults described compassionate caregivers who helped them turn their lives around as valuing their humanness and life potential. These compassionate caregivers were practical, consistent, and solution-focused, and older prisoners described them as responsible and resourceful. Their helpful guidance ranged from counseling for personal growth to referrals or advocacy for needed medications, programs, or services. When these useful qualities were present, some older adults described feeling loved, cared for, and motivated to change their lives. Being in the presence of a loving or caring person, and learning to love and care for themselves, was pivotal in the expansion of their positive attitude and overall well-being.

Caring and Justice

The world, as we have created it, is a process of our thinking. It cannot be changed without changing our thinking.
　—Albert Einstein

Caring is often described as feeling or showing care and compassion. A person with a caring attitude is warm, sensitive, and considerate toward others. A caring person speaks respectfully, offers a handshake or a hug, and uses direct or indirect eye contact appropriate to that cultural tradition. The person to whom the care is directed feels cared for by the giver of that care. This process of giving and receiving care is associated with the heart, that is, "having a heart."

A growing body of research suggests that the heart can be imagined as being a second brain in the chest; it is an information processing center that is, in some ways, similar to the brain. The heart can learn, remember, and act independently of the brain, and it can send signals that connect to key areas of the brain—the amygdala, thalamus, and hypothalamus—that regulate human emotions and perceptions.[1]

The brain seems to be innately sensitive and receptive to the heart "energy" of others. Studies conducted at the HeartMath Research Institute have found that a heart-to-heart connection may be made between one person and another person (or animal). The heart's electromagnetism can affect and even synchronize with another person's brain waves when they are as much as five feet apart.[2] An example of heart-to-heart/brain wave communication is the skin-to-skin time newborns have with their primary caregivers, which helps them regulate their breathing patterns, heart rhythms, blood sugar, and body temperature.[3] This type of electromagnetic communication may be part of our evolutionary development and meant to enhance interpersonal communication and survival of the species.

Empathy

Incarcerated and formerly incarcerated older adults often described the importance of feeling listened to by another concerned person, someone who understood their experience and did not judge them for it. *Empathy* is a key aspect of demonstrating caring; it refers to the ability to understand and share the feelings of another as if that person is standing in the other's shoes.[4] Research on emotions defines empathy as the capability to sense other people's emotions as well as imagine what they might be thinking (cognitive) or feeling (affective). *Cognitive empathy* demonstrates that a person has a perspective-taking ability and can identify and understand other people's emotions; *affective empathy* refers to a person's sensations and feelings in response to another's emotions, enabling the person to mirror the emotions of that person. The empathic individual may feel stress, fear, or guilt even though the other person did not verbalize it.

Empathy has been identified in dogs and other animals as well as in humans. Whether a person performs an empathic action or observes someone else doing so, the same therapeutic effect is felt. Scientists hypothesize that these two different empathy pathways may be due to the activation of mirror neurons. Empathy triggers an understanding between two individuals, but it falls short of a person feeling the pain and suffering of someone else and being compelled to act on that feeling.[5] Martin Luther King Jr. and Mahatma Gandhi are two notable examples of civic leaders in whom empathy was elevated to the level of compassion in action.

Compassion and Unconditional Love

The Latin root of the word "compassion" means "co-suffering." *Compassion* is when a person "feels for another" and has a strong desire to do something to alleviate the person's suffering. Some older adults in prison showed compassion to younger incarcerated people by helping them, and the elders also appreciated the compassion shown to them by other caregivers. A compassionate caregiver is sensitive to the emotional pain or suffering of another. However, when compassion is thought of in a cognitive sense, such as fairness, justice, and interdependence, it is described as rational sound judgment.[6]

Unconditional love describes affection or love without any limitations. It is sometimes associated with altruism or complete love. *Altruism* is an action that benefits someone else. The definitions of unconditional love vary across cultures and disciplines, but all commonly agree that unconditional love represents love that is boundless, consistent, and not based on conditions.[7] For example, unconditional love of a parent for a child means loving the child no matter what he or she thinks, says, or does. If a child has a different viewpoint or does something that is not acceptable, the parent still loves the child despite that condition. For a person to give unconditional love, the person must first love him- or herself. Unconditional love may be shared between family members, by groups with a common goal, or by religious or spiritually minded people or groups. Despite hurt, betrayal, or relational discord, the love of these individuals is steadfast, dogged, and unchangeable.[8]

Justice

True peace is not merely the absence of war; it is the presence of justice.
—Jane Addams

Justice forms the other half of a caring justice worldview. To understand the relationship between care and justice, we must explore the history and shifting meanings of the concept of justice. In the United States, *justice* is the quality of being just, impartial, or fair and the conformity to truth, fact, or reason. The dictionary defines justice as "the maintenance or administration of what is just especially by the impartial adjustment of conflicting claims or the assignment of merited rewards or punishment."[9]

Throughout history and across cultures and disciplines, justice has been associated with truth, rationality, balance, order, harmony, law, morality, ethics, fairness, equity/equality, and religion. The polar opposites include injustice, chaos, violence, immorality, disparities, inequalities, and evil doing (negative behavior). During the rise of industrialization in the early twentieth century, the social aspects of justice and equality were paramount. The pursuit of social and distributive justice was advanced in philosophy, theology, and religion. In the study and application of the law, procedural justice entailed an effort to understand the processes and outcomes, and to improve the legal mechanisms that could ensure equality and fairness.

Responsibility for justice has been placed on the individual and on society. John Rawls and Erin Kelly described two basic principles of justice: justice as fairness and justice as just arrangements.[10] This theory of justice places some responsibility on society to create conditions that provide access to justice for all people. *Justice as fairness* entails each person having an equal right to basic liberties. *Just arrangements* provide for an even social and economic playing field with access to justice and resources for all. The just arrangements a society makes should provide the greatest benefits to the least advantaged people, for example, those living in poverty or older people. These arrangements should be attached to institutions that can ensure open access to conditions of fair and equal opportunity.

Rawls and Kelly suggest that one role of society is to *redress* inequalities and shift the balance of contingencies in the direction of equality. Rawls and Kelly believe that distributive principles for material goods and services and nonmaterial social goods, such as opportunity and power, should be grounded in an egalitarian view. They envision a just society as one in which everyone's basic needs are met, the competence of each person is maximized, and unnecessary stress and threats to well-being are minimized.[11]

The extent to which societal institutions, such as the U.S. justice system, can provide a just arrangement for equality has been questioned. One problem is that attorneys, judges, and legislatures often get caught up more in procedure than in achieving justice for all. The adage "justice delayed is justice denied" applies to the burdensome procedures, lack of sufficient courts, a system clogged with meritless cases, and using courts to settle matters that could be resolved by negotiation. The imbalance between court privileges obtained for the wealthy and for people of modest means, the use of delay and "blizzards" of unnecessary paper by large law firms, and judges who fail to cut through the underbrush of procedures all erode justice.

The social justice movement in the United States has deep roots in the Judeo-Christian religious tradition, the philosophical principles of Plato and Aristotle, and Western political theorists such as John Rawls. Throughout our history, the association of faith with social justice has been present, but social justice was commonly viewed as an abstract ideal that intersected with values related to what is good, desirable, and moral. This discourse has extended to how to achieve a right relationship for the individual in the social environment.[12]

The social work profession was born during the rise of industrialization in the early twentieth century in response to the large number of societal ills.[13] Their intervention was considered a form of socially responsible community practice and advocacy. Most social workers were women, and they practiced in settlement houses in urban and impoverished communities, providing a range of services and advocacy to community members, such as youth education, day care, food, and civic engagement and education for those most impoverished in the community. The movement focused on addressing the social-environmental conditions of those living in poverty, new immigrants, and wayward delinquent youth living in substandard conditions.[14] These workers were society's housekeepers, and they sought social reform by following what they referred to as "social gospel." Their moral mission was to speak out about the social justice issues of their times, such as poverty, poor working conditions, incarceration, women and children's rights, and war and peace, and to seek community and legislative level change. The motto of the settlement house was "research, residence, and reform."[15]

Social work leaders Jane Addams and Florence Kelly are often remembered for their advocacy efforts that led to systemic reforms in juvenile justice and development of the juvenile court system in the 1890s in Chicago, Illinois. This court innovation was soon adopted worldwide. They also advocated for workers' rights, child labor rights, mother and child rights, and world peace. These women leaders were morally compelled to do good and to help alleviate the pain and suffering of those underrepresented in society. It was a form of faith in action. Jane Addams embodied a type of moral justice based on the idea that "action is indeed the sole medium of expression for ethics." They used innovative practices to get the direct viewpoints of those less powerful in society, to invite participation by those most affected to gain understanding and resolution of social problems, to construct new forms of social belonging, respect, and participation, and to hold to a vision of a caring and just world.[16]

In the next section, we draw for historical precedence and new collective insights about how we might visualize and co-construct a caring justice world. We draw innovative perspectives from humanistic and transcendental psychology, physics, and Eastern medicine to facilitate new ways of thinking that foster fresh solutions.

Caring Justice: Visualizing Its Inner and Outer World

Issues involving aging, trauma, and the level of access to care and justice affects individuals, families, organizations, communities, and even entire cultural groups. An unbalanced system with wide-scale cruelty, abuse, and neglect is the result of a society's incapacity to share values of kind-heartedness and equality. Experiences of the psychological and moral injury of injustice run deep inside the historical psyche of humanity. Each person has his or her own idea about what justice looks like, and society at large has a variety of notions and interpretations of the meaning of justice.

In contemporary times, the focus has been on oppression and imbalanced interrelationships, and the question of care versus justice as punishment are of paramount concern. In response to the increase in the aging, sick, and dying prison population, some people may choose to cope with it by shutting down (or remain shut down to) their innate sense of justice by using ignorance, denial, or justification. Other people may feel an innate sense of justice and hear an ethical calling that compels them to act.

Justice is both a personal and a collective experience, and it is critical to understand how individual and collective consciousness and subjective viewpoints shape relationships between the self and other systems. The term "consciousness" often refers to a transcendental characteristic of the human mind. Most thought centering around consciousness comes from the fields of philosophy, psychology, psychiatry, physics, and neurobiology. Consciousness has been described as a state or quality of awareness regarding internal or external existence (table 8.1). For an individual, the subjective aspect is that the person has the ability to experience, feel, or sense an existence of the self or a higher self or soul.[17] The individual's subjective realities, such as thoughts and emotions, are "what I experience." In turn, these internal mental and emotional worldviews influence external behaviors, "what I do," which are objective and observable by the person and those who witness it.

Understanding the personal and collective conscious and the archetypal images of the feminine and masculine—mother and father (caregivers) and son and daughter (care receivers)—is helpful in understanding the concepts of care and justice. The concepts of personal and collective consciousness and archetypes were introduced by Carl Jung, a Swiss psychiatrist. He asserted that the human psyche comprises three parts: the ego, the personal unconscious, and the collective unconscious. The *ego* represents the conscious mind

TABLE 8.1 Individual and collective consciousness

	Internal	External
Individual	**Consciousness**	**Behavior**
	What I Experience.	*What I Do.*
	Subjective realties: self and consciousness, psychological development, states of mind, thought, emotions, and will (e.g., internal self and worldviews)	Objective realties: self and consciousness, psychological development, states of mind, thought, emotions, and will (e.g., compassion, justice advocacy, or violence and abuse, victim or offender)
Collective	**Culture**	**Systems**
	What We Experience.	*What We Do.*
	Intersubjective realities: shared values, culture and worldview, webs of culture, communication, relationships, norms, boundaries, customs (e.g., gender, racial/ethnic cultural groups, patriarchal culture)	Interobjective realities: social systems and the environment, visible societal structures, economic system, social system, justice system, political orders and structures (e.g., health care, victim services, prisons)

and is responsible for feelings of identity and continuity; the *personal uncon-scious* holds individual memories, including suppressed memories; and the *collective unconscious* is an inherited psychological template that contains all the collective knowledge and experiences humankind share. Jung believed that individuals inherit archetypes in much the same way they inherit instinctive patterns of behavior.[18]

Jung described archetypes as inborn tendencies that influence human behavior and personalities. These archetypes may appear in our dreams, art, religion, music, or literature, especially in mythology. Four archetypes are relevant to understanding the care and justice model: the persona, anima/animus, shadow, and self. The *persona* is the actor or mask; it is the outward face, a conformity archetype that changes according to the different roles an individual has in society (e.g., mother, father, professional, politician, daughter, son, student).[19]

The *anima/animus* reflects our male and female biological sexes. The psyche of a woman contains masculine aspects (the animus archetype), and the psyche of a man contains feminine aspects (the anima archetype). The *shadow* is the animal side of an individual's personality, a source of creative and destructive energies. Possible shadow aspects of the wounded mascu-line are aggressive impulses, unacknowledged biases and prejudices, envy, greed, and hate. Possible shadow aspects of the wounded feminine are being needy, dependent, passive aggressive, and jealous. The *self* is the archetype of psychic totality and unity, and it resides between ego-consciousness and the unconscious. The realization of the self is what individuals strive for during the individuation process.[20]

According to Jung and other theorists, a significant drawback in the male-dominated patriarchy of Western civilization revolves around cultural norms that stop men and women from developing the positive aspects of their feminine and masculine sides, especially as it relates to caregiving. This collec-tive repression has been expressed as a wounded masculine or animus and a wounded feminine or anima. Cultural repression against fully developing these gender aspects has resulted in a blockage for both men and women, which makes it impossible for them to embrace the totality of who they are and their capacities to give and receive care. This has led to devaluation of the positive feminine (e.g., inner knowing, the good mother) and positive masculine (e.g., the good and responsible father) qualities and to the predominance of the per-sona (the mask) of negative aspects of the collective feminine and masculine.

Society's beliefs and moral values about criminality determine the theory of punishment in that society, and these beliefs generally spread into the political arena. For example, in the United States in the 1960s, the judicial and execu-tive branches of the government designed sentencing laws with rehabilitation as the primary goal. During the politically conservative era of the 1980s and

1990s, lawmakers took much of that power away from the judicial and executive branches, and the main goal of this period was to get "tough on crime." Retribution, incapacitation, and deterrence became the dominant model, and rehabilitation was no longer a priority.[21]

We have now reached a critical point in time. Our old ways of thinking about criminality have not led to lasting solutions. We have lost sight of prison being a place of "corrections," in which people who broke the ethical and legal norms of their communities would have an opportunity to address the underlying root causes for their behavior.[22] Harsher approaches, such as deterrence, incapacitation, and retribution, are suggestive of a punishing father using corporal punishment, social deprivation, and revenge, and an absent mother. The strategy of deterrence through fear of or actual punishment to reduce or eliminate undesirable behavior may be doing more damage than good to the group of traumatized people who come to the attention of the criminal justice system. The incapacitation approach (out of sight out of mind) places people in a secure environment where they cannot cause additional harm to people or property, but recidivism rates demonstrate the failure of this approach. The retribution approach emphasizes providing the punishment they deserve for causing harm to others.[23]

The cumulative result of these strategies is an increasing number of frail and sick older inmates who can no longer maintain the pace of the prison regime. The increasing older adult prison population demonstrates that the criminal justice system has not achieved the objective of rehabilitating wrongdoers to keep the general public safe. The punishing father is not consistent in showing care to his wayward children. A more caring rehabilitative approach, such as that favored in earlier corrections models, is needed.[24] Many prisons lack the age-specific programming necessary to address the unique needs of older adults.[25] Clearly the system is out of balance. It is time for a new vision: an integrative paradigm of care with justice that honors the safety and well-being of people of all ages.

To this end, we offer the caring justice partnership paradigm, which is a philosophy and a way of life (figure 8.1). It integrates principles of care, justice, balanced scales, and partnership between the archetypal energies of the feminine (expressive) and the masculine (instrumental). The concepts of care and justice require the positive aspects of both feminine and masculine archetypes, that is, feeling and demonstrating love and concern for another's well-being (feminine aspect) and taking inspired yet thoughtful action (masculine aspect). These aspects apply to individuals, but they can be applied to systems as well, such as the correctional system, to assess whether its actions are in balance with the positive of the masculine and feminine. If out of balance, the shadow aspects of the masculine (e.g., misuse of power and control, neediness, passive aggression, manipulation) can alert us that an adjustment is needed.

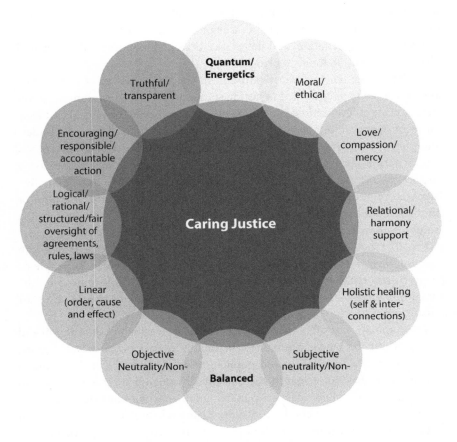

8.1 Caring justice partnership paradigm, philosophy, and way of life

The Energy Behind Care and Uncaring and Justice and Injustice

Everything is energy and that's all there is to it. Match the frequency of the reality you want, and you cannot help but get that reality. It can be no other way. This is not philosophy. This is physics.

—Albert Einstein

Everything that exists is part of a vast and invisible field of energy[26] that contains all possible realities and is molded by individuals' thoughts and feelings. The unique energy of the human body is made up of particles or vibrations formed by atoms and their subatomic particles. The concepts of care and justice are images in the personal and collective unconscious that live in individuals' minds in the form of thoughts and emotions, which are also energy. According to the laws of physics and the observer effect of those in society, a new idea or thought paradigm can become reality in the physical world through imagination and focused observation. That is, we can create a caring justice world that first occurs in the minds and hearts of individuals.

When imagining a caring justice worldview, two concepts organize the relationship between care and justice: quantum justice and balanced justice. They are reviewed in the following pages.

Quantum Justice

Any changes within us or in our environment must start at the quantum level. We refer to this unseen inner world of the subconscious or unconscious mind as *quantum justice*. The outer reality eventually must be affected and modified to reflect this internal blueprint. In essence, changing a belief from "I am not worthy" to "I am worthy" will eventually lead to a shift in an individual's sense of self-worth. For example, if a person perceives the environment as unsafe and threatening, he may react violently as a form of self-protection, whereas a person who feels loved and cared for may respond with loving kindness to another person. The human and collective mind is constantly changing, and the broad concepts of justice and care have shifted in meaning across time and space, affecting the way humans have responded to care and justice. In the past two centuries, the debate between who is deserving of justice has swung along a continuum between conservative (punishment) and liberal (care and rehabilitation) poles.

Physics offers a new perspective on the energy that fuels human action. A person's inner perspective often entails thoughts and feelings that guide his or her activities, behaviors, and interactions in their external world. The same process is true for the collective dominant cultural perspective about care and justice that informs the thoughts and emotions of a collective response to health and justice matters. Quantum energy represents the blueprint (or logic model) of physical reality. Any time an individual's energy patterns are modified, there will be a modification in the individual's reality. Care and justice concepts also involve interrelationships between individuals, society, and the natural world. Lasting positive changes in the criminal justice system must come first from a transformation at the quantum level of energy, or the inner mind of individuals, then behavioral change will follow.

We currently have ethical dilemmas regarding substandard health care for incarcerated people, use of the death sentence, and a large number of aging people becoming ill and dying in prison. Not everyone in society supports this punitive criminal justice approach. Our conscious and subconscious thoughts affect reality. If enough people believe in a different approach and practice it in their own consciousness, a new positive mental map can transform our thinking and influence manifested reality.[27]

Individuals within family units/cells make up society and are connected to the world and the universe. If these units of society are unwell, that will be reflected not only in society but also on the world and universal order. The caregivers beliefs, feelings, and intentions affect those of the care receivers. The dominant vibrations of society caregivers are most beneficial when their vibration is high and positive, especially when working with individuals processing the physical, mental, emotional, and spiritual aftermath of trauma. In essence, wherever the mind goes the energy follows.

When applied to health or criminal justice, a focused mind is most important. Creating a mental map of an ill older adult or a criminal offender in a state of wellness will foster an improved state for that person. Joseph described how support and encouragement from an incarcerated older adult helped him change his perspective on his life. If the other person receives this positive projection, that person has the potential to rise to that image. If a care receiver is not yet strong enough in self-love to reject a negative or biased mental image, that projection may have a negative effect.

Perhaps, the most challenging aspect in conceptualizing quantum energetics is the idea of vibration and the fluidity of what seems to be concrete matter, such as the human body or the prison's physical building structure. Reality is similar to watching a film or video in which individual frames appear to run seamlessly. Our material bodies and the universe flicker in and out of existence at the speed of light, and our nervous system cannot process these quantum events at the speed at which they are happening. Therefore, the nervous system decodes the energy into the experience of solid three-dimensional bodies.

Perhaps most interesting of all is how individuals are visualized in the context of their relationships and the world. According to quantum entanglement theory, *all humans* are a part of a larger *quantum field*. When there is a change in one aspect of the system, such as the individual, it affects all other aspects of the system. When applied to individuals and societies, this theory suggests that whatever we do unto others, we are also doing unto ourselves.[28] If we hurt others, we also hurt ourselves. If we are good to others, such as being helpful and compassionate, we receive goodness in return. This concept also challenges the notion of retribution and punishment. If others are suffering in prison, those of us free in society vicariously experience that suffering. If we forgive someone else for their transgressions, we also have freed ourselves. These notions turn our current approach to criminal justice matters upside down. Our current criminal justice system is overtaxed and overcrowded, and many communities remain unsafe. Might we try a new approach that is guided by a balance of care and kindness?

Balanced Justice

Balanced justice is the second overarching organizing concept of the caring justice paradigm. Many areas of life require us to pay attention to balance. For example, balancing self and others is necessary to have an interdependent as opposed to codependent relationship. Work-life balance often refers to giving equal attention to work and leisure. The remnants of the association of balance with care and justice can be seen in the statue of Lady Justice found at many courthouses. She holds a scale in one hand (balance), has a blindfold over her eyes (impartiality), and holds a double edge sword (authority) in the other hand.

The focus on justice has evolved and is increasingly associated with a related concept, equality. But equality and fairness are subjective concepts, and they may change over time based on society's definitions. In the caring justice approach, balanced justice represents equality among diverse individuals, groups, and cultures. Equality signifies commonality between a group of persons, objects, processes, or circumstances. For example, although our differences have led to conflict and oppression by the dominant group over subordinate groups, our commonalities include similar life experiences, the use symbols, and the capacity for self and other awareness. Instead of focusing on differences, individuals and groups could focus on their similarities to build a collective consensus that incorporates aspects of a caring justice world into daily life, bringing relationships between individuals, families, communities, and the external world into balance.[29]

Restorative justice addresses the relational aspects of crime and can provide this balance. The restorative justice model, in which healing is balanced with accountability, community safety, and competency development, addresses the identified parties affected by the crime: those victimized, those who committed the offense, and the community as a whole.[30]

Caring Justice Partnership Paradigm

The caring justice partnership paradigm incorporates the complementary concepts of care and justice. It is a visionary blueprint that can be applied for personal and relational growth and evolution as well as for community and societal change to solve the social and environmental problems that continue to plague our society. The aging prison population crisis is just one symptom of an outdated thought paradigm of patriarchy, conflict, separation, power, and control. The new blueprint we offer can be used by individuals, partners, families, communities, and the collective to realize a caring justice world (see figure 8.1). The caring justice model uses the universal symbol of the circle to represent the power of the masculine/feminine interchange. The masculine principles are represented by the fiery life-giving force of the sun (left side of circle). By day its powerful light travels to the earth enhancing life and growth. At night we are reminded of the feminine power of the moon (right side of circle) and the ripples of the encircling waters of the earth, which give and sustain life.

The circle has been associated with notions of totality, the self, wholeness, original perfection, infinity, eternity, timelessness, and all cyclical movements.[31] The masculine and feminine principles can be expressed by individuals and the collective along a continuum between the polarities of feminine/expressive and masculine/instrumental ways of thinking, feeling, and doing (see text box). Feminine and masculine meet in the center to balance self and collective expression. It is important to emphasize that these feminine and masculine traits live within each of us and influence our thoughts, feelings, actions, and relational interactions. Anyone can tap into these energies, such as unconditional self-love, respect, and worthiness or rational thinking and logical decision making. Individuals, societies, and the collective may expressive these aspects anywhere on the continuum.

We define the feminine/expressive major aspect or principle as the universal and inherent archetypal subjective awareness counterpart, and the balance to the objective. In comparison, we define the masculine/instrumental major aspect or principle as the universal and inherent archetypal objective awareness counterpart, and the balance to the subjective. The masculine and feminine archetypal energies are located within all people and systems and manifest through individual or collective thoughts, feelings, actions, and beliefs (see text box).

Caring Justice Partnership Paradigm: A Mental Emotional Model for Personal and Relational Evolution

Overarching Organizing Principles: Quantum Justice and Balanced Justice

Feminine/Expressive Polarity	Masculine/Instrumental Polarity
Feminine/Expressive: universal and inherent archetypal energy, subjective awareness counterpart, and balance to objective masculine/instrumental justice, within all people and systems that manifest through individual or collective thoughts, actions, and beliefs	Masculine/Instrumental: universal and inherent energy, objective awareness counterpart, and balance to feminine/expressive justice, within all people and system that manifest through individual or collective thoughts, actions, and beliefs

Feminine/Expressive Major and Minor Aspects

Moral/Ethical Major Aspect
Minor Aspects
- Heart-centered
- Unconditional love
- Compassionate
- Nurturing
- Merciful
- Flexibility
- Kindness
- Humility
- Dignity and respect (self, others, the natural world)
- Receiver, receptive, providing inner resources

Actions/Interactions Major Aspect
Minor Aspects
- Relational, interdependent
- Seeks harmony and equality
- Weighs all options via the heart
- Diplomatic
- Discerning
- Supportive and healing
- Analyzes the whole and sum of its parts

Self and Worldview Major Aspect
Minor Aspects
- Right brain driven (emotions)
- Process oriented
- Collective-focus (society responsible to citizens)
- Matriarchal/horizontal shared power/control
- Holistic-bigger picture, interconnections, integration, togetherness, merging
- Creative/innovative/births ideas
- Subjective awareness
- Subjective neutrality (nonjudgmental)
- Intuitive way of knowing
- 'Being
- Intentionality
- Illogical/circular thinking
- Emotions are powerful
- The rule of natural law and moral rightness
- Collective empowerment

Masculine/Instrumental Major and Minor Aspects

Moral/Ethical Major Aspect
Minor Aspects
- Mind-centered
- Logical/rational thought and thinking
- Judicious decision making/impartial
- Honor/honesty/honorable/worthiness
- Disciplined, structured, order
- Inner strength of will, leadership
- Authority in service of protection, oversight of agreements, rules, laws, policies
- Truthful/transparent/integrity/trustworthy
- Giver, giving/providing outer resources

Actions/Interactions Major Aspect
Minor Aspects
- Practical, procedural
- Conscious action and use of power
- Thoughtful, judicious decision making and planning
- Encouraging, teach/teacher, reinforce
- Responsibility, accountability, independence
- Structured/consistent/dependable
- Oversees rules, laws, and their administration

Self and Worldview Major Aspect
Minor Aspects
- Left brain driven (intellect)
- Outcome oriented
- Individualistic-focused (self-responsibility)
- Patriarchal/hierarchical/vertical power/control
- Linear (order, cause-effect), Inter-independence, separateness, individuality
- Action-driven (doing)/materializes ideas
- Objective awareness (observable)
- Objective neutrality (nonjudgmental)
- Rational way of knowing
- Puts intentions into action
- Logical/rational processes
- Thoughts and actions are powerful
- Rule of laws (legal justice) established by the authorities of a community
- Self-empowerment

In the caring justice partnership model (CJPM), the positive expression of feminine and masculine aspects are equal in importance for personal development of the true self (the whole person). For example, an individual who has achieved wholeness integrates and balances the positive aspects of the masculine and feminine in every aspect of his or her daily life. Integration is important for building and maintaining healthy love and other types of relationships. In a partnership in which both parties are whole in their own selves, neither is dependent on the other to complete their wholeness. This is a partnership of interdependence, not codependence. This model also can be applied to societies that strive to make their communities and the service systems, institutions, and organizations within them healthy and safe for people of all ages. Feminine compassion requires masculine help to devise and implement the plan.

The internal energetic and balancing aspects of caring justice consist of feminine and masculine archetypal energies. Individuals and systems exist along a continuum between these two archetypes. For example, the criminal justice system, and society in general, has chosen to express approaches to crime in extreme and unbalanced ways, such as stricter sentencing policies that fail to recognize the effect these policies have on individuals, families, and communities.

A balanced criminal justice system would access the positive aspects of both feminine and masculine energies, integrating the feminine heart-centered compassionate aspect of justice with the masculine logical mind-centered aspect, taking into account the highest good for all. Balancing masculine and feminine aspects will result in wholeness, equality, and personal power infusing the criminal justice system.

Three major characteristics represent the caring justice partnership virtues: moral/ethical, actions/interactions, and self/worldview. These characteristics inform the expressive and instrumental activities when building caring and just partnerships. The feminine expression of morality/ethics draws from the reflective thoughts and feeling realm of intuition and "beingness." The higher feeling level and practice of unconditional love, compassion, nurturance, mercy, humility, dignity, and respect are expressed as the feminine archetype washes over care and justice with waves of unconditional love. Even the most hardened criminals are deserving of love and care, and people affected by hurt, harm, and crime can be brought together for support and healing. The masculine/instrumental expression of morality/ethics draws on moral and ethical principles of the mind regarding order, authority, and truthfulness. Logical decision making reduces the emotional fever, such as a fear of diversity or the systemic biases that led to mass incarceration. To correct the U.S. criminal justice system that disproportionately confines racial/ethnic minorities to long prison sentences, the balance between masculine and feminine aspects of care and justice is paramount. Through mind-centeredness, logical/rational thinking, and judicious decision making, all options are weighed in addressing inner and interpersonal conflicts to turn relationships from discord to harmony. In tandem, these two energies reach a center point of impartialness and neutrality.

The second characteristic is actions/interactions. Feminine/expressive actions and interactions are guided by a holistic approach toward personal inner growth and interdependence. Diplomacy, support, and healing dominate in matters of care and justice. Masculine/instrumental actions brings a practical and procedural aspect to the partnership to assist in moving forward the feminine/masculine mutual agenda of self-powered partnerships. The positive masculine is independent and highly responsible and accountable in his actions, reactions, and interactions, providing consistency and dependability to complement the emotional expression of the feminine. The structured, dependable, and encouraging authority figure is a most needed aspect for many individuals who find themselves involved in the criminal justice system. The positive masculine archetype offers encouragement, mentoring, and positive reinforcement to others, especially to young adults confused about their life direction.

The third major characteristic is self/worldview. The feminine/expressive archetype is right-brain driven, tapping into emotions and intuition and being process-oriented and focused on the collective. The power of feminine leadership rests on equality and sharing, striving for togetherness, harmony, and love between and among humans and the natural world. The masculine/instrumental archetype is left-brain driven, drawing from the intellect to understand and respond to relationships. For example, a parent or judge would take into account mitigating factors such as a history of physical and emotional abuse, lack of access to community resources, or systemic discrimination that influenced the thoughts, feelings, and behaviors of a child or a defendant. While the feminine pays attention to the process, the masculine is more outcome oriented and emphasizes self-control in encounters with the world. The feminine and masculine perspectives working together influence the type of disciplinary action a judge may choose. These options might include rehabilitation as an alternative to incarceration to address the root cause of the problem as opposed to criminal conviction and a long prison sentence.

When the feminine and masculine are in harmonious partnership, the energy of egalitarianism, respect, and balance prevails. Individuals, partners, and systems peacefully interact, and the whole is greater than the sum of its parts and is forward moving. Balanced and judicious decision-making processes are exemplified in the teachings of the Iroquois Nation as told by Oren Lyons (Seneca), faith keeper, Onondaga Nation:

> The Peacemaker taught us about the Seven Generations. He said, when you sit in council for the welfare of the people, you must not think of yourself or of your family, not even of your generation. He said, make your decisions on behalf of the seven generations coming, so that they may enjoy what you have today.

Final Reflections

In this chapter, we explored the inner and outer aspects of the age-old concepts of care and justice. We are at a crossroads. The old ways of doing things have not solved our problems of poverty, crime, violence, and abuse, nor have they reduced the gender, race, and class divide or health disparities. We offered a caring justice philosophical way of life as a new way of thinking and feeling about the same old social problems.

The caring justice partnership paradigm offers the opportunity to be creative within broad parameters. The current crisis of mass incarceration of diverse older people in America began with moral panic during the1970s and 1980s, the get tough on crime era. A collective fear of crime was rampant, and politicians and media used our fears related to race, violent expressions of masculinity, vulnerability expressions of feminism, fear of crime, aging, death and dying, and diversity and difference to capitalize on their own self-interested agendas. Visualize yourself there as you reflect on these questions:

1. Would you have supported the punitive and stricter sentencing policies?
2. Would you have supported long or life sentences in which people would age and die in prison?
3. If you were aware of the often inhumane conditions of confinement, would you have supported this choice?

Now think about our current situation and the wide-scale community trauma and increases in the aging prison population. How might Iroquois teachings and a caring justice approach inform your decision-making process today? What might be one or two positive or negative consequences of your recommendations thirty or forty years into the future?

Thank you for sharing your thoughts, feelings, and visualizations. The caring justice partnership paradigm offers broad principles and guidelines so individuals, groups, communities, nations, and the collective can be creative in how they choose to express it. As we underscored in this chapter, caring justice is a philosophy and a way of life. In the next chapter, we draw from the knowledge and wisdom of older adults in prison and present models and programs that integrate care and justice.

CHAPTER 9

ACCEPTING THE GIFT OF LIFE

Incarcerated Older Adults' Prescription for Living Longer,
Happier, and Healthier Lives

*A human being is a part of the whole called by us universe, a part limited
in time and space. He experiences himself, his thoughts and feelings as
something separated from the rest, a kind of optical delusion of his consciousness. This delusion is a kind of prison for us, restricting us to our
personal desires and to affection for a few persons nearest to us. Our task
must be to free ourselves from this prison by widening our circle of compassion to embrace all living creatures and the whole of nature in its beauty.*

—Albert Einstein

In this chapter, we explore ways in which older people in prison can
teach us how to co-create a caring justice world. Narratives and other
findings in this chapter are based on the Hartford Prison Study of 2010
(see chapter 3). Building on coping and resilience among older adults in prison,
we examine how biopsychosocial, structural, and spiritual medicine interact to
promote benevolent and holistic well-being for individuals, family, and communities. We next draw from Western and Eastern knowledge and practices to
explore the internal and external pathways that influence health, wellness, and
compassionate behaviors of older adults in prison. We conclude the chapter by
sharing self-caring contemplative, responsible, restorative, and peaceful practices
that facilitate living a long, healthy, and happy life even under prison conditions.

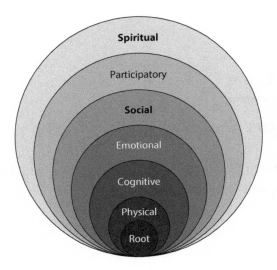

9.1 Domains of coping practice for well-being among older adults in prison

People of all ages who have suffered trauma may experience challenges in the physical, mental, emotional, social, and spiritual domains. Evidence suggests that older adults in prison who use coping resources targeting these domains have better health in later life than those who do not. Coping resources fall into the following domains: root, physical, cognitive, emotional, social, spiritual, participatory, and multidimensional (figure 9.1).

Some older adults felt appreciation for being able to meet their basic needs in prison, and others used physical coping resources, such as exercise or taking medication. Older adults reported using cognitive coping practices, such as finding peace within (thinking positive, optimism), making healthy choices, reading books or other written materials, and playing games or mind exercises such as completing puzzles. One incarcerated older adult found optimism and inner peace by meditating. Others described emotional coping through prison program offerings such as supportive emotional counseling or anger and stress management programs that taught alternative emotions to anger, worry, and anxiety. Other activities that evoked emotional wellness included listening to music, writing/journaling, or engaging in play and pleasurable experiences.

Social coping consisted of interactions with family, friends, peers in prison, and program participation. Being in touch with family members was described as one of the most important external social coping strategies for some incarcerated older individuals. Spirituality was both an internal and external expression of coping. Some focused on their internal connection with God and attended a religious service. Others thought of spirituality as praying or being of service to others. Participatory coping was described as self-empowerment and leadership. Several older adults were involved in leadership positions, taking classes or vocational training for personal advancement, teaching, leading a book club, or prison advocacy. Some activities were multidimensional and tapped multiple coping domains, such as making art or playing music or practicing yoga.

Coping Practices That Support Well-Being for Older Incarcerated Adults

Domains	Description	Sample Quotes
Root	Meeting basic needs/ foundation: food, clothing, safety, grounded in love/ family	"I try to be secure in myself." "I stay busy." "I avoid confrontation." "I think about my family a lot." "I stay away from negative influences." "At least I have three hots and a cot."
Physical	Exercise (yard, run/walk, sports), medication	"I work out to relieve my stress." "I became a jogger and sprinter at 56 years old. I run five miles per day and sprint 105 yards every other day." "In prison, I get the medication and treatment I need to survive and feel much better."
Cognitive	Finding peace within, meditate, thinking positive, making healthy choices, puzzles, read	"I try to think positive and try to meditate and read a great deal to take my mind off worries."
Emotional	Supportive emotional counseling, anger and stress management, music (listening), writing/ journaling, play and pleasure	"I participate every Monday in a group therapy Cage Your Rage program" (10 weeks). "I write about experiences to process my thoughts and feelings." "I have fun."
Social	Interaction with family, friends, or peers in prison, program participation	"I keep in touch with family members."

Domains	Description	Sample Quotes
Spiritual	Church, God, pray, service to others	"I pray to God and go to church regularly here." "I attend religious services, offer my prayers, and try as much as I can to be faithful to my oaths as a Muslim."
Participatory	Leadership, taking classes or vocational training for personal advancement, teaching, leading a book club, advocacy	"I lead a bereavement group for other inmates." "I am a paralegal and seek justice for people in prison."
Multidimensional	Making art or music, yoga	"I do yoga, doctor, I do yoga."

Our body of research on trauma, coping, and well-being among older adults in prison support these findings. Incarcerated older people who engaged in a variety of biopsychosocial, structural, and spiritual coping practices, especially to reduce stress-related symptoms, reported higher levels of physical and mental well-being compared to those who did not (see chapter 6). In particular, older adults who reported having a more positive worldview of self and others were less likely to report a history of recidivism and prison disciplinary infractions than their counterparts who reported fewer coping resources. These findings are consistent with empirical evidence that coping resources can prevent or ameliorate the adverse effects of traumatic and stressful life experiences and well-being.

We are still learning why the biopsychosocial, structural, and spiritual aspects of coping have a multidimensional therapeutic effect on trauma or stress and well-being in individuals and the collective. In this chapter, we explore this idea further, drawing from Western and Eastern traditions of coping to understand how worldview might influence the self's physical, mental, emotional, behavioral, and spiritual health and wellness. We begin with the role of energy and balance in this cognitive and emotional mind, body, and spirit interrelationship.

The Role of Energy and Balance in Health and Wellness

Multidimensional biopsychosocial, structural, and spiritual practices are consistent with Western complementary medicine that originated in the East and has historically focused on energy and balance as keys to health and well-being.

Although you may doubt that these practices could be implemented in the duress of the prison environment; nonetheless, it is important to note that in the path toward enlightenment individuals develop their skills not only in appropriate environments and life situations but also in challenging and even inhospitable environments. In this section, we illustrate how resilient older adults' coping resources can be mapped to the seven major energy centers in the body, known as *chakras* in Eastern cultures.

The role of energy and balance explain the presence of health, wellness, and peace or its absence in personal and collective ills such as physical and mental illness and crime and violence. Energy is often thought of as a subtle and malleable substance and is referred to as life force energy or *chi*. Energy can be easily manipulated by the thoughts and emotions of an individual and can be influenced by others' thoughts and emotions. Internal positive or negative characteristics will manifest in accordance with the nature of the thoughts experienced. This imprinting process is similar to the negative worldview older adults in prison reported learning as children, such as "you are no good like your father" or "the world is not a safe place." Fear and guilt may place an individual at risk of victimization or revictimization or at risk of engaging in criminal behavior. Unraveling these false truths about one's thoughts and emotions will eventually lead to personal authenticity or the true self, a process in which mental, emotional, and behavioral patterns shift, creating a more positive outlook.

Eastern philosophy references cosmic energy and consciousness (Shiva and Shakti) as the forces that create balance in the world. *Shakti* represents feminine energy and the dynamic forces that move through the universe. Feminine energy is responsible not only for creation but also for being an agent of change and restoration of balance. Masculine energy, *Shiva*, represents consciousness and the unchanging, unlimited, and unswayable observer. It is only when Shiva and Shakti combine that creation, movement, and action arise. In other words, energy without consciousness is blind, aimless, ignorant, and disordered; it needs consciousness to give it content, form, and direction. And consciousness without energy is dormant power that cannot be the cause of anything.[1] Understanding the energetic aspects of life and body are critical nurturing it to function as a whole. Energy also helps to explain the biopsychosocial, structural, and spiritual determinants of health and justice that have fueled many local and global societal ills: climate change, multisystemic oppression and violence, and the growth of the aging prison population.

Human Body and Its Different Layers

The human body is composed of different layers of energy, also called bodies: spiritual body, mental body, emotional body, etheric body, and the physical

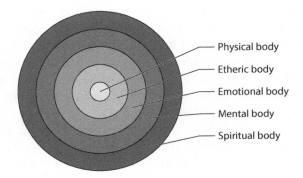

9.2 The different layers of energy in the human body

body (figure 9.2). Essentially, we are all energy and use the physical body to function in the material realm; that is, within the physical body is the core of spirituality that is the driver of the physical body throughout our lifetime.[2] The *etheric body* is one of the conduits that connect with the spirit. However, this connection depends on how clear the etheric body is of negativity and negative elementals.

The etheric body is the external energy system for the physical body, and it is the densest energy system in human beings. The etheric body has three major components: meridians, energy centers, and the aura. The meridians are energetic rivers and tributaries. They are responsible for delivering small energy streams to the energy centers, the aura, and ultimately to the physical body. The aura generally extends about 1 inch off the body, but it can extend farther away from the physical body depending on the positive or negative vibration patterns of the body. The colors of the aura reflect the level of thinking of the person. As the etheric body delivers energy to the physical body, it enables individuals to generate their life experiences.[3] The etheric and physical bodies complement each other, and they need to be cared for and nurtured so that an individual can achieve a healthy and happy life.[4]

Etheric matter is an elastic-like substance that permeates all space, including the human body. Because the etheric body is made of matter less dense than the human body but more dense than the emotional, mental, and spiritual bodies, it serves as a vehicle to convert subtle emotional, mental, and spiritual energy into more dense energy that can be manifested in the physical world. It also serves as a filter for different patterns of energy that come from the environment so that the physical body is nurtured appropriately.[5] Cleansing and healing the etheric body may be a coping strategy to heal not only the physical body but also the emotional, mental, and spiritual bodies, which, in turn, is necessary for lasting physical healing.

Energy Centers

Another important aspect of understanding the relationship of consciousness (thoughts and feelings) to aging, health, and justice, are the energy centers. The human body is composed of *energy centers* or vortexes, and they come in many sizes and frequencies. There are 114 energy centers in the body, but we focus only on the seven energy centers that govern the primary aspects of individuals. If all seven are balanced, the individual will experience physical, emotional, and psychological well-being and empowerment and optimal functioning. If not, the individual will experience fluctuations in the energy centers that may result in suboptimal functioning.

In Eastern philosophy, these energy centers are called chakras, which in Sanskrit means wheel or circle of life. They are represented by the seven primary colors of the rainbow, and they vibrate or spin at different frequencies. Energy centers are positioned throughout the length of the body approximately 3 inches from each other, beginning at the base of the spine and ending at the top of the head (figure 9.3).[6] These seven energy centers are the root (EC-1), sacral (EC-2), solar plexus (EC-3), heart (EC-4), throat (EC-5), brow (EC-6), and crown (EC-7).

Table 9.1 details the basic focus, color, gender, and balance qualities, elements, anatomical location, basic rights and needs, senses, and signs and symptoms of the seven energy centers. The table also lists imbalances in the physical,

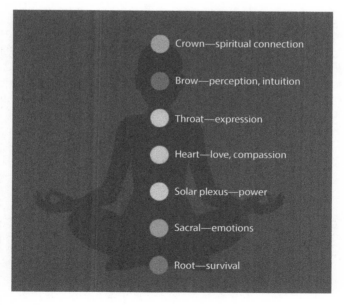

9.3 The seven main energy centers (chakras) in the human body

TABLE 9.1 Energy centers (EC) awareness tool for personal and collective evolution

Qualities	Root EC	Sacral EC	Solar Plexus EC	Heart EC	Throat EC	Brow EC	Crown EC
Basic Focus/Function	Survival, physical existence, basic needs, safety, & security	Emotions, sexuality intimacy	Power & identity	Love, connection, compassion	Communication, life purpose, authentic expression	Clear perspective & intuition	Connection to spirit and wisdom
Coping Resources (*Older Adults in Prison*)	Root/physical	Emotional/physical	Participatory	Emotional/social	Cognitive/social	Cognitive/spiritual	Spiritual
Color	Red	Orange	Yellow	Green	Blue	Indigo	Violet
Gender Balance Qualities	Masculine	Feminine	Masculine	Feminine	Masculine	Feminine	Feminine & masculine
Elements	Earth	Water	Fire	Air	Ether	Light (EWFA)	None
Anatomic Location	Tailbone base	Pelvis/sacrum	Solar plexus	Chest center	Throat center	Brow center	Crown
Basic Right	To be	To feel	To act	To love	To express	To perceive	To know
Basic Need	Safety & security	Creative expression, emotion awareness/ intimate connection	Personal empowerment	To love and be loved	Expressing one's truth	Connection with higher self	Oneness with the divine
Sense	Smell	Taste	Sight	Touch	Hearing	Intuition/sixth sense	None

TABLE 9.1 (*Continued*)

Qualities	Root EC	Sacral EC	Solar Plexus EC	Heart EC	Throat EC	Brow EC	Crown EC
Signs and Symptoms of a Balanced Energy Center	Feeling secure, stable, independent, earth grounded, belonging, accomplished, and peaceful, money, safety, and shelter; vitality, prosperity, patient, tenacious, successful	Emotions, creativity balance between feminine and masculine energies, joy and pleasure in life, healthy relationships, sensuality and sexuality, adaptability	Feeling in control, confident, strong self-esteem and self-worth, knows when to surrender and to take action, natural leader, inner strength, strong will, clarity, and courage	Feeling loved, compassionate, understanding, empathetic, possessing self-acceptance, forgiveness, kindness, and gratitude	Speak one's truths, need and desires, being able to express oneself, having a sense of inner freedom, and good communication skills, good oral communicator	In tune with the physical and material world, ability to make decisions, being open-minded; being able to access inner wisdom, intuition, and creativity	Ability to establish spiritual connection, sense of oneness, wholeness, inner connection. sense of clarity and harmony, happiness, good health, and wisdom
Signs and Symptoms of Physical Imbalances	Bowel, blood, or bone disorders; obesity, walking problems, frailty	Genital, sexual, fertility issues; hip or sacroiliac problems; bladder issues, dehydration, prostrate or ovarian cancer	Digestion issues; kidney or liver problems, ulcers, chronic fatigue	Lack of energy, asthma, heart or lung problems, immune disorders	Neck stuffiness, teeth/gum issues, TMJ, thyroid or hearing problems	Headaches, migraines, nightmares, lack of intuition, allergies, sinus issues	Confusion, spaciness, disconnected from self, others, and higher self
Signs and Symptoms of Psychological/ Emotional, Social, Spiritual Imbalances	PTSD, materialism, anorexia, anxiety, hypervigilant, chronic fear, shame worry, instability, hopeless humiliation, blame, depression inertia	Sexual disorders, fear of intimacy, repressed emotions, emotional dysregulation, repressed sexuality, blame, relationship problems, including violence, neglect, abuse	Indecisive, insecure, timid and needy. rageful, low self-esteem, bullying	"Heartless" grief, hatred of self and other, disconnection, self-absorbed, lack of empathy or compassion or concern for humans, the environment, in the extreme: "evilish"	Lying, an impostor or fraud, trickster, talks loud and too much, doesn't listen, lack of purpose, malingering, Tourette's syndrome, stuttering, mutism	Poor judgment bipolar disorder, psychosis	Depression, dementia

(*continued*)

TABLE 9.1 (*continued*)

Qualities	Root EC	Sacral EC	Solar Plexus EC	Heart EC	Throat EC	Brow EC	Crown EC
Signs and Symptoms of Behaviors Associated with Imbalance	Stealing, financial exploitation, physical abuse perpetration or victimization, revictimization	Emotional abuse, sexual abuse perpetration or victimization, revictimization	Fearless, disempowered abuse survivor, hostage taking, hyperactive-power and control	Antisocial behavior, dictator, despot, terrorism, serial killer	Fraud, verbal abuse/psychological abuse, terroristic threat, perjury	Manipulation, extortion, financial exploitation	Religious driven genocide and terrorism
Potential Coping Activities (*Older Adults in Prison*)	Seek social welfare benefits, safe housing, employment, financial or job training, gardening, nature walks, exercise, meditation, brain exercises for optimal physical functioning (e.g., puzzles)	Creative brainstorming, creative visualization, use of imagination, engage in play and pleasurable activities (games), emotional expression through the arts or participation in groups intimate relationships	Fearless expression of the authentic self, participatory leadership, facilitate groups, develop programs to help other people, teach others, self-advocacy or advocacy on behalf of others, self-defense training, martial arts, building self-esteem and physical and emotional strength, public speaking	Engage in loving and compassionate activities, personal relationships with a partner or family, volunteer for social causes	Speak your truth whether alone or with others, practice thinking before you speak or act, clearly speak with love, kindness, and truth, practice listening, meditation, journal, write, communicate in groups	Connect with nature, the earth, the beach, solitude and solitary meditation, connect with inner-knowing and spirit, engage in spiritual support groups or organizations with likeminded others	Meditation, use repetitive sounds or words, like mantras, engage in spiritual support groups or organizations with likeminded others

TABLE 9.1 (*continued*)

Qualities	Root EC	Sacral EC	Solar Plexus EC	Heart EC	Throat EC	Brow EC	Crown EC
Positive Affirmations for All Energy Centers	I am grounded, safe, and secure. I am stable, strong, and healthy.	I am creative and adaptable. I am playful and emotionally open. I love intimacy and life's pleasures.	I can do anything I set my mind to. I am powerful and I use it wisely. I think clearly and laugh often.	I am loving and lovable. I am compassionate and I forgive. I am a source of healing in the world.	I know my truth and I share it. I am driven by my deepest purpose. I am a great communicator and I listen well.	I follow my inner guidance. I always see the big picture. I follow my dreams.	I am intelligent and aware. I am one with everything. I am a source of the divine. I live in the now.
Maslow's Hierarchy of Needs	**Physiological Needs:** Bodily needs, breathing, food, water, sleep, etc. **Safety & Security Needs:** Security of body, education, employment, resources, morality, family, health property, freedom from violence in the home or community, shelter	**Love/Belonging:** Child bonding with caregivers, important relationships in childhood and sexual intimacy in adulthood (family bonding, friendships, and intimate partners)	**Esteem:** self-worthiness and dignity, confidence, achievement, respect by others	**Esteem/Social:** Unconditional self-love and relational love, such as important social relationships and connection with nature	**Esteem/Social:** Authentic self-expression and communication, positive self-talk, positive relational communication	**Self-Actualization:** Morality, creativity, spontaneity, self-awareness, personal growth, self-assertiveness and fulfilling one's potential	**Self-Actualization:** Self-awareness, personal growth, self-assertiveness and fulfilling one's potential

psychological, emotional, social, behavioral, and spiritual domains as well as behaviors associated with imbalance and associated positive affirmations. We also mapped the coping resources and activities of incarcerated older adults and their associated energy centers.

The first energy center (root EC) is related to basic survival, physical existence, basic needs, safety, and security. Based on their life histories, many incarcerated older adults reported growing up in poverty-ridden or low-income homes and neighborhoods, with family and community discord, and violence similar to their current experience of prison. This suggests that many individuals in prison have imbalanced root energy centers. This may include internal negative messages regarding self-worth, their ability to support themselves via legitimate ends, and their right to safety and security. High rates of physical, emotional, mental health, social, spiritual, and behavioral well-being may signify balance or imbalance in one more of their energy centers.

Older adults in prison who internalized negative messages throughout their life have yet to reframe this false notion into a truthful notion, that is, that they are deserving and have rights to safety and security. People in the community who are homeless, penniless, or have a serious mental illness may steal or commit a petty crime to go to jail or prison where at least they have access to their basic needs: food, water, shelter, and medical and mental health care. The community must improve access to services for people of all ages to interrupt the pipeline to prison. We must provide access to practical programs and psychological and emotional counseling for people in prison to address all levels of their root issues.

Designing interventions that address these seven domains will address the unique needs not only of older adults in prison but also of those in the community, and health, wellness, and public safety will then abound.

Energy and Levels of Consciousness

Knowing yourself is the beginning of all wisdom.

—Aristotle

The levels of consciousness model can help us understand the process of personal evolution in individuals who have overcome adversity, such as resilient older adults in prison who have demonstrated that it is not only possible to survive but also to thrive despite any condition. Many of them used coping practices to improve their well-being, self-awareness, and personal growth. Despite inhumane treatment, the divine human spirit will rise to the occasion and demonstrate the personal power and will of the unchained resilient mind. As we move forward in visualizing and realizing a caring justice world, it will behoove us to imagine how we can move from a trauma consciousness that resonates with victimhood, bondage, and disempowerment to a loving kindness consciousness that encourages growth, liberation, and empowerment. In shifting our personal and collective way of experiencing the world, it is helpful to visualize a map that can take us from point A to point Z.

To this end, we draw on the groundbreaking work of David Hawkins and the levels of consciousness process model. To develop the levels of consciousness, Hawkins applied an empirically validated method that used muscle-testing techniques of applied kinesiology.[7] The model maps the association, interaction, and progression of emotions, thoughts, behaviors, consciousness levels, life, and worldviews that influence personal and collective consciousness (table 9.2). The range of the Hawkins scale is arbitrary and the numbers are subjective, from 1–1,000 megahertz, a unit of frequency equal to one million hertz. The numbers on the scale represent logarithmic (log) calibrations (measurable vibratory frequencies on a scale that increases to the tenth power) of human consciousness levels and the life views or perspectives from which they operate.

Levels of Consciousness

Level 4 Zone

- Emotion: Bliss/ineffable
- Level: Peace (600)
- Enlightenment (700–1,000)
- Life Views: Perfect/is
- Energy Level: 700+ pure Tao
- 1,000 Omega ultimate consciousness

Level 3 Zone

- Emotion: Love (500), gratitude (510), joy (540)
- Consciousness Level: Reverence, serenity
- Energy Level: Synchronicity and extraordinary outcomes

Level 2 Zone

- Emotion: Understanding
- Consciousness Level: Reason (400)
- Life View: Meaningful
- Energy Level: Peak performance without stress (flow-freedom-power)

Level 1 Zone

- Emotion: Affirmation, trust, willingness, acceptance
- Consciousness Level: Courage (200), neutrality (250), optimism (310), forgiveness (350)
- Life View: Feasible, satisfaction, hopeful, harmonious
- Energy Level: Happy and productive

Out of the Zone

- Stuck in lower level negative emotions: Craving, hate, scorn
- Desire (125), Anger (150), Pride (175)
- Energy Level: Hyperactivity

Out of the Zone

- Stuck in the lowest levels of negative emotions: humiliation, blame, despair, grief, regret
- Consciousness Level: Shame (20), guilt (30), apathy (50), grief (75), fear (100)
- Life View: Miserable, evil, hopeless, tragic, frightening
- Alpha Point: Bondage, victimhood, disempowerment
- Energy: Inertia

TABLE 9.2 Levels of consciousness

Level of Consciousness	Logarithm (log)	Life View	Emotion	Type of Expression
Levels 0–100: Bondage, Victimhood, and Disempowerment				
Shame	20	Miserable	Humiliation	Suicidality, homicide, hate crimes
Guilt	30	Evil	Blame	Suicidality, lack of accountability, criminal behavior
Apathy	50	Hopeless	Despair	Homelessness, petty crimes, numbness
Grief	75	Tragic	Regret	Negative thoughts/ emotions

Fear	100	Frightening	Anxiety	Fearful/ anxious thoughts/ emotions, self-defense crimes, paranoia
Level 101–199				
Desire	125	Disappointing	Craving	Addictive behaviors (substance abuse, sex, alcohol, gambling, etc.)
Anger	150	Antagonistic	Hate	Abusive behaviors, violence, use of force
Pride	175	Demanding	Scorn	Racism, nationalism, terrorism, religious fundamentalism
Level 200–499				
Courage	200	Feasible	Affirmation	Individuals seek personal growth and empowerment, true power
Neutrality	250	Satisfaction	Trust	Satisfaction with life, leisure, necessary for attaining unconditional love
Willingness	310	Hopeful	Optimism	Optimism, willpower, self-discipline
Acceptance	350	Harmonious	Forgiveness	Creative, empowered self to change
Reason	400	Meaningful	Understanding	Reasoning abilities, desire for knowledge, meaningful contributions through science and medicine
Level 500–1000				
Love	500	Benign	Reverence	Charity work, express unconditional love, only wishes the welfare of the community
Joy	540	Complete	Serenity	Flow-freedom-power, unshakable happiness
Peace	600	Perfect	Bliss	Still state of mind
Enlightenment	700–1000	Is	Ineffable	Pure Tao humanity blends with divinity

Note: Based on the Hawkins Levels of Consciousness Scale.

Hawkins's levels of consciousness scale can be used as a tool to generate self-awareness and guidance for individuals and groups on their personal growth journey. If used in prisons with both incarcerated people and staff, the idea of prisons can be transformed from the inside to the outside. Chambers of punishment could be transformed into houses of healing and retreat, helping individuals who struggle with untreated traumatic residue move from victimhood, bondage, and disempowerment to a divine selfhood, liberation, and empowerment. Through the development of self and other love, awareness, forgiveness, and discipline, the adverse behaviors (committing crimes) can be reduced or even eliminated.

The consciousness scale begins at the alpha level, representing bondage, victimhood, and disempowerment, which contracts to 100 or less. At the 540–600 level, the flow of freedom and power is expanded, and at 700–999 it is pure Tao energy, or a state of liberation or moksha. Individuals reach omega ultimate consciousness at 1,000 and become one with divinity. Many resilient older adults in prison operate at a level of empowerment or higher. They released negative emotions or thought patterns, such as victimhood, fear, and anger, replacing them with positive emotions and thoughts and engaging in productive behaviors. These states included attitudes, feelings, and thoughts related to satisfaction and contentment, inner peace, empowerment, taking responsibility, being of service to others, and being positive about their present and the future.

For example, Joseph described going through life in a fearful and angry emotional state and believing that the world is a dangerous place and could not be trusted (see chapter 4). In response, he created a reactionary false-self Angry state (150) in which he viewed himself as the "baddest bad ass" and used brute force to prove it. Based on the mentoring advice of an older adult in prison, Joseph was able to take his true source of power back, embracing the loving view of a power greater than himself. As if waking from a bad dream, he accepted self-love and his authentic and strong masculine courage and heart-driven leadership capacities. The older adult in prison was the first to see Joseph's true potential, and Joseph rose to the occasion to accept this vision of himself. This pivotal event powerfully influenced Joseph, who was able to shift from a consciousness of Anger (150) and disempowerment (use of brute force) to a higher level of Courage (200) and empowerment.

Many individuals in the criminal justice system have a history of traumatic early life experiences and may have emotions and worldviews that place them at risk of victimization or reactionary behavior. As a wise elder shared with us in the introduction, this is a family and community issue. If we as a society create the loving and safe space for positive personal growth, an authentic caring justice world will flourish. In the meantime, we have a personal and collective responsibility to participate in healing, a remedy for the criminalization and mistreatment of individuals in the criminal justice system.

Personal and Collective Transformation: Toward the Power of the Positive Being

Individuals can shift their consciousness level by shifting their thoughts, feelings, and behaviors. In fact, the largest personal and spiritual growth occurs between the 200 and 500 levels of consciousness. At the level of Courage (200), a significant shift can occur from a lifestyle that once was destructive, hurtful, and harmful to themselves or others to one that is constructive, life-promoting, and loving and helpful to others. Many of the stories of older adults in prison and after their release demonstrate this positive perspective as well as the actions of care providers who practiced nonjudgmental and responsible care:

> The only thing I'd say about prison is it can be a learning experience if you use it for that. It's negative, but it doesn't have to stay negative, because a lot of good, there's a lot of positive that can come out to it.
>
> I mean, at the end of the day it's about doing what I can do to help myself. It's a process, it really is. To me it is a system within itself. Doing what I can do for myself, then my family, then that immediate community.

The stories told by incarcerated older adults illustrate how many of them went from the levels of bondage, victimhood, and disempowerment (before and during prison) to levels of courage, neutrality, willingness, and acceptance (during prison and after release). These inner transformations relied on their willingness and courage to practice introspection and gradually change not only their thoughts and emotions but also their vibrational levels. Joseph and a formerly incarcerated older adult put it this way:

> Years of self-evaluation and solitary contemplation have given me the answers to what happened and what I had to do to get ahold of the monster in control of me. There are some people I've dealt with to get an understanding and the assistance to become somewhat healed and on the road to becoming a man I'd want to be friends with.
>
> The difficulty for me at first was changing my mind-set. With me when I get stressed it's so much easier just to think and jump and go back to the old behaviors. So, I think to stay out you really got to change how you deal with your issues, how you deal with the stress.

According to Hawkins, 85 percent of the people on the planet live below the level of Courage (200), and only 4 percent of humans have ever achieved the level of Love (500). The 200 or less level consists of negative affect/emotional states, and this majority is kept in balance by the positive cognitive worldview of the remaining 15 percent of the collective (those who log 200 or higher). The levels of consciousness are constructed so that each incremental level results in a significant increase in energy and power. Hawkins states that the level of energy of a person who calibrates at the level of Peace and Bliss (600) has the power to equalize the lower level frequencies of 10 million people who calibrate below 200. The Reason (400) level of consciousness refers to individuals who are guided by the sciences, linear thinking, rationality, and the visible and mechanistic world of matter and form. Hawkins noted that scientific luminaries such as Aristotle, Newton, Freud, and Einstein had scores in the upper 400 range.

Level 500 is Love, representing an unconditional love and a way of "being" in the world. This level is difficult to achieve and requires a shift from the linear, verifiable realm to the nonlinear, formless, spiritual realm. The ego is focused on the visible objective world, and the spiritual dimension of unconditional love often alludes those operating from a completely objective focus. Due to this challenge, many individuals are stalled from higher development, which in turn affects collective higher development. According to Hawkins, a person's level of consciousness is steady, changing by an average of five points across the life span. However, some individuals are motivated or inspired to seek greater self-awareness: survivors of trauma, persons redemptive of how they have treated others, persons interested in personal and collective transformation, or persons who have consciously or unconsciously chosen the opposite. In these cases, the consciousness level may increase or decrease hundreds of points in a single lifetime, especially with supported intervention. We revisit the words of wisdom from the unchained mind of Mr. J:

> I once was a Fool but now I' am Wise!
> I once was Blind but now I see!
> I once was Deaf but now I Hear!
> I once was Ignorant but now I use Intelligence!
> YOU have your PhD, but I have the Knowledge and Inspiration that comes
>   from a Higher Power, the one and only True GOD!
> A Mind is a terrible thing to waste, so is the Soul!

These words suggest that self-love and acceptance of one's divinity know no boundaries and can be found anywhere and inside anyone who is open to the marvelous possibility of what appear to be impenetrable prison walls. Those of us looking in to prison from the outside might see beams of light shining through the shadows of prison darkness. Those inside the prison looking out might see that we are prisoners of our community on earth. Half the time we hide in the shadows of dark nights outside of prison. Our own shadows can be camouflaged, if only for a short while. We can use flickers of light to see our own reflection and open us to the possibility of learning what older adults in prison can teach us about the pathways to health, wealth, and happiness in a free world. In valuing one's own wisdom, you tap into the true joy of singing the liberation love song of your soul. With arms wide open and hands forward as if ready to receive, the butterflies of joy awake like a dormant caterpillar let loose to fly. As you revel in what was once lost, you are the pure white light of an imprisoned mind and heart set free and the embodiment of a caring justice inner world. Once a freedom fighter, you are now a freedom lover.

Accepting the Gift of Life: Recipes for Living a Longer, Healthier, and Happier Life

In this section, we highlight the naturally occurring self-care and empowerment activities engaged in by older adults to promote their health and well-being under the challenging conditions of confinement. Many of them wanted to participate in our studies to share their wisdom and experiences; they selflessly want to give back to others the gift of life.

Perhaps no one knows the meaning and preciousness of life better than the incarcerated. Here is what they tell us about life:

> Live each moment to the fullest.
> Love yourself more than love can love.
> You are beyond self-esteem; you are the esteemed self.
> Choose to thrive despite the conditions.
> Find the higher purpose and follow it upward.
> Be creative within confinement.
> Be the person in prison who sings.
> Be the person in the community who listens and sings back.

The self-care and empowerment activities discussed here were demonstrated in quantitative and qualitative research to promote health, well-being, and positive behaviors among individuals in a prison setting, but these activities can help anyone anywhere. These recommendations are consistent with the 2012 United Nations Office on Drugs and Crimes handbook on the reintegration of offenders.[8]

Accepting the Gift of Life" is a self-love empowerment program based on activities older adults recommended as being helpful to them in managing challenging conditions of stress in prison or after their release. It also includes organizational and community level interventions that older adults

recommended. Their self-directed and care activities fall within the following areas: contemplative practices, social determinants of collective health
practices, and trauma healing programs.

Contemplative Practices in Prison and in the Community

*The greatest discovery of my generation is that a human being can alter his life
by altering his attitudes of mind.*

—William James

Contemplative practices include meditation, yoga, centering prayer, and
mindfulness that promote individual and collective self-awareness, patience,
compassion, and concentration. These practices can help individuals and communities identify the root of personal and social problems and find creative ways
to eliminate them, bringing about positive transformations in organizations and
social institutions such as prisons.[9] The number of contemplative practices being
used as holistic health interventions for people with different physical and mental health conditions has increased. Contemplative practices can be effective for
a number of conditions, including but not limited to cardiovascular disease,
posttraumatic stress, vascular disease, anxiety, fibromyalgia, stress reduction,
chronic pain management, cognitive deficits, and asthma.[10] These practices have
been studied for their effect on physical and mental well-being and also for
individuals' subtle energy bodies and energy centers, or chakras.[11] The positive
effects of contemplative practices go beyond physical and mental improvements,
realigning energy centers that create physical and mental imbalances. Here are
some examples of contemplative practices for individuals or groups.

- **Mindfulness** has its roots in Buddhist meditation and refers to "being in the
  present moment." Mindfulness can be practiced by individuals anywhere.
  It is based on (a) paying attention to breathing patterns, mainly when feeling intense emotions; (b) noticing what is being sensed in a given moment;
  (c) recognizing that thoughts and emotions are fleeting and do not define us;
  (d) tuning into the body's sensations; and (e) finding micro moments of mindfulness during the day in which we can reset our focus and sense of purpose.
- **Meditation** is a mind and body practice that focus on interactions among
  the mind, body, and behavior.[12] There are different forms of meditation, and
  individuals can meditate as little as five minutes a day and gradually increase
  their meditation time. Examples of meditation practices are loving-kindness
  meditation, breath awareness meditation, self and collective affirmations
  or mantra meditation, and Zen meditation. Self and collective affirmations,

or mantra practice, involve creation and repetition of words or phrases that reflect what you are trying to achieve. For example, if you are trying to be in the present moment, you can say out loud or mentally: "No regrets for the past. No fears for the future. I am living in the here and now."[13]

- **Yoga** is another mind and body practice rooted in Indian philosophy that began as a spiritual practice but has become popular as a way of promoting physical and mental well-being. Popular yoga styles in the United States such as Iyengar, Bikran, and Hatha yoga include physical postures (*asanas*), breathing techniques (*pranayama*), and meditation (*dyana*). A 2017 study of prison yoga programs in Swedish correctional facilities reported positive effects on incarcerated individuals' emotional well-being and on risk factors associated with recidivism, such as impulsivity and antisocial behavior.[14] The Prison Yoga Project has offered free yoga books for incarcerated individuals since 2010, and they can be requested by mail: The Prison Yoga Project, P.O. Box 426, San Quentin, CA 94964.

- **Self-compassion** refers to individuals' awareness of their own pain and suffering and their understanding that even though suffering and pain is hard, it is a normal human experience. Other crucial components of self-compassion are individuals' abilities to direct feelings of kindness and care toward themselves and to focus their attention and energy on how they might ameliorate their pain. Growing evidence supports self-compassion as an important predictor of well-being and resilience. When practiced, it may activate an individual's soothing system, which calms overactive threat and drive systems responsible for difficult emotions related to anxiety, anger, or depression.[15] Individuals can use a self-compassion break exercise to become mindful of suffering, normalize this experience (It is difficult, but part of life.), and state an intention to be kind, patient, and accepting.

- **Self-forgiveness** is an important aspect of self-compassion because it acts to soothe the body, mind, and soul from the pain caused by shame, facilitating the overall healing process.[16] A successful example of self-forgiveness practice applied in the criminal justice system is the RESTORE Forgiveness Project in the UK. The program's goal is to support incarcerated individuals in their process of change toward crime desistance.[17]

- **Gratitude** is a way of acknowledging the good in life. The state of gratitude prompts individuals to go beyond themselves and connect to other people, nature, or a higher power.[18] Practicing gratitude may have a positive impact on physical and mental health. Keeping a gratitude journal was connected to less stress, improved quality of sleep, and emotional awareness.[19] Simple gratitude exercises include keeping a gratitude journal, counting your blessings, thanking someone mentally, and prayer.[20]

- **Religious teachings and prayer** are contemplative practices that are practiced in the prison system. The Liberation Prison Project provides incarcerated people with spiritual advice, teachings, books, and other materials that explore the practice of Buddhism.[21]

- **Physical exercise and sports** are critical components for the physical and mental well-being of incarcerated individuals. Moving the body in a focused way, such as stretching and strengthening exercises, has an effect similar to meditation and other contemplative practices. Cardiovascular plus resistance training and high-intensity strength training have produced significant gains in incarcerated individuals' cardio-respiratory capacity, reducing the risk of cardiovascular disease. These results suggest that supervised exercise interventions or sports could significantly improve the health status of incarcerated people.[22]

- **Creative arts** of all varieties are used in prison: visual arts, listening or playing music, creative writing, reflective journaling, and reading. A contemplative element of engaging in the arts helps individuals better understand themselves in relation to others and their environment. Research suggests that the use of arts in prison and with justice-involved individuals improves health and well-being, increases pro-social behavior, and reduces recidivism.[23]

- **Peer support and mentoring** is consistent with the recommendations for promising practices highlighted in the 2012 report by the United Nations Office on Drugs and Crime.[24] Older incarcerated adults shared the importance of one-on-one support and mentoring and peer support groups such as AA, NA, and group counseling (facilitated by a peer mentor).

- **Personal and collective advocacy** may range from information and assistance for individual inmates to systemic monitoring or large-scale litigation. Personal level advocacy encompasses informal advocacy within a prison, systemic advocacy with corrections officials, and coordination with community stakeholders and policy makers. Some older incarcerated adults reported that they served as informal paralegals to help other incarcerated people with legal issues they were experiencing. As a collective, people in prison can file a class action lawsuit. A powerful example was a class action suit for mental health treatment filled by two hundred prisoners against the New Jersey Department of Corrections (NJDOC) in 1996. After a careful audit, the NJDOC identified areas that could be improved and budgeted $16 million to be spent on mental health treatment for incarcerated individuals.[25] The Center for Prisoner Health and Human Rights, the ACLU, and Human Rights Watch are national watchdog organizations that advocate for and with people in prison.

- **Reiki self treatment** is another promising contemplative practice, not only in hospitals and community centers but also in prisons. It is a Japanese form of hands-on energy healing in which stagnant energy is redistributed. People can be taught basic strategies to do their own Reiki self-treatment. It has been reported to be helpful in decreasing stress-related health problems.[26]

Social Determinants of Collective Health Practices

The social determinants of collective health practices that older adults in prison participated in or recommended include education, employment, and vocational training; trauma healing programs; and civic engagement and education.

- **Housing, health care, and basic rights/needs:** Older people in prison and after their release have the right to and need of safe and affordable housing compliant with Americans with Disabilities Act requirements. Access to quality health care while in and after their release is critical, especially for older adults with chronic health-care needs. When released, older prisoners need access to supplies for basic survival such as healthy foods, clothing, toiletries, and social welfare benefits (e.g., Medicare, Medicaid, SSI). These recommendations are consistent with the American Psychological Association's consensus statement and with the Nelson Mandela Rules.[27]
- **Systemic reforms** were suggested by older adults in prison that supported national and international recommendations for reforms of systems and laws and policies. Systems reforms included providing culturally responsive care and interprofessional and intersectional collaboration among agencies that service people involved in the justice system. Law and policy reforms included changes to health, housing, and mental health policies that adversely affect individuals involved in criminal justice matters.[28]
- **Learn from countries that "see and do it differently."** Several older adults shared learning from best practice models by our world neighbors, such as Norway, Sweden, and Germany.[29]
- **Education, employment, and vocational training** are necessary offerings in prison as well as in the community. The right to education and the right to work foster the willingness and ability of incarcerated adults to lead a fulfilling and self-supporting life upon release from prison. Educational programs in prison should aim to develop the full potential of each incarcerated individual to minimize the negative impact of incarceration and institutionalization and to improve prospects for reunification in the community. These skills are essential to reduce recidivism and ultimately to improve public safety.[30]

Trauma Healing Programs

Older adults in prison also understood that an entire organization, such as prison, or an entire community would be needed to heal the results of the wrongdoing that has occurred. A number of strategies can be employed to do this important work.

- **Peace and reconciliation** programs have been engaged in by many incarcerated and formerly incarcerated older adults. They often practice inner peace using self-focused contemplative activities as well as group-oriented peace and reconciliation activities. The Prison of Peace program aims to reduce violence and promote peaceful conflict resolution among incarcerated individuals. It was developed by two lawyers and a mediator for use with incarcerated women serving long or life sentences in a California prison. The program offers intensive workshops that address the art of communication and conflict resolution, enabling incarcerated individuals to foster safer and more peaceful lives while in custody and upon release. Different levels of workshops are offered, including peacemaker, mediator, mentor, and trainer. Participant who complete all required levels are eligible to lead future workershops.[31] Restorative justice programs in prison and in the community focus on the harm that has been done to people and relationships; obligations and liabilities are addressed with wrongdoers, victims, and the community in an effort to heal the harm and put things right.[32]
- **Seeking safety** is an organizational level evidence-based model that can be used in group or individual counseling to treat survivors with co-occurring trauma and substance use disorders. This model does not ask individuals to delve into their emotionally distressing trauma narratives.[33]
- **Sanctuary** is an organizational and community level trauma intervention model to reduce trauma. The aim is to reduce stress and violent incidents and to improve the overall well-being for all those affected.[34]
- **Trauma and community healing** is exemplified through the Linking Human Systems (LINC) approach, which is based on a theory of resilience for individuals, families, and communities collectively facing crisis, trauma, and disaster. Families and communities forge linkages that increase resiliency within systems. The model's goal is to mobilize "natural change agents" to establish connections with outside social support systems that can empower communities to reconnect and identify resources for healing.[35] The LINC model is an innovative, social justice–oriented approach. After experiencing a traumatic event, communities are at risk of becoming disconnected and isolated. This situation may particularly affect diverse families that are already facing health disparities, chronic poverty, discrimination, and other structural barriers. Systemic therapists can use the principles outlined in the LINC model to facilitate healing at a community level, including communities in which populations are difficult to engage using a traditional approach.[36]
- **Civic engagement and education** is a useful strategy to increase interaction, integration, and inclusion of diverse groups in the community, including

formerly incarcerated older adults. Offering civic education in the form of moral and ethics education may foster a common ground on how to develop nurturing and meaningful bonds among families and community members. Community members can help underserved groups in the community or in prison. Tithing and volunteer activities are beneficial through both the act of giving and of receiving the gift. Here are some suggestions for getting involved in volunteerism with prisons: volunteerism with Volunteers of America Correctional Reentry Center; be a Pen-Pal (www.writeaprisoner. com); donate books (www.prisonerpenpals.com/booksbehindbars.html); donate to community prison and reentry programs (www.prisonlit.org /donate/ or www.prisonfellowship.org/donate/).

- **Training staff and professionals** in the criminal justice system should learn many of the techniques described in the Accepting the Gift of Life program, especially those related to compassion and forgiveness. Developing compassion and forgiveness in the criminal justice system and also within each of us is a critical step toward a world with fewer competing and inconsistent values.[37]

Our wise elders have alerted us to a new way of approaching the gift of life. The human spirit has often been tested, and it has ascended like the phoenix rising from the fiery ashes of hatred and pain. Perhaps it is time to embark on a new way of testing diversity and difference using heart-centered actions grounded in unconditional love and acceptance. Let's see how high the human spirit can rise to create a caring justice world filled with peace, justice, truth, harmony, and balance. Now that would be a new way of responding to the same old problem.

CHAPTER 10

REALIZING A CARING JUSTICE WORLD

Promising Global Practices for Justice-Involved Older Adults

It is said that no one truly knows a nation until one has been inside its jails. A nation should not be judged by how it treats its highest citizens, but its lowest ones.

—Nelson Mandela

Over the past two decades we have seen some signs of realizing a caring justice world. National and international movements in corrections and in the community have emerged, and they are asking for programs, initiatives, and policies that foster the physical, mental, social, spiritual, economic, and legal well-being of older adults and their families. In this chapter, we highlight some promising practices. We conclude with recommendations for how local and global communities can collaborate to build a caring justice world that includes older adults involved in the criminal justice system and their families and communities. It is our hope that this chapter inspires other individuals, communities, and government agencies who have specific responsibilities to serve older and justice-involved people.

Growth in institutional or community programming has often been a response to the recognition that older adults in prison derive little value from prison programming designed to target younger incarcerated adults' needs. These programs offer education, vocational training, and employment opportunities, and they were aimed at reducing offending behavior.[1] In the United States, more than 3,000 (5 percent) incarcerated people age 50 or older die in prison annually, and the need for more geriatric and palliative care services is a growing concern.[2]

Worldwide some innovative geriatric programs in prisons and in community reintegration are consistent with a caring justice philosophy. Both the incarcerated and formerly incarcerated older adults and concerned correctional and community organizations have demonstrated heart-centered actions, such as providing compassionate care to the older, sick, and dying in prison and after release. Promising prison and community practices include comprehensive case management services for medical, mental health, substance abuse, family, social services, housing, education or vocational training, spiritual counseling, exercise and creative arts programs, employment, and retirement counseling. Program-specific aspects include one or more of the following: age and cognitive capacity environmental modifications (including the use of segregated units), interdisciplinary staff and volunteers trained in geriatric correctional care, complementary medicine, and specialized case coordination along with family and inmate peer supports and volunteers, mentoring, and self-help advocacy group efforts. (Please see the text box for programs highlighted in this chapter.)

Promising International Practices and Programs

We classified global programs based on whether they are prison-based programs in corrections facilities or community-based programs that provide inpatient or outpatient programs. Programs that serve justice-involved older adults across the globe are located in the United States (e.g., True Grit Program), the United Kingdom (e.g., RECOOP), Canada (e.g., RELIEF), and other international locations. This information can be used to inform responses to the aging prison crisis at local and global levels.

Prison- and Community-Based Programs and Initiatives for Justice-Involved Older Adults

Corrections/Prison-Based Programs: Inpatient/Outpatient	Community-Based Programs: Inpatient/Outpatient
True Grit	60 West Nursing Home
The Gold Coat Program	The Aged Care and Rehabilitation Unit

Corrections/Prison-Based Programs: Inpatient/Outpatient	Community-Based Programs: Inpatient/Outpatient
The Unit for Cognitive Impairment (UCI)	Reintegration Effort for Long-Term Infirm and Elderly Federal Offenders' Program (RELIEF)
NYS DOCCS Discharging Planning Unit (DPU)	Senior Ex-Offender Program (SEOP)
Other Prison Hospice Units/Programs	Resettlement and Care for Older Ex-Offenders (RECOOP)
Chronic Disease Self-Management Education (CDSME)	Restore Support Network
Long-Term Offender Program (LTOP)	Area Agencies on Aging (AAA)
The Coyote Ridge Assisted-Living Unit	Aging Without Bars
The Kevin Waller Unit	Project for Older Prisoners (POPS)
National and International Initiatives	
Families Against Mandatory Minimums (FAMM)	
From Prison to Peace: Learning from the Experience of Political Ex-Prisoners	

International Prison-Based Programs

Inpatient/Outpatient Programs

Older adults in prison have complex, co-occurring health and mental health care needs (see chapter 5). As a natural part of the aging process, older adults in prisons have higher rates of chronic illnesses and disabilities, such as heart and lung diseases and dementia, compared to incarcerated younger adults. Minor to serious mental health and substance abuse issues are commonplace in prison populations, especially among older adults.[3] Perhaps the most significant mental health issue of aging in prison is accelerated cognitive decline. Poor health behaviors coupled with the prison environment place older adults at increased risk for age-related mental health problems, especially dementia, that result in the loss of physical and cognitive capacities and death.[4] To address incarcerated older adults' needs, inpatient skilled nursing or geriatric units, hospice programs, and outpatient chronic health, mental health, and social service programs have been developed internationally, especially in the United States.

True Grit Program (Nevada). This is a prison-based structured living program that attempts to foster older prisoners' well-being. The mission statement of True Grit is "no more victims." It is set in a geriatric sociocultural environment and was designed to enhance physical health (creative arts and recreational and physical therapy activities), mental and social well-being (group and individual therapy), human agency and empowerment (self-help modalities), spiritual well-being (a prison chaplain and volunteers), and successful community reintegration (discharge planning). Eligibility criteria include:

- Age 55 or older (with no upper age limit)
- No full-time work or school (part-time school is acceptable)
- Willingness to participate in all program activities, including correctional programs that target individual criminogenic factors
- Compliance with a formal contract specifying the rules and regulations governing behavior and grooming standards

Originally established for men, an additional program site has been added for women. Rather than just providing a safe and healthy environment within the prison for older adults, True Grit became a mechanism for bridging the chasm between prison and the community. It was gradually transformed into a rehabilitation and community reintegration initiative.[5]

Research suggests that the program is effective in increasing psychological and social well-being.[6] For instance, preliminary quantitative analysis shows a zero percent recidivism rate of participants who were released from prison. In addition, the qualitative data from True Grit participants suggests that they view the program as an invaluable part of their lives, helping them cope with daily prison stress and enabling them to offer restitution for their crimes.[7]

Gold Coat Program: Dementia Unit. Perhaps the best known U.S. prison dementia program is at the Men's Colony in San Luis Obispo, California. In the dementia unit, other inmates or "peer supports" provide services to dying incarcerated people. This is particularly important because prisons are often dangerous environments, and incarcerated people with cognitive disorders are vulnerable to victimization. The availability of a hospice with peer support can provide protection for these inmates.[8] The program aides are prisoner volunteers or "social aides" who have at least ten years of exemplary behavior and who have received training in dementia caregiving. Their responsibilities include making sure inmate patients receive medical care, providing social support, helping with daily tasks, and protecting them. Prisoner volunteers receive supervision by a clinical psychologist, and the clinical team addresses challenges such as how volunteers should respond to patients who are experiencing hallucinations. In addition, the clinical supervisor is always available for emotional support for issues that might affect volunteers, such as a death in the family, going through a parole hearing, or other problems.[9]

Unit for Cognitive Impairment (UCI, New York). This well-known prison dementia unit in Beacon, New York, is a thirty-bed unit located on the third floor of the Regional Medical Unit in Fishkill Correctional Facility. This is the only formal UCI in New York State, and they receive transfers from other prisons. The UCI houses individuals with health conditions that contribute to cognitive decline such as Alzheimer's disease, HIV, AIDS, TBI, Huntington's disease, and mental illnesses such as schizophrenia. The atmosphere of the unit is similar to a hospital, and all rooms have an open-door policy 24/7 unless the patient is under special supervision. Staff consists of doctors, psychiatrists, social workers, psychologists, registered nurses, nursing assistants, correction staff, and a recreational officer. The recreational officer acts as a liaison with community agents through the parole process to ensure a seamless transition for patients back to their families. The UCI administration emphasizes the importance of training for security, civilian, and clinical staff, and all staff levels receive an initial forty-hour training session delivered by the local chapter of the Alzheimer's Association. Nursing educators also provide the same training to new staff and in refresher courses. As part of their therapeutic care, the UCI provides patients with activities such as music, poetry, and pet therapy.[10]

State Discharge Planning Unit (DPU, New York). The New York State Department of Corrections and Community Supervision (NYS DOCCS) has recently established a Discharge Planning Unit (DPU). The DPU consists of four nurses and one social worker who are supervised by a chief medical officer. The DPU is responsible for the discharge planning of the general population with two chronic health conditions or one serious condition. The DPU teams also work in tandem with the DOCCS medical parole coordinator to set up a discharge plan. Other individuals and organizations involved in transitional care planning include DPU staff, family members or assigned surrogates or guardians, and community service providers such as visiting nurses for home placement or a staff member at an assisted living or skilled nursing facility. If an individual is on parole, a parole officer is also involved. Service providers, especially skilled nursing homes, who collaborate directly with NYS DOCCS help provide smooth care transitions, including holding a bed and having access to medical equipment needed for patients, such as wheelchairs and oxygen.[11]

Prison Hospices

Hospices are another practice innovation now available inside of correctional facilities. Hospice and end-of-life care is provided to incarcerated people with life-limiting illnesses. There are approximately seventy-five prison hospice programs in the United States, and six of them are in the Federal Bureau of Prisons. These prison hospice programs vary from very informal to a formal structure. Some programs have an established hospice unit and a fully staffed interprofessional team to care for prisoners. In contrast, other programs are much less formal with no established unit and minimal staff who care for the dying person.

Some prison hospice programs include a peer-support model in which fellow inmates assist the dying. Only twenty out of seventy-five units use inmates as volunteer workers. Cloyes and colleagues[12] emphasized that the participation of prisoner volunteers is not only cost-effective but also provides more comprehensive and personalized end-of-life care than that provided by health care staff only. Inmates who volunteer have reported an increased sense of purpose in prison life, and others see the opportunity as a way to "pay back" for their crimes. Prison volunteers receive education and development in how to provide end-of-life peer care and are provided with formal and informal mentoring and ongoing peer support.

Among the prison hospices in the United States, scholars have said that the Angola Prison Hospice in Louisiana is a model program that should be replicated in prisons across the country. Prospective volunteers undergo extensive training, including basic education in pathophysiology, the dying process, the hospice philosophy, and basic clinical competencies. Volunteers are initially shadowed by more experienced workers and are given supervised hands-on training in addition to ongoing training and educational development. Medical and corrections staff are available to answer prison volunteers' questions, and staff play a critical role in helping these volunteers to become skilled and knowledgeable. Prison volunteers provide most of the hospice patient care and psychosocial support because family members of inmate patients normally are not active participants in the hospice care process.[13]

Outpatient Programs

In addition to prison-based inpatient units, several outpatient programs target incarcerated older adults and the seriously ill. These programs include chronic disease management, community reintegration or reentry preparedness programs, and assisted living programs.

Chronic Disease Self-Management Education Program (Virginia). This is an evidence-based disease self-management program developed by Stanford University that is administered in prison. This six-week workshop offers prisoners new tools and builds on their skills to better deal with symptoms, manage common problems, and participate more fully in life. Long-term research shows that the program improved energy, physical activity, psychological well-being, partnerships with physicians, health status, and self-efficacy. Participants experienced reduced fatigue, pain symptoms, emergency room visits, hospital admissions, and hospital length of stay. In addition, national findings showed lower health costs and lower health care use. There have been twenty-one workshops in Virginia correctional facilities since 2012, and 78 percent of the 283 attendees completed the program.[14]

Long-Term Offender Program (California). This is a voluntary program that provides services in individual and group settings to address substance use disorder, criminal thinking, anger management, family relationships, denial management, and victim impact. Individuals receiving services are offenders who are subject to the Board of Parole Hearings (BPH) parole suitability process. The program's goal is to reduce reoffending by providing cognitive behavioral treatment programming to address criminogenic needs and risks. The program is tailored according to each individual's needs, and its duration varies accordingly. Offenders must have an assessed criminogenic need and be one to five years away from a BPH suitability hearing.[15]

Coyote Ridge Assisted Living Unit (Washington State). This unit is for incarcerated older adults and persons with disabilities. The unit has capacity to house seventy-four inmates who are segregated from the general prison population. Two nurses are assigned twenty-four hours a day, seven days a week. Eligibility criteria include an inmate's disability and being a minimum-security risk.[16]

Kevin Waller Unit (Australia). This assisted living unit is for prisoners who do not require skilled nursing home care. Operated by Correctional Services New South Wales, Australia, patients who do not require inpatient-based supportive care at the Aged Care and Rehabilitation Unit are cared for here. The Kevin Waller Unit has fifteen beds and provides elderly offenders with independent living in segregation from the general prison population.[17]

Other Useful Prison Resources

Other prison resources that guide internal and external monitoring of the conditions of confinement with relevance to community-based treatment include the Nelson Mandela Compliance Assessment and the Age Action Alliance-UK.

Nelson Mandela Rules Compliance Assessment. The United Nations has published a checklist for internal inspection of prisons for compliance with the Nelson Mandela Rules.[18]

Age Action Alliance-UK. A monitoring guide published by the Age Action Alliance offers a checklist to monitor appropriate conditions of confinement for older adults in prison.[19]

Community-Based Practices and Programs

A number of international community-based programs assist incarcerated adults with community reintegration and reentry. These programs are critical for the smooth transition of release for older incarcerated adults, which may pose significant challenges. For example, older adults who served long prison sentences may experience institutionalization (i.e., not knowing how to survive outside of prison).[20] Community reintegration success for older adults may be compounded by other physical or mental health issues; lack of family and peer support; substance use; lack of available community medical, mental health, and substance abuse services; lack of financial resources or access to social welfare benefits (including retirement); suitable housing options, such as assisted living and nursing homes; and available transportation.[21]

Some older adults released from prison have limited functional capabilities and may need assistance with activities of daily living, such as taking care of their personal hygiene and clothing. Other seriously or terminally ill older adults may need long-term institutional care, such as placement in a nursing home or hospice care in the community to address their palliative and end-of-life care.[22] Community reintegration or reentry programs are essential to help incarcerated and formerly incarcerated adults face the challenges of reentry. The stigma of incarceration, aligned with a limited work history and aging, can significantly reduce employment prospects for elderly former prisoners. Most aging prisoners do not have family or a community network to return to, which leaves them with limited options.[23] However, some promising programs and initiatives specifically target incarcerated older adults released from prison.

60 West Nursing Home (Connecticut). The Connecticut legislature created a nursing-home-release parole in 2013. This privately owned nursing home's mission is to provide specialized care, dignity, and acceptance for their residents. Patients go through a comprehensive screening process and are not accepted if they seem to pose a risk to the public.[24] This innovation has been considered a role model for other states to follow because it proves that a partnership between private ownership and the state can efficiently meet the state's needs and be a catalyst for reforming the criminal justice system nationwide. This program has gained notoriety because it is the first facility in the United States to gain approval from the Centers for Medicare and Medicaid Services for federal nursing home funding to meet the needs of older incarcerated adults.

Aged Care and Rehabilitation Unit (Australia). This is an inpatient facility for older offenders who require long-term supported care. Operated by the Justice Health & Forensic Mental Health Network, the community-based unit is located at Long Bay Hospital, New South Wales. The unit is equipped with fifteen beds and provides palliative care to both male and female offenders. Patients receive comprehensive assessment and treatment planning, and they are provided with daily rehabilitation activities such as gardening, bingo, table tennis, air hockey, and computer games.[25]

Reintegration Effort for Long-Term Infirm and Elderly Federal Offenders (RELIEF) Program (Canada). Established in 1999, this program was developed to facilitate the transition of elderly and infirm prisoners into the community.

The program addresses the hospice care needs of elderly and infirm former prisoners (who are screened and provided with hospice care training). Based on human rights and social justice values of dignity, the worth of the person, and respect for the dying, former prisoners and caregivers provide compassionate peer support to fellow former inmates who are dying.[26] Clients and caregivers are housed in four self-contained, six-bedroom houses that are accessible to wheelchairs and walkers. Clients' needs are assessed on a regular basis to determine the level of intervention and support required, with patients assigned to one of three houses that offer high, medium, or low levels of attendant care.

All participants must be eligible for release on Day Parole, have a sincere desire to participate in the program, and be supported by their case management team. Clients must have some mobility. Caregivers must be trained, or supported for training, and committed to providing care in the program for a specified period of time.[27]

Reentry-Focused Organizations, Programs, and Initiatives

Several community-based organizations and programs around the world address the well-being of older adults prior to and after their release from prison. We review these programs as well as some innovative community-based advocacy programs that support older adult prisoners.

Senior Ex-Offender Program (SEOP, California). Based in San Francisco, this was the first community reintegration program in the United States that focused on the unique needs of older adults released from jails and prisons. Their mission was to restore ex-offenders' self-respect using social modeling, compassionate care, and providing guidance and mental health and other services. This wraparound model connects senior ex-offenders to counseling, certified addiction specialists, behavioral health services, and basic necessities such as clothing and hygiene products. The program also helps secure transitional housing, which gives ex-offenders a chance to live in the community with support systems. To qualify, individuals must be over age 50, have been incarcerated, or are about to be released from prison. The program also helps participants find solutions to the challenges they may face. The goal is to give elderly formerly incarcerated people an opportunity for a new start through referrals to needed services and other social supports.[28]

Resettlement and Care for Older Ex-Offenders Program (Recoop, England). This community-based program promotes older adults' health and well-being by providing comprehensive care, resettlement, and rehabilitation services for incarcerated and formerly incarcerated older adults. The program provides support services, advocacy, financial advice, mentoring on employment and training, and advice on housing and health that enable ex-offenders to take control of their lives, remain free from reoffending, and minimize social isolation.[29] The program addresses nine pathways to rehabilitation that can reduce reoffending among older adults: attitudes, thinking, and behavior; accommodation; drugs and alcohol; children and families; health; education, training, and employment; finance, benefits, and debt; abuse; and prostitution.

Transition 50+ Resettlement Program (England). This program offered by Recoop addresses specific resettlement needs of individuals over the age of 50. The goals are to provide justice-involved older adults with appropriate knowledge and skills to support a positive resettlement experience and prevent reoffending.[30] Eligibility criteria include being 50 years or older, approaching retirement or perhaps looking for voluntary work rather than actively seeking employment, having health or social care needs, and having received longer sentences and are more likely to be institutionalized. Length of time still to serve is not a barrier. The Justice Select Committee and the Prisons Inspectorate recognized the South West prison services for having good practice models in 2013.[31]

Restore Support Network (England). This community-based program promotes the health and well-being of older adults (50+ years) exiting prison. Formerly incarcerated older adults, in coordination with corrections staff, provide peer mentoring and social support to older adults at various stages of their journey. It is a holistic, community-focused program that emphasizes offender responsibility for older adults reentering the community with aging-related needs.[32] This holistic program provides the following advantages:

- Prior to release from prison a "through the gate" support worker helps determine the social, health care, and resettlement pathway best suited to the inmate. Needs and goals are documented in the inmate's My Own Pathway to Care. This gives the individual access to services while in prison and after release.
- A personal support worker in the community reviews the My Own Pathway to Care plan and assesses the risks and coordinates the need for different levels of community services. Levels of support in the community vary from advice and advocacy to intensive mentoring and care support for a person who is considered high risk.
- Presentencing using the My Own Pathway to Care approach is also suitable for older people appearing in court for sentencing.
- Supported accommodation in each region is ensured through collaboration with other agencies in a national network to provide for older people with convictions and special care needs, including vulnerable groups such as women who have suffered from abusive relationships.

Program effectiveness was measured through the analysis of 327 older individuals who had criminal convictions and were supported by the program for a ten-year period (2003–2013). One of the key findings was that more than two-thirds of older prisoners did not receive enough information or documentation to access local services prior to their release from jail. A follow-up study of forty-one individuals who received one-to-one support in 2015–16 found that 5 percent had reoffended or been recalled. In 2017, Public Health England released a guidance to commissioners stating that the Restore Support Network approach was an example of good practice.[33]

Area Agencies on Aging (Schuyler County, New York). After assessing the needs of individuals being released from jail, the Schuyler County Office for the Aging partnered with the probation and parole departments to help meet transportation needs of these individuals. The program provides a paid driver and a volunteer who transport formerly incarcerated older adults to their appointments, such as parole, counseling, and health care. The Probation Department also strives to keep recently released individuals informed of the services offered by the Schuyler County Office and the Disability Resource Center. These initiatives are funded with Older Americans Act transportation grants. Program effectiveness has been ascertained through client reports and staff commitment, and many inmates have independently reached out to the Area Agencies on Aging for help.[34]

Aging Without Bars (Virginia). This program, based in Arlington, Virginia, provides a six-week, person-centered, educational community reintegration workshop. It is offered to incarcerated people over age 50 prior to their prison release to assist their transition into the community. The program also connects inmates to case management services before they are released from jail. This program is the result of a collaboration among jail intake staff, community partners, and the Area Agencies on Aging.[35]

Community Advocacy and Supports

Two community advocacy initiatives founded in the United States foster the well-being of justice-involved older adults and provide additional support to older incarcerated adults.

Project for Older Prisoners (POPS). This law school–based advocacy program addresses the rights and needs of incarcerated older adults. Law student volunteers assist individual low-risk prisoners older than age 55 in obtaining paroles, pardons, or alternative forms of incarceration. When an assessment for risk of recidivism is low, students locate housing and support for prisoners and help prepare their case for a parole hearing. Established in 1989 at Tulane Law School, in 2003 POPS expanded its programs across the United States to address advocacy issues for the growing aging prisoner population.[36]

Families Against Mandatory Minimums (FAMM, Washington, DC). Founded in 1991, this national advocacy organization promotes fair and effective

criminal justice reforms to make our communities safe, including compassionate release of loved ones. The organization's mission is "to create a more fair
and effective justice system that respects our American values of individual
accountability and dignity while keeping our communities safe." It strives to
promote change through the voices of those who face unjust sentencing and
its negative effects. Public education and targeted advocacy are key elements
of its success to date. Since 1991, more than 312,000 people have benefited from
sentencing reforms championed by FAMM.[37]

U.S. National Initiatives

In addition to the advocacy programs discussed previously, several noteworthy
U.S. initiatives and policies assist incarcerated older adults, including federal
and state laws allowing for compassionate release.

   Area Agencies on Aging (AAAs). Since passage of the Older Americans Act
in 1973, AAAs have been operating in communities across the United States to
assist incarcerated and formerly incarcerated older adults. Their mission is to
preserve the independence and dignity of older adults by providing services and
supports that enable them to remain in their homes and communities as long as
this is feasible.[38] Services include planning and program development, information and assistance, home and community-based services, caregiver support,
transportation, counseling, employment services, senior center activities, and
adult day care. AAAs have been addressing the aging prisoner population's
needs based on supports already provided to the broader aging population.
Engagement with the criminal justice system includes connecting older prisoners with appropriate services that support healthy aging during incarceration
and assistance with transitional reentry so former prisoners develop the necessary skills to avoid reoffending.

   Federal and State Compassionate Release Laws. Early release provisions
for elderly and severely ill inmates are meant to address prison overcrowding,
increase budgets, and avoid civil rights lawsuits,[39] but compassionate release
laws are underutilized in state and federal institutions. The Sentencing Reform
Act, established in 1984, permits the release of federal inmates due to "extraordinary and compelling circumstances" that were not foreseeable or present at
the time of sentencing.[40] Requests for compassionate release can be based on
medical or nonmedical circumstances.[41]

   Federal criteria for compassionate release due to medical circumstances
requires inmates age 65 and older to have served at least 50 percent of their
sentence. Older adults must be suffering from chronic or serious medical
conditions related to the aging process, experiencing deteriorating mental
or physical health that substantially diminishes their ability to function in a

correctional facility, and affirm that conventional treatment promises no sub-stantial improvement to their mental or physical condition. Compassionate release due to nonmedical circumstances is available for inmates sentenced for an offense that occurred on or after November 1, 1987 (e.g., "new law"), who are age 70 or older, and who have served thirty or more years of their term of imprisonment.[42]

The request for federal release is a slow process; almost four hundred appli-cations received between 2013 and 2017 are still pending a decision by the Bureau of Prisons. Inmates initiate their request with a petition to the warden, presenting the circumstances that warrant consideration, a release plan, and explaining how medical costs will be covered.[43] When the warden approves the petition, it goes to the Bureau of Prisons where the medical director reviews the record and approves it. The petition is then sent to the deputy attorney general, who may approve or object to it. If approved, the request goes to a judge who makes the final decision.[44]

Other Federal Initiatives. Other federal initiatives that support former prisoners' reentry into the community are the Federal Interagency Reentry Council, the Office of Personnel Management, and the Department of Justice's Road Map to Reentry, which implement principles to ensure that the reentry process is addressed from the moment prisoners enter the system until their exit. Other initiatives have come from the Department of Housing and Urban Development Supporting America's Aging Prisoner Population: Opportunities & Challenges for Area Agencies on Aging. Guidance on Fair Housing Act standards excludes the use of arrest records in making public housing deci-sions. And the Department of Health and Human Services clarified that indi-viduals in halfway houses and on probation or parole are eligible for Medicaid as long as they meet eligibility criteria. To provide better services to veterans with involvement in the criminal justice system, the Department of Veterans Affairs is participating in events at the Bureau of Prison facilities and the VA medical centers.[45]

From Prison to Peace in Northern Ireland

From Prison to Peace is an educational program developed to explore ways in which political ex-prisoners in Northern Ireland can use their experience to engage with youth and remove the mythical elements of the conflict and the prison experience. The program is part of a wider initiative administered by the Community Foundation for Northern Ireland and partially funded by the European Union. Its main goals are to prevent youth from becoming involved in or returning to violence; demonstrate alternative ways of dealing with con-flict; and present youth with different perspectives on the conflict through the shared experience of politically motivated ex-prisoners. A Citizenship Working Group of support groups formed by political ex-prisoners from loyalist and republican constituencies developed a school-based educational program for students ages 14 to 16. The program includes ten classroom lessons and conversations with politically motivated ex-prisoners. Evidence suggests that this program has had a positive effect on youths' knowledge, attitudes, and behaviors.[46]

Final Reflections

This chapter reviewed promising programs and initiatives for justice-involved older adults that are consistent with a caring justice philosophy. These innovations are designed to respect the worthiness, dignity, and well-being of incarcerated older adults, and they exemplify justice and fairness. Other countries are also adopting innovations that exemplify justice and fairness. In Uruguay, house arrest is allowed for convicted individuals age 70 and older who do not have serious offenses. This legislation also includes a provision for house arrest for seriously ill incarcerated people.[47] India has established an open prison for incarcerated older adults with life sentences so they can maintain family and community contact and belonging. The open prison program allows older "lifers" to be moved to a minimum-security prison, live with their families, and obtain a job of their choice within prescribed limits. And the Netherlands has a buddy system for incarcerated individuals diagnosed with AIDS that is similar to a U.S. program. These buddies provide support services in the prison and in the community.[48] Correctional systems in Norway, Sweden, and Germany also have instituted humane practices that benefit incarcerated people of all ages.[49]

As illustrated in this chapter, the caring justice movement is growing as international awareness of the plight and proliferation of older adults in prison has captured the hearts and minds of many concerned citizens. Correctional and community-based settings both locally and globally are in a unique position to address the rights and needs of older adults in prison. Vision has moved into action, and promising programs and initiatives are developing in corrections and community-based settings. The United Nations suggests that the time to act on this crisis is now; no elder anywhere in the world should be treated unjustly, including those in prison.

Recommendations

These recommendations are stepping stones for communities seeking solutions that address issues of the expanding justice-involved older adult population, especially those with dementia and serious and terminal illnesses. Responding to the aging prison population also can address health and public safety issues that may affect all individuals, families, and community well-being.

1. Conduct government and independent mixed methods health, crime prevention, and intervention studies to identify biopsychosocial and structural factors that influence health and criminal justice outcomes across the life course. Evaluate the effectiveness of health and wraparound services for promoting healthy aging and pro-social behavior. Include country or regional analyses of all stakeholders, including incarcerated and formerly incarcerated older adults and their family members, relevant service providers, policy makers, and the wider community.

2. Conduct institutional and community-based needs assessments for the provision of forensic geriatric and other services for dementia and serious health and mental health issues that may increase in a geriatric population. This includes exploring local needs for and the effectiveness of geriatric professionals in the fields of psychiatry, psychology, social work, and law.

3. Conduct cost-benefit analyses of tax savings to the general public if alternatives are instituted to remove older adults from criminal justice settings that were not designed to house them.

4. Develop or refine prison or community-based discharge planning unit programs and residential facilities for justice-involved older people and their families, including for those individuals with serious mental and physical health issues, such as dementia and terminal illnesses. These program development opportunities may include adopting or modifying innovative prison or community practice models already in existence with an age-specific or intergenerational component.

5. Evaluate existing aging, intergenerational, and peace and reconciliation programs for their capacity to address the rights and needs of justice-involved older adults at all stages of the criminal justice trajectory (police, courts, probation, prison, and prison release/parole).

6. Regularly update and disseminate information about the development and evaluation of existing health, social, and criminal justice programs that target justice-involved older adults and their families and communities. This information should be in the form of publicly available reports that are readily available for interested stakeholders.

7. Develop or refine criminal justice and community staff training for professionals that includes forensic geriatric assessment and treatment and reentry preparedness. Training is needed in all service settings: law enforcement, the courts, probation, prison, community corrections, social services, physical health, mental health, and substance use settings.

8. Assess prison and community-based residential care facilities for accessibility for a population of older people released from prison and for the unique

legal needs of justice-involved older adults, especially those with cognitive impairments (dementia) or terminal illnesses.

9. Develop a regional aging and justice task force of all community stakeholders to improve the intersectoral or cross-sectoral provision of services to the justice-involved aging population and their families that at minimum includes health, mental health/addictions, aging, social service, and criminal justice agencies.

10. Assess and revise international, national, and state and local laws that affect incarcerated and formerly incarcerated older adults, especially geriatric and compassionate release policies that would transfer care from corrections to community-based family members or service providers. A monitoring mechanism that assesses implementation effectiveness should drive improvements.

Communities that take collective action on one or more of these recommendations can contribute significantly toward community capacity building to realize caring justice.

In the beginning, only incarcerated older adults and their family members wished for and imagined a better way. Soon concerned citizens began to feel compassion and moral outrage over the treatment of vulnerable and sick older people in prison. Programs and legal advocacy efforts first imagined in the minds of caring people were gradually designed and implemented, turning a vision into reality. In a caring justice world, it is the heart in consort with the mind that creates the vision and guides the hands creating it. In this book, we have given you a look behind prison walls and introduced you to a number of incarcerated older adults. Now you know that you, too, are part of their story and they of ours. We have come full circle.

Imagine a world full of healthy people and communities living in peace and prosperity. Gandhi was once imprisoned for his political beliefs, and in his wise later years, he said: "An eye for an eye will make the whole world blind." In another breathe he concluded that "the day the power of love overrules the love of power, the world will know peace." We urge you to visualize the world through the eyes of love. Now imagine that.

AFTERWORD

In the Wake of the Coronavirus

On March 11, 2020, the World Health Organization declared a novel coronavirus, COVID-19, to be a global pandemic. Today's news is replete with reports of the increased vulnerability of older adults and individuals with compromised immune systems, including those confined in prisons. People in prison, in close proximity to each other, are considered at high risk of rapidly spreading the virus, and the federal government is considering releasing nonviolent incarcerated older adults. Most people have lost their sense of safety and security as the health, social, economic, and political landscapes are seemingly in disarray. Countries across the globe have instituted lockdowns to protect families and communities. Public discourse and social media are spreading fear and the need for disconnection from one another.

In this text, we offered a new way of looking at the same old problems. We suggested that most of us live in an invisible prison, having not yet realized who we truly are as individuals and as a collective. Aging people in prison shared their stories and showed us the pathway to the divine. Currently, we are literally practicing social isolation. We can use this time, as some incarcerated older adults did, to embrace the solitude and discover who we truly are at our core. Take a deep breath, look in a mirror, and say you are loved, followed by the reply, I am loved. This is the unconditional you, and the unconditional we.

We have entered a brave new world, one in which we can reclaim personal and universal love. Recognize the power of the subconscious and the power to influence among things we do not see. This is the quantum aspect of justice, bringing the shadow into the light. We are all interconnected: What happens to one of us, happens to all of us. Older adults in prison practiced detached observation of the lower emotions and behaviors related to fear, shame, hatred, and violence and chose to move to unconditional love. Recovery and transformation is a multidimensional process in which we can thrive individually and collectively. We can create a caring justice world that recognizes the divinity in one another, and we can work through the messiness of being human. Start with simple choices, such as loving and forgiving yourself and those around you. The power inside each of us can influence us all. The older adults in prison taught us so much. Let's let their love for us go viral. By releasing ourselves, we will release them.

The halo of the sun is called a *corona*. Let's let the sunshine in.

Select Resources

World Health Organization, "Rolling Updates on Coronavirus Disease (COVID-19)," updated March 23, 2020, https://www.who.int/emergencies/diseases/novel-coronavirus-2019/events-as-they-happen

United States Department of Health and Human Services, "HHS Coronavirus Disease 2019 (COVID-19) Updates" updated March 23, 2020. https://www.hhs.gov/about/news/coronavirus/index.html

Cranley, E. (2020). "Trump is considering releasing elderly, 'totally nonviolent' offenders from federal prisons amid coronavirus outbreak," March 23, 2020 https://www.businessinsider.com/trump-consider-coronavirus-executive-order-federal-prisons2020-3

APPENDIX 1

Co-Constructed Community Project Methods

The study was conducted in two phases from September 2013 to August 2014. The study was approved by the Fordham University Institutional Review Board (IRB) to meet the ethical standards for research with vulnerable populations.

Phase One: Service Providers

In phase one, community corrections staff in a northeastern region of the United States who provide services to adults age 50 and older on parole or community supervision were invited to participate in an online questionnaire about their views and practices with older adults on parole (or community supervision). Participants were invited to complete a confidential survey if they met the following inclusion criteria: individual is a professional who has provided services for at least three months to parolees age 50 and older. Service providers were asked to complete the questionnaire using the secure internet survey service, Survey Monkey.

The principal investigator was given permission to email seventy-six community corrections program administrators who then forwarded the study announcement and invitation to their frontline staff. The following four-step Dillman, Smyth, and Christian[1] mail survey method was used to invite participants to take part in the study: (1) In step one [week 1], an email study announcement was sent. (2) In step 2 [week 2], an email invitation to participate in the study was sent. (3) In step 3 [week 3], an email thank you and reminder was sent.

(4) In step 4 [week 4], a final email thank you and reminder was sent. Sixteen frontline staff who met the study criteria responded to the survey. Participants were asked a series ten questions about their perspective on factors that facilitated or created barriers to the successful community reintegration of older adults.

Phase Two: Formerly Incarcerated Older Adults

In phase two of the study, adults age 50 and older who were released from prison within the past five years were recruited to participate in the survey. The research team posted an announcement and invitation describing the study on the bulletin boards of regional correctional community service providers and parole offices. Informational handouts were available directly below the posted study announcement, with an invitation for potential participants to review and, if interested, voluntarily respond to the research team by phone or mail. Each of the thirty-one participants who responded to the announcement met with members of the research team to learn more about the study and to provide informed consent to participate in the study. The one-on-one, ninety-minute, semistructured, in-depth interviews were held in a private office of a community program that was easily accessible by public transportation. The interviews were administered by the principal investigators and two trained MSW students with personal histories of incarceration. The interview schedule was divided into three parts: participants experiences before, during, and after prison. Participants were asked about their life course experiences of family and community and what factors facilitated or created barriers to their successful reintegration. The interviews were recorded using a digital audio recorder and were transcribed verbatim. Participants who completed the interview were offered a thirty-dollar gift card for their participation.

Data Analysis

The qualitative data from service providers and formerly incarcerated older adults was analyzed using Tutty, Rothery, and Grinnell's[2] qualitative data analysis coding scheme. The first step involved identifying meaning units'(or in vivo codes) from the data. First-level codes were assigned to the data to accurately reflect the writer's exact words (e.g., family, community, care). Second-level coding and first-level meaning units were sorted and placed in their respective categories (e.g., facilitators to success). A constant comparative strategy was used to ensure meaning unit codes were classified by similarities and differences and carefully analyzed for relationships, themes, and patterns. The categories were examined for meaning and interpretation. Conceptually clustered matrices and diagrams were constructed to detect patterns, themes, and relationships within and across categories.[3]

APPENDIX 2

___

COMING OUT OF PRISON STUDY

LGBTQ+ OLDER ADULTS' EXPERIENCES BEFORE, DURING, AND AFTER PRISON

Research Design

In 2013–14, the authors used a qualitative longitudinal research design to gather data from a sample of ten LGBTQ+ adults age 50 and older released to New York City from New York State prisons. The study was approved by the Fordham University Institutional Review Board and met the criteria for research with vulnerable populations, such as elders and ex-prisoners.

To recruit LGBTQ+ older adults, the research team posted an announcement and invitation flier that described the study on the bulletin boards of regional correctional community service providers and parole offices. The flier included the principal investigator's contact information for potential LGBTQ+ older adults who were interested in finding out more about the study. Once LGBTQ+ older adults were identified, snowball sampling methods were used to recruit LGBTQ+ older adults. Ten LGBTQ+ older adults agreed to participate in the study and provided their informed consent. All LGBTQ+ older adult participants were between the ages of 50 and 65. The sample consisted of five gay men (black=3 and Latino=2), one bisexual man (white=1), and four lesbians (black=3, white=1).

Data Collection

Longitudinal data were collected using focus groups (Time 1; T1). One month later, one-on-one in-person interviews were conducted (Time 2; T2). In the first phase of the study, two ninety-minute focus groups with five LGBTQ+ older adults were conducted with formerly incarcerated LGBTQ+ elders (men=3; women=2). All interviews were conducted in a private group room at the principal investigator's office building. A trained researcher assistant moderated the focus groups. The focus group's semistructured interview consisted of ten open-ended questions and follow-up probes that asked about the LGBTQ+ older adults' life experiences before, during, and after prison. The focus groups were taped using a digital audio recorder and were transcribed verbatim. As an incentive, a thirty-dollar gift card was given to each focus group participant.

One month later (T2), each participant met with a trained interviewer to elicit further information in a follow-up in-person, one-on-one, ninety-minute, in-depth interview. All ten interviews were held in a private room at the principal investigator's office building. The semistructured interview was divided into three parts that asked LGBTQ+ older adults more detailed questions about their personal and social experiences before, during, and after prison. The interviews were taped using a digital audio recorder and were transcribed verbatim. The LGBTQ+ older adults were offered a thirty-dollar gift card for their participation for each interview completed.

Data Analysis

The focus group and in-person interviews were analyzed using Tutty, Rothery, and Grinnell's constant comparative data analysis methods.[1] The first step of the analysis involved identifying meaning units (similar to in vivo codes) from the data. First level codes were assigned to the data to accurately reflect the writer's exact words (e.g., true self, homo thug). Second level coding and first level meaning units were sorted and placed in their respective categories (e.g. going in or coming out of prison). A constant comparative strategy was used to ensure meaning unit codes were classified by similarities and differences and carefully analyzed for relationships, themes, and patterns. A conceptually clustered diagram was constructed to detect patterns and themes and develop a process model.[2]

Formerly Incarcerated LGBTQ+ Elders Recommendations for System Reform

These recommendations for system reform come directly from formerly incarcerated LGBTQ+ elders in their own words. They offer suggestions on how corrections and community service providers and policy makers can improve the system for LGBTQ+ elders released from prison.

Adoption of More Affirming Services and Policies

- We need to reform the whole criminal justice process. Like the intake process in prison. I don't know if they do it like that as some type of scare tactic or what. The way they intake is like they can give you like a very negative outlook on life in prison. And if you're not an open-minded person, you can go through your whole sentence being in fear. I think they need to be a little bit more compassionate on intake because if you're full of fear, you're not open to anything, you know. So you go in jail or prison and you think you got to fight or you got to do this. It's just not true. You don't have to fight your way through jail. It's like anything in life. If you're not educated about the situation, it can be bad.
- I believe that if people had better, like if there was better planning for people that's coming out of prison system, a lot of them wouldn't be going back to jail. A lot of them would change their ways, and they would become productive members of society, LGBTQ+ or not.

Nondiscrimination and Special Population Considerations

- And one of the things you were talking about in jail that really needs to change, gays in prison should be able to safely go to school. Right now they can't. They'd be attacked. In prison, they need to separate the jobs for older and people that's younger. I worked in a mess hall, and that's a hard job, and, you know, if you're up in age and you got your, you know, the older you get, the more aches and pains you have, you know, and working in the mess hall, I don't see it being good for somebody that's 55 or 60.
- They need to have senior citizen things up there in prison for people that are senior citizens, I mean, because when you're old, I mean, everybody gets old. I mean, already you're forgetful in the mind and stuff like that. You get senile and stuff like that, you know. Um, they should have just a, I can't say, um, a certain place, but, I mean, they should have something for seniors too, you know, because—How can you put a 60-something-year-old man in with the regular population of 15- and 16-year-old kids? I wish they would have places for people who are of that age, something to do for them and something to keep their mind on the right thing, you know, where they won't get into trouble or get hurt.

Reentry Access to Culturally Responsive Safe and Affordable Housing and Social Services

- Cheaper housing, housing, affordable housing, connected to a therapist, connection to treatment. All these things—Affordable treatment because now safe housing is essential in being able to successfully adjust back into the community. Living in a high crime area, that has a majority of unemployed or underemployed residents that may be socially stigmatized, will reduce the ability to manage. In addition, some of these areas have high rates of victimization of residents, and easy access to illegal activities and drugs. Adding identification as LGBTQ+ can exacerbate community discrimination and oppression.

- Specific services for people who are at least age 50 or older, LGBTQ+, and formerly incarcerated. For programs, we need them more affirming. See everyone says we need something for the gays, something for the, no, we need a firm thing so we can integrate and learn to live.

Mental Health and Social Needs

- More activities, more sponsoring of something for the LGBTQ+ seniors. We don't have anything. Even if they go into regular senior citizen. Senior citizens are just like kids. They are just [as] biased as kids so, you know, just more resources for us.
- We need a lot with diabetes because a lot of our seniors are coming down with it, especially the black and Puerto Ricans because we are limited to our resources of eating, you know.

Justice and Policy Advocacy Opportunities

- For policies, I would change stop and frisk of course. And there is no law but their treatment of gays. They have no respect for gays. There's nothing in line that they can say they are breaking and not doing, it's just their treatments toward especially the gay men, and I can't even say lesbians. There's very few cops that will be angry with lesbians, but all cops are angry in treatment of gay people or trans people. It's just horrible.
- One of the things that we should always have is someone in the LGBTQ+, in like on the returning is access to a lawyer. They should have an LGBTQ+ person, affirming person to defend us because we get no defense by regular attorneys. Now, I mean that's one time that will probably predict some things and coming out we can work on that end but going in, I need somebody like, they don't even want to talk to you. We need yeah, LGBTQ+ representation of lawyers, otherwise they may not want to talk to you or really understand or help you.
- We need to have the opportunity to be more visible and have our voices heard. What better way to let people and professionals know what needs to change for LGBTQ+ elders.

NOTES

Introduction

1. "Why Keep the Old and Sick Behind Bars?," editorial, *New York Times*, January 3, 2017, https://www.nytimes.com/2017/01/03/opinion/why-keep-the-old-and-sick-behind-bars.html.
2. Tina Maschi and Ronald H. Aday, "The Social Determinants of Health and Justice and the Aging in Prison Crisis: A Call for Human Rights Action," *International Journal of Social Work* 1, no. 1 (2014): 15, doi:10.5296/ijsw.v1i1.4914; Tina Maschi and Judith Baer, "The Heterogeneity of the World Assumptions of Older Adults in Prison: Do Differing Worldviews Have a Mental Health Effect?," *Traumatology* 19, no. 1 (2013): 65–72, doi:10.1177/1534765612443294.
3. Wendy Sawyer and Peter Wagner, "Mass Incarceration: The Whole Pie 2019," Prison Policy, 2019, https://www.prisonpolicy.org/reports/pie2019.html.
4. *New York Times*, "Why Keep the Old and Sick Behind Bars?"
5. Bureau of Justice Statistics, "Prisoners in 2016," 2016, https://www.bjs.gov/index.cfm?ty=pbdetail&iid=6187.
6. "Old Behind Bars: The Aging Prison Population in the United States," Human Rights Watch, 2012, http://www.hrw.org/reports/2012/01/27/old-behind-bars; Katie Stone, Irena Papadopoulos, and Daniel Kelly, "Establishing Hospice Care for Prison Populations: An Integrative Review Assessing the UK and USA Perspective," *Palliative Medicine* 26, no. 8 (2011): 969–78, doi:10.1177/0269216311424219.
7. Martha H. Hurley, *Aging in Prison* (Durham, N.C.: Carolina Academic Press, 2014).
8. Bureau of Justice Statistics, "Prisoners in 2016," 2.
9. Tina Chiu, "It's About Time: Aging Prisoners, Increasing Costs, and Geriatric Release," Vera Institute, 2010, https://www.vera.org/publications/its-about-time-aging-prisoners-increasing-costs-and-geriatric-release.

10. Doris James and Lauren Glaze, "Mental Health Problems of Prison and Jail Inmates," Bureau of Justice Statistics, 2006, https://www.bjs.gov/content/pub/pdf/mhppji.pdf; Tina Maschi, Samantha L. Sutfin, and Brendan O'Connell, "Aging, Mental Health, and the Criminal Justice System: A Content Analysis of the Literature," *Journal of Forensic Social Work* 2, no. 2–3 (2012): 162–85, doi:10.1080/1936928x.2012.750254; Tina Maschi and Adriana Kaye, "Responding to the Crisis of Aging People in Prison: Promising Corrections and Community Practices," *Advancing Corrections: Journal of the International Corrections and Prisoners Association* 7 (2019): 151–60.

11. Tina Maschi, Keith Morgen, Kimberly Westcott, Deborah Viola, and Lindsay Koskinen, "Aging, Incarceration, and Employment Prospects: Recommendations for Practice and Policy Reform," *Journal of Applied Rehabilitation Counseling* 45, no. 4 (2014): 44–55, doi:10.1891/0047-2220.45.4.44.

12. Tina Maschi, Deborah Viola, and Fei Sun, "The High Cost of the International Aging Prisoner Crisis: Well-Being As the Common Denominator for Action," *The Gerontologist* 53, no. 4 (2012): 543–54, doi:10.1093/geront/gns125.

13. Ann Carson and William Sabol, "Prisoners In 2011," Bureau of Justice Statistics, 2011, https://www.bjs.gov/content/pub/pdf/p11.pdf.

14. Maschi et al., "Aging, Incarceration, and Employment Prospects," 44.

15. Matthew Davies, "The Integration of Elderly Prisoners: An Exploration of Services Provided in England and Wales," *International Journal of Criminology* 1 (2011): 1–32.

16. Tina Maschi and Lindsay Koskinen, "Co-Constructing Community: A Conceptual Map for Reuniting Aging People in Prison with Their Families and Communities," *Traumatology* 21, no. 3 (2015): 208–18, doi:10.1037/trm0000026.

17. Nick Mesurier, "Supporting Older People in Prison: Ideas for Practice," Age UK Services, 2011, https://www.ageuk.org.uk/documents/en-gb/for-professionals/government-and-society/older%20prisoners%20guide_pro.pdf?dtrk=true.

18. "Old Behind Bars."

19. Tomris Atabay, "Handbook on Prisoners with Special Needs," United Nations Office on Drugs and Crime, 2009, https://www.unodc.org/pdf/criminal_justice/Handbook_on_Prisoners_with_Special_Needs.pdf; Maschi and Kaye, "Responding to the Crisis of Aging People in Prison," 150.

20. American Civil Liberties Union, "At America's Expense: The Mass Incarceration of the Elderly," June 2012, https://www.aclu.org/report/americas-expense-mass-incarceration-elderly.

21. W. Dai and F. Yu, "The Correction of Old Prisoners: A Sociological Study," *China Prison Journal* 4 (2011): 25–29.

22. Stan Stojkovic, "Elderly Prisoners: A Growing and Forgotten Group Within Correctional Systems Vulnerable to Elder Abuse," *Journal of Elder Abuse & Neglect* 19, no. 3–4 (2007): 97–117, doi:10.1300/j084v19n03_06; Atabay, "Handbook on Prisoners with Special Needs."

23. Tina Maschi, Jung Kwak, Euojong Ko, and Mary B. Morrissey, "Forget Me Not: Dementia in Prison," *The Gerontologist* 52, no. 4 (2012): 441–51, doi:10.1093/geront/gnr131.

24. Tina Maschi, Carolyn Bradley, and Kelly Ward, *Forensic Social Work: Psychosocial and Legal Issues in Diverse Practice Settings* (New York: Springer, 2009).

25. Maschi, Bradley, and Ward, *Forensic Social Work*, 11.

26. Craig Haney, "The Psychological Impact of Incarceration: Implications for Post-Prison Adjustment," 2001, https://aspe.hhs.gov/basic-report/psychological-impact-incarceration-implications-post-prison-adjustment.

27. Maschi and Kaye, "Responding to the Crisis of Aging People in Prison," 154.

28. John S, Wilson and Sharen Barboza, "The Looming Challenge of Dementia in Prisons," *Correct Care* 24, no. 2 (Spring 2010): 12–15, https://www.ncchc.org/filebin/images/Website _PDFs/24-2.pdf.

29. Stojkovic, "Elderly Prisoners," 100.

30. Haney, "The Psychological Impact of Incarceration."

31. Maschi, Sutfin, and O'Connell, "Aging, Mental Health, and the Criminal Justice System," 162.

32. Tina Maschi, Deborah Viola, and Lindsay Koskinen, "Trauma, Stress, and Coping Among Older Adults in Prison: Towards a Human Rights and Intergenerational Family Justice Action Agenda," *Traumatology* 21, no. 3 (2015): 188–200, doi:10.1037 /trm0000021.

33. Maschi, Viola, and Koskinen, "Trauma, Stress, and Coping," 190.

34. Mesurier, "Supporting Older People in Prison."

35. Maura Ewing, "When Prisons Need to Be More Like Nursing Homes," The Marshall Project, 2015, https://www.themarshallproject.org/2015/08/27/when-prisons-need-to -be-more-like-nursing-homes.

36. "Community," *Merriam-Webster*, 2019, https://www.merriam-webster.com/dictionary /community.

37. American Civil Liberties Union, "At America's Expense."

38. "Old Behind Bars."

39. Chad Kinsella, "Corrections Health Care Costs," Council of State Governments, January 2004, http://www.csg.org/knowledgecenter/docs/TA0401CorrHealth.pdf.

40. Hurley, *Aging in Prison*, 25.

41. Maschi and Koskinen, "Co-Constructing Community," 210.

42. Maschi and Koskinen, "Co-Constructing Community," 212.

1. An Ounce of Prevention Is Worth a Pound of Cure

1. Help Age International, "International Human Rights Law and Older People: Gaps, Fragments and Loopholes," August 2012, https://social.un.org/ageing-working-group /documents/GapsinprotectionofolderpeoplesrightsAugust2012.pdf.

2. Tina Maschi, Deborah Viola, and Lindsay Koskinen, "Trauma, Stress, and Coping Among Older Adults in Prison: Towards a Human Rights and Intergenerational Family Justice Action Agenda," *Traumatology* 21, no. 3 (2015): 188–200, doi:10.1037 /trm0000021.

3. Tomris Atabay, "Handbook for Prisoners with Special Needs," United Nations Office on Drugs and Crime, 2009, https://www.unodc.org/pdf/criminal_justice/Handbook_on _Prisoners_with_Special_Needs.pdf.

4. American Civil Liberties Union, "At America's Expense: The Mass Incarceration of the Elderly," 2012, https://www.aclu.org/report/americas-expense-mass-incarceration -elderly; Justice Policy Institute, "The Ungers, 5 Years and Counting: A Case Study in Safely Reducing Long Prison Terms and Saving Taxpayer Dollars," November 15, 2018, http://www.justicepolicy.org/research/12320; Thailand Institute of Justice, "Home Page," http://www.tijthailand.org/main/en/home; Attabay, "Handbook for Prisoners with Special Needs," 10.

5. Tina Maschi, Deborah Viola, and Fei Sun, "The High Cost of the International Aging Prisoner Crisis: Well-Being as the Common Denominator for Action," *The Gerontologist* 53, no. 4 (2012): 543–54, doi:10.1093/geront/gns125; Ann Carson and William Sabol,

"Prisoners in 2011," Bureau of Justice Statistics, 2011, https://www.bjs.gov/content/pub/pdf/p11.pdf.

6. Penal Reform International and Thailand Institute of Justice, "Global Prison Trends 2018," April 1, 2018, https://www.prisonlegalnews.org/news/publications/penal-reform-international-thailand-institute-justice-global-prison-trends-2018/.

7. Tina Maschi, "Why I Am in Prison: One Older Man's Prison Parable as Society's Collective Lesson," Justia Agenda, 2013, http://justiaagenda.com/policy-campaigns/.

8. Tina Maschi, Deborah Viola, Keith Morgen, and Lindsay Koskinen, "Trauma, Stress, Grief, Loss, and Separation Among Older Adults in Prison: The Protective Role of Coping Resources on Physical and Mental Well-Being," *Journal of Crime and Justice* 38, no. 1 (2013): 113–36, doi:10.1080/0735648x.2013.808853.

9. Maschi, "Why I Am in Prison," 10.

10. Janice Denehy, "Thinking Upstream About Promoting Healthy Environments in Schools," *The Journal of School Nursing* 17, no. 2 (May 2001): 61, https://journals.sagepub.com/doi/10.1177/105984050101700201.

2. Intersecting Perspectives on Aging, Diversity, Difference, and Justice

1. Bureau of Justice Statistics, "Prisoners in 2016," 2016, https://www.bjs.gov/index.cfm?ty=pbdetail&iid=6187.

2. Bureau of Justice Statistics, "Prisoners in 2016"; Craig Haney, "The Psychological Impact of Incarceration: Implications for Post-Prison Adjustment," 2001, https://aspe.hhs.gov/basic-report/psychological-impact-incarceration-implications-post-prison-adjustment; Tina Maschi, Samantha L. Sutfin, and Brendan O'Connell, "Aging, Mental Health, and the Criminal Justice System: A Content Analysis of the Literature," *Journal of Forensic Social Work* 2, nos. 2–3 (2012): 162–85, doi:10.1080/1936928x.2012.750254; Robin J. Wilson, Janice E. Picheca, and Michelle Prinzo, "Evaluating the Effectiveness of Professionally-Facilitated Volunteerism in the Community-Based Management of High-Risk Sexual Offenders: Part Two. A Comparison of Recidivism Rates," *The Howard Journal of Criminal Justice* 46, no. 4 (2007): 327–37, doi:10.1111/j.1468-2311.2007.00480.x; Stan Stojkovic, "Elderly Prisoners: A Growing and Forgotten Group Within Correctional Systems Vulnerable to Elder Abuse," *Journal of Elder Abuse & Neglect* 19, nos. 3–4 (2007): 97–117, doi:10.1300/j084v19n03_06; Cindy Struckman-Johnson and David Struckman-Johnson, "A Comparison of Sexual Coercion Experiences Reported by Men and Women in Prison," *Journal of Interpersonal Violence* 21, no. 12 (2006): 1591–1615, doi:10.1177/0886260506294240.

3. John Gramlich, "The Gap Between the Number of Blacks and Whites in Prison Is Shrinking," Pew Research Center, 2019, https://www.pewresearch.org/fact-tank/2019/04/30/shrinking-gap-between-number-of-blacks-and-whites-in-prison/.

4. Bureau of Justice Statistics, "Prisoners in 2016," 2; Haney, "The Psychological Impact of Incarceration"; Maschi, Sutfin, and O'Connell, "Aging, Mental Health, and the Criminal Justice System," 164; John Wilson and Sharen Barboza, "The Looming Challenge of Dementia in Prisons," Correct Care, 2010, https://www.ncchc.org/filebin/images/Website_PDFs/24-2.pdf; Stojkovic, "Elderly Prisoners," 100; Struckman-Johnson and Struckman-Johnson, "A Comparison of Sexual Coercion Experiences," 1592.

5. Bureau of Justice Statistics, "Prisoners in 2016," 3; Haney, "The Psychological Impact of Incarceration"; Maschi, Sutfin, and O'Connell, "Aging, Mental Health, and the Criminal

Justice System,"165; Wilson and Barboza, "The Looming Challenge of Dementia in Prisons," 25; Stojkovic, "Elderly Prisoners," 101; Struckman-Johnson and Struckman -Johnson, "A Comparison of Sexual Coercion Experiences," 1593.

6. See note 5.
7. See note 5.
8. See note 5.
9. See note 5.
10. See note 5.
11. Tina Maschi, Deborah Viola, and Lindsay Koskinen, "Trauma, Stress, and Coping Among Older Adults in Prison: Towards a Human Rights and Intergenerational Family Justice Action Agenda," *Traumatology* 21, no. 3 (2015): 188–200, doi:10.1037 /trm0000021.
12. D. A. Andrews and James Bonta, "Rehabilitating Criminal Justice Policy and Practice," *Psychology, Public Policy, and Law* 16, no. 1 (2010): 39–55, doi:10.1037/a0018362.
13. Kimberle Crenshaw, "Demarginalizing the Intersection of Race and Sex: A Black Feminist Critique of Anti-Discrimination Doctrine, Feminist Theory and Anti-Racist Politics," *University of Chicago Legal Forum* (1989): article 81989, https://chicagounbound .uchicago.edu/cgi/viewcontent.cgi?article=1052&context=uclf.
14. Crenshaw, "Demarginalizing the Intersection of Race and Sex," 142; Yvette Murphy, *Incorporating Intersectionality in Social Work Practice, Research, Policy, and Education* (Washington, D.C.: National Association of Social Workers, 2009).
15. Robert P. Mullaly, *Challenging Oppression and Confronting Privilege*, 2nd ed. (Ontario, Canada: Oxford University Press, 2017), 39.
16. David Gil, *Confronting Injustice and Oppression* (New York: Columbia University Press, 1987), 50; Mullaly, *Challenging Oppression and Confronting Privilege*, 42.
17. Mullaly, *Challenging Oppression and Confronting Privilege*, 44.
18. Bureau of Justice Statistics, "Prisoners in 2016," 2.
19. Vera Institute, "Research Confirms That Entrenched Racism Manifests in Disparate Treatment of Black Americans in the Criminal Justice System," 2018, https://www.vera .org/newsroom/research-confirms-that-entrenched-racism-manifests-in-disparate -treatment-of-black-americans-in-criminal-justice-system.
20. Mullaly, *Challenging Oppression and Confronting Privilege*, 45.
21. Mullaly, *Challenging Oppression and Confronting Privilege*, 48.
22. Mullaly, *Challenging Oppression and Confronting Privilege*, 52.
23. Hussein Abdilahi Bulhan, *Frantz Fanon and the Psychology of Oppression* (Charlesbourg, Québec: Braille Jymico, 2011).
24. Marion Young, "Five Faces of Oppression," *Philosophical Forum* 19, no. 4 (1988): 27–290.
25. Maschi, Sutfin, and O'Connell, "Aging, Mental Health, and the Criminal Justice System," 162.
26. Young, "Five Faces of Oppression," 55.
27. Tina Maschi, Deborah Viola, and Fei Sun, "The High Cost of the International Aging Prisoner Crisis: Well-Being as the Common Denominator for Action," *The Gerontologist* 53, no. 4 (2012): 543–54, doi:10.1093/geront/gns125.
28. Maschi, Viola, and Sun, "The High Cost of the International Aging Prisoner Crisis," 543.
29. Maschi, Viola, and Sun, "The High Cost of the International Aging Prisoner Crisis," 544.
30. Maschi, Viola, and Sun, "The High Cost of the International Aging Prisoner Crisis," 545.
31. Glen Elder, Monica Kirkpatrick Johnson, and Robert Crosnoe, "The Emergence and Development of Life Course Theory," in *Handbook of the Life Course*, ed. Jeylan T. Mortimer and Michael J. Shanahan (Boston, Mass.: Springer, 2003), 3–19; Martha C.

Nussbaum, "Beyond the Social Contract: Capabilities and Global Justice," *Oxford Development Studies* 32, no. 1 (June 2003): 3–18, doi:10.1080/1360081042000184093.

32. Hans-Werner Wahl, Susanne Iwarsson, and Frank Oswald, "Aging Well and the Environment: Toward an Integrative Model and Research Agenda for the Future," *The Gerontologist* 52, no. 3 (2012): 306–16, doi:10.1093/geront/gnr154.

33. World Health Organization, "Constitution of the World Health Organization," accessed November 28, 2019, http://apps.who.int/gb/bd/PDF/bd47/EN/constitution-en.pdf?ua=1.

34. Ronald H. Aday, *Aging Prisoners* (Westport, Conn.: Praeger, 2003); Tina Maschi, Jung Kwak, Eujeong Ko, and Mary B. Morrissey, "Forget Me Not: Dementia in Prison," *The Gerontologist* 52, no. 4 (2012): 441–51, doi:10.1093/geront/gnr131.

35. Tina Maschi and Judith Baer, "The Heterogeneity of the World Assumptions of Older Adults in Prison: Do Differing Worldviews Have a Mental Health Effect?," *Traumatology* 19, no. 1 (2013): 65–72, doi:10.1177/1534765612443294; Tina Maschi, Sandy Gibson, Kristen M. Zgoba, and Keith Morgen, "Trauma and Life Event Stressors Among Young and Older Adult Prisoners," *Journal of Correctional Health Care* 17, no. 2 (2011): 160–72, doi:10.1177/1078345810396682.

36. Elder, Johnson, and Crosnoe, "The Emergence and Development of Life Course Theory," 14; Leonard I. Pearlin, Scott Schieman, Elena M. Fazio, and Stephen C. Meersman, "Stress, Health, and the Life Course: Some Conceptual Perspectives," *Journal of Health and Social Behavior* 46, no. 2 (2005): 205–19, doi:10.1177/002214650504600206.

37. Glen H. Elder, *Children of the Great Depression* (Chicago, Ill.: University of Chicago Press, 1974).

38. Robert Agnew, "A Longitudinal Test of the Revised Strain Theory," *Journal of Quantitative Criminology* 5, no. 4 (1989): 373–87, doi:10.1007/bf01062560; Pearlin, Schieman, Fazio, and Meersman, "Stress, Health, and the Life Course," 205.

39. Agnew, "A Longitudinal Test of the Revised Strain Theory," 373.

40. Catherine E. Ross and John Mirowsky, "Neighborhood Disadvantage, Disorder, and Health," *Journal of Health and Social Behavior* 42, no. 3 (2001): 258, doi:10.2307/3090214.

41. Ross and Mirowsky, "Neighborhood Disadvantage, Disorder, and Health," 258; Robert J. Sampson and John H. Laub, "Crime and Deviance over the Life Course: The Salience of Adult Social Bonds," *American Sociological Review* 55, no. 5 (1990): 609, doi:10.2307/2095859.

42. Patricia McGrath Morris, "The Capabilities Perspective: A Framework for Social Justice," *Families in Society: The Journal of Contemporary Social Services* 83, no. 4 (2002): 365–73, doi:10.1606/1044-3894.16.

43. McGrath Morris, "The Capabilities Perspective: A Framework for Social Justice," 53.

44. Nussbaum, "Beyond the Social Contract," 5.

45. Nussbaum, "Beyond the Social Contract," 8.

46. United Nations Office on Drugs and Crime, "Handbook on Prisoners with Special Needs," 2009, https://www.unodc.org/pdf/criminal_justice/Handbook_on_Prisoners_with_Special_Needs.pdf.

47. United Nations, "The Universal Declaration of Human Rights," 1948, http://www.un.org/en/documents/udhr/.

48. United Nations, "The Universal Declaration of Human Rights"; United Nations, "Standard Minimum Rules for the Treatment of Prisoners," 1977, http://www2.ohchr.org/english/law/treatmentprisoners.htm; United Nations, "Report of the United Nations High Commissioner for Human Rights," 2012.

49. Urie Bronfenbrenner, *Ecology of Human Development* (Cambridge, Mass.: Harvard University Press, 2009).

50. Bronfenbrenner, *Ecology of Human Development*, 56.

51. Nancy Hooyman and Asuman Kiyak, *Social Gerontology: A Multidisciplinary Perspective* (Needham Heights, Mass.: Allyn & Bacon, 2007).

52. Hooyman and Kiyak, *Social Gerontology*.

53. Sheldon Cohen and Thomas A. Wills, "Stress, Social Support, and the Buffering Hypothesis," *Psychological Bulletin* 98, no. 2 (1985): 310–57, doi:10.1037//0033-2909.98.2.310; Sheldon Cohen, Benjamin H. Gottlieb, and Lynn G. Underwood, "Social Relationships and Health," in *Measuring and Intervening in Social Support* (New York: Oxford University Press, 2000) 3–25.

54. Sampson and Laub, "Crime and Deviance over the Life Course," 609.

55. Emily Greenfield, "Using Ecological Frameworks to Advance a Field of Research, Practice, and Policy on Aging-in-Place Initiatives," *The Gerontologist* 52, no. 1 (2011): 1–12, doi:10.1093/geront/gnr108.

56. Paul Glasziou, "Evidence-Based Medicine: Does It Make a Difference?," *British Medical Journal* 330, no. 7482 (2005): 92–93, doi:10.1136/bmj.330.7482.92-b.

57. Crenshaw, "Demarginalizing the Intersection of Race and Sex," 142.

58. Murphy, *Incorporating Intersectionality in Social Work Practice*, 30.

59. Wilson, Picheca, and Prinzo, "Evaluating the Effectiveness of Professionally-Facilitated Volunteerism," 327.

60. Andrews and Bonta, "Rehabilitating Criminal Justice Policy and Practice," 39.

61. Andrews and Bonta, "Rehabilitating Criminal Justice Policy and Practice," 39.

62. Tina Maschi and Adriana Kaye, "Responding to the Crisis of Aging People in Prison: Promising Corrections and Community Practices," *Advancing Corrections: Journal of the International Corrections and Prisoners Association* 7 (2019): 151–60.

3. Trauma and Diversity Among Older Adults in Prison

1. Tina Maschi, Deborah Viola, and Keith Morgen, "Unraveling Trauma and Stress, Coping Resources, and Mental Well-Being Among Older Adults in Prison: Empirical Evidence Linking Theory and Practice," *The Gerontologist* 54, no. 5 (2013): 857–67, doi:10.1093/geront/gnt069.

2. Tina Maschi and Dweeja Dasarathy, "Social Determinants and Mental Health Among Older Adults in the Criminal Justice System," in *Psychiatric Ethics in Late-Life Patients*, ed. Meera Balasubramaniam, Aarti Gupta, and Rajesh R. Tampi (New York: Springer, 2019), 185–88.

3. Johan Galtung, "Violence, Peace, and Peace Research," *Journal of Peace Research* 6, no. 3 (1969): 167–91, doi:10.1177/002234336900600301.

4. Iris Marion Young, "Five Faces of Oppression," *Philosophical Forum* 19, no. 4 (1988): 270–90.

5. Tina Maschi, Judith Baer, Mary Beth Morrissey, and Claudia Moreno, "The Aftermath of Childhood Trauma on Late Life Mental and Physical Health: A Review of the Literature," *Traumatology* 19, no. 1 (2013): 49–64, doi:10.1177/1534765612437377.

6. SAMHSA-HRSA Center for Integrated Health Solutions, "Trauma". Retrieved from https://www.integration.samhsa.gov/clinical-practice/trauma.

7. World Health Organization, "Violence Against Women," November 29, 2017, https://www.who.int/news-room/fact-sheets/detail/violence-against-women.

8. Thema Bryant-Davis and Carlota Ocampo, "Racist Incident–Based Trauma," *The Counseling Psychologist* 33, no. 4 (2005): 479–500, doi:10.1177/0011000005276465.

9. T. N. Alim, E. Graves, T. A. Mellman, N. Aigbogun, E. Gray, W. Lawson, and D. S. Charney, "Trauma Exposure, Posttraumatic Stress Disorder and Depression in an African-American Primary Care Population," *Journal of the National Medical Association* 98, no. 10 (October 2006): 1630–36.

10. Maschi and Dasarathy, "Social Determinants and Mental Health Among Older Adults in the Criminal Justice System," 185–88.

11. SAMHSA-HRSA Center for Integrated Health Solutions, "Trauma."

12. Tina Maschi, Keith Morgen, Kristen Zgoba, Deborah Courtney, and Jennifer Ristow, "Age, Cumulative Trauma and Stressful Life Events, and Post-Traumatic Stress Symptoms Among Older Adults in Prison: Do Subjective Impressions Matter?," *The Gerontologist* 51, no. 5 (2011): 675–86, doi:10.1093/geront/gnr074.

13. Valerie Jenness, Cheryl Maxson, Kristy Matsuda, and Jennifer Summer, *Violence in California Correctional Facilities: An Empirical Examination of Sexual Assault* (Irvine: University of California Center for Evidence-Based Corrections, 2007).

14. Jody Marksamer and Harper Tobin, *Standing with LGBT Prisoners: An Advocate's Guide to Ending Abuse and Combatting Injustice* (Washington, D.C.: National Center for Transgender Equality, 2014).

15. Maschi, Viola, and Morgen, "Unraveling Trauma and Stress, Coping Resources, and Mental Well-Being Among Older Adults in Prison," 857.

16. Maschi, Baer, Morrissey, and Moreno, "The Aftermath of Childhood Trauma on Late Life Mental and Physical Health," 49–64.

17. SAMHSA-HRSA Center for Integrated Health Solutions, "Trauma."

18. American Psychiatric Association, *Diagnostic and Statistical Manual of Mental Disorders: DSM-5* (Arlington, Va.: American Psychiatric Association, 2013).

19. Glen Elder, Monica Kirkpatrick Johnson, and Robert Crosnoe, "The Emergence and Development of Life Course Theory," in *Handbook of the Life Course*, ed. Jeylan T. Mortimer and Michael J. Shanahan (Boston, Mass.: Springer, 2019), 3–19; Leonard I. Pearlin, Scott Schieman, Elena M. Fazio, and Stephen C. Meersman, "Stress, Health, and the Life Course: Some Conceptual Perspectives," *Journal of Health and Social Behavior* 46, no. 2 (2005): 205–19, doi:10.1177/002214650504600206.

20. Chaya S. Piotrkowski, "Gender Harassment, Job Satisfaction, and Distress Among Employed White and Minority Women," *Journal of Occupational Health Psychology* 3, no. 1 (1998): 33–43, doi:10.1037/1076-8998.3.1.33.

21. Tina Maschi, "Trauma and Violent Delinquent Behavior Among Males: The Moderating Role of Social Support," *Stress, Trauma, and Crisis* 9, no. 1 (2006): 45–72, doi:10.1080/15434610500506233.

22. Joy DeGruy, *Post Traumatic Slave Syndrome: America's Legacy of Enduring Injury and Healing* (Milwaukie, Ore: Uptone Press, 2005).

23. Michelle Sotero, "A Conceptual Model of Historical Trauma: Implications for Public Health Practice and Research," *Journal of Health Disparities Research and Practice* 1, no. 1 (2006): 93–108.

24. Cynthia Wesley-Esquimaux and Magdalena Smolewsk, *Historic Trauma and Aboriginal Healing* (Ontario, Canada: Aboriginal Healing Foundation, 2004).

25. Michelle Alexander, *The New Jim Crow: Mass Incarceration in the Age of Colorblindness* (New York: New Press, 2019).

26. Bessel A. Van der Kolk, Alexander C. McFarlane, and Lars Weisæth, *Traumatic Stress* (New York: Guilford Press. 2007).

27. Van der Kolk, McFarlane, and Weisæth, *Traumatic Stress*.
28. Van der Kolk, McFarlane, and Weisæth, *Traumatic Stress*; James D. Bremmer, "Traumatic Stress: Effects on the Brain," *Dialogues in Clinical Neuroscience* 8, no. 4 (2006): 445–61; Michael D. De Bellis and Abigail Zisk, "The Biological Effects of Childhood Trauma," *Child and Adolescent Psychiatric Clinics of North America* 23, no. 2 (2014): 185–222, doi:10.1016/j.chc.2014.01.002.
29. See note 28.
30. See note 28.
31. See note 28.
32. Maschi, "Trauma and Violent Delinquent Behavior Among Males," 45; Maschi, Viola, and Morgen, "Unraveling Trauma and Stress, Coping Resources, and Mental Well-Being Among Older Adults in Prison," 857; Tina Maschi, Deborah Viola, and Lindsay Koskinen, "Trauma, Stress, and Coping Among Older Adults in Prison: Towards a Human Rights and Intergenerational Family Justice Action Agenda," *Traumatology* 21, no. 3 (2015): 188–200, doi:10.1037/trm0000021.
33. K. M. Abram, J. J. Washburn, L. A. Teplin, K. M. Emanuel, E. G. Romero, and G. M. McClelland, "Posttraumatic Stress Disorder and Psychiatric Comorbidity Among Detained Youths," *Psychiatric Services* 58, no. 10 (October 2007): 1311–16, doi:10.1176/appi.ps.58.10.1311; Brigette A. Erwin, Elana Newman, Robert A. McMackin, Carlo Morrisey, and Danny G. Kaloupek, "PTSD, Malevolent Environment, and Criminality Among Criminally Involved Male Adolescents," *Criminal Justice and Behavior* 27, no. 2 (2000): 196–215, doi:10.1177/0093854800027002004; Carolyn Wolf Harlow, "Prior Abuse Reported by Inmates and Probationers," Bureau of Justice Statistics, April 11, 1999, http://www.bjs.gov/index.cfm?ty=pbdetail&iid=837.
34. Doris J. James and Lauren E. Glaze, "Mental Health Problems of Prison and Jail Inmates," Bureau of Justice Statistics, September 2006, http://www.ojp.usdoj.gov/bjs/mhppji.htm; Harlow, "Prior Abuse Reported by Inmates and Probationers," 2.
35. Harlow, "Prior Abuse Reported by Inmates and Probationers," 3.
36. Maschi, "Trauma and Violent Delinquent Behavior Among Males," 45; Lena J. Jäggi, Briana Mezuk, Daphne C. Watkins, and James S. Jackson, "The Relationship Between Trauma, Arrest, and Incarceration History Among Black Americans," *Society and Mental Health* 6, no. 3 (2016): 187–206, doi:10.1177/2156869316641730; Micah E. Johnson, "Trauma, Race, and Risk for Violent Felony Arrests Among Florida Juvenile Offenders," *Crime & Delinquency* 64, no. 11 (2017): 1437–57, doi:10.1177/0011128717718487.
37. Johnson, "Trauma, Race, and Risk for Violent Felony Arrests," 1437.
38. Andy Hochstetler, Daniel S. Murphy, and Ronald L. Simons, "Damaged Goods: Exploring Predictors of Distress in Prison Inmates," *Crime & Delinquency* 50, no. 3 (2004): 436–57, doi:10.1177/0011128703257198.
39. Maschi, Viola, and Koskinen, "Trauma, Stress, and Coping Among Older Adults in Prison," 188–200.
40. Ronald H. Aday and Jennifer J. Krabill, "Older and Geriatric Offenders: Critical Issues for the 21st Century," in *Special Needs Offenders in Correctional Institutions*, ed. Lior Gideon (Thousand Oaks, Calif.: Sage, 2019), 203–32; Tina Maschi, Deborah Viola, Mary T. Harrison, William Harrison, Lindsay Koskinen, and Stephanie Bellusa, "Bridging Community and Prison for Older Adults: Invoking Human Rights and Elder and Intergenerational Family Justice," *International Journal of Prisoner Health* 10, no. 1 (2014): 55–73, doi:10.1108/ijph-04-2013-0017.
41. Maschi, Morgen, Zgoba, Courtney, and Ristow, "Age, Cumulative Trauma and Stressful Life Events, and Post-Traumatic Stress Symptoms Among Older Adults in Prison," 675.

4. "I Try to Make the Best of It": A Look Inside the Resilient Minds of Older Adults in Prison

1. Tina Maschi, Keith Morgen, Kristen Zgoba, Deborah Courtney, and Jennifer Ristow, "Age, Cumulative Trauma and Stressful Life Events, and Post-Traumatic Stress Symptoms Among Older Adults in Prison: Do Subjective Impressions Matter?," *The Gerontologist* 51, no. 5 (2011): 675–86, doi:10.1093/geront/gnr074.

2. Maschi, Morgen, Zgoba, Courtney, and Ristow, "Age, Cumulative Trauma and Stressful Life Events," 675.

3. K. M. Abram, J. J. Washburn, L. A. Teplin, K. M. Emanuel, E. G. Romero, and G. M. McClelland, "Posttraumatic Stress Disorder and Psychiatric Comorbidity Among Detained Youths," *Psychiatric Services* 58, no 10 (2007): 1311–16, doi:10.1176/appi .ps.58.10.1311; Elizabeth Cauffman, Shirley Feldman, Jaime Watherman, and Hans Steiner, "Posttraumatic Stress Disorder Among Female Juvenile Offenders," *Journal of the American Academy of Child & Adolescent Psychiatry* 37, no. 11 (1998): 1209–16, doi:10.1097/00004583-199811000-00022.

4. American Psychiatric Association, *Diagnostic and Statistical Manual of Mental Disorders: DSM-5* (Arlington, Va.: American Psychiatric Association, 2013).

5. Ronnie Janoff-Bulman, *Shattered Assumptions* (New York: Free Press, 1992); Chaya S. Piotrkowski, "Gender Harassment, Job Satisfaction, and Distress Among Employed White and Minority Women," *Journal of Occupational Health Psychology* 3, no. 1 (1998): 33–43, doi:10.1037/1076-8998.3.1.33.

6. S. Kelly Avants, David Marcotte, Ruth Arnold, and Arthur Margolin, "Spiritual Beliefs, World Assumptions, and HIV Risk Behavior Among Heroin and Cocaine Users," *Psychology of Addictive Behaviors* 17, no. 2 (2003): 159–62, doi:10.1037/0893-164x.17.2.159; Tina Maschi, Keith Morgen, George Leibowitz, and Jo Rees, "Exploring the Relationship Between Cumulative Trauma and Recidivism Among Older Adults: Does Race and Offense History Matter?," *Traumatology* 25, no. 1 (2019): 11–20, doi:10.1037/trm0000167.

7. Maschi, Morgen, Leibowitz, and Jo Rees, "Exploring the Relationship Between Cumulative Trauma and Recidivism Among Older Adults," 11.

8. Ronnie Janoff-Bulman, "Assumptive Worlds and the Stress of Traumatic Events: Applications of the Schema Construct," *Social Cognition* 7, no. 2 (1989): 113–36, doi:10.1521 /soco.1989.7.2.113.

9. Tina Maschi, Deborah Viola, and Keith Morgen, "Unraveling Trauma and Stress, Coping Resources, and Mental Well-Being Among Older Adults in Prison: Empirical Evidence Linking Theory and Practice," *The Gerontologist* 54, no. 5 (2013): 857–67, doi:10.1093/geront/gnto69.

10. Richard G. Tedeschi and Lawrence G. Calhoun, "Posttraumatic Growth: Conceptual Foundations and Empirical Evidence," *Psychological Inquiry* 15, no. 1 (2004): 1–18, doi:10.1207/s15327965pli1501_01.

11. Stephen Joseph and P. Alex Linley, "Positive Adjustment to Threatening Events: An Organismic Valuing Theory of Growth Through Adversity," *Review of General Psychology* 9, no. 3 (2005): 262–80, doi:10.1037/1089-2680.9.3.262.

12. Tedeschi and Calhoun, "Posttraumatic Growth," 262–80; Janoff-Bulman, "Assumptive Worlds and the Stress of Traumatic Events," 113–36.

13. Ronnie Janoff-Bulman and Irene Hanson Frieze, "A Theoretical Perspective for Understanding Reactions to Victimization," *Journal of Social Issues* 39, no. 2 (1983): 1–17, doi:10.1111/j.1540-4560.1983.tb00138.x.

14. K. Forest, "The Role of Critical Life Events in Predicting World Views: Linking Two Social Psychologies," *Journal of Social Behavior & Personality* 10, no. 2 (1995): 331–48; Ronnie Janoff-Bulman and Hillary J. Morgan, "Victims' Responses to Traumatic Life Events: An Unjust World or an Uncaring World?," *Social Justice Research* 7, no. 1 (1994): 47–68, doi:10.1007/bf02333822.

15. Janoff-Bulman, *Shattered Assumptions*, 87.

16. Janoff-Bulman, *Shattered Assumptions*, 89.

17. Janoff-Bulman, *Shattered Assumptions*, 89.

18. Janoff-Bulman, *Shattered Assumptions*, 89.

19. Janoff-Bulman and Frieze, "A Theoretical Perspective for Understanding Reactions to Victimization," 1–17.

20. Janoff-Bulman and Frieze, "A Theoretical Perspective for Understanding Reactions to Victimization," 1–17; Richard Rogers, "The Uncritical Acceptance of Risk Assessment in Forensic Practice," *Law and Human Behavior* 24, no. 5 (2000): 595–605, doi:10.1023/a:1005575113507.

21. Janoff-Bulman and Frieze, "A Theoretical Perspective for Understanding Reactions to Victimization," 8.

22. Tina Maschi and Judith Baer, "The Heterogeneity of the World Assumptions of Older Adults in Prison: Do Differing Worldviews Have a Mental Health Effect?," *Traumatology* 19, no. 1 (2013): 65–72, doi:10.1177/1534765612443294.

23. M. Susan Marting and Allen L. Hammer, *Coping Resources Inventory Manual Revised* (Menlo Park, Calif.: Mind Garden, 2014).

24. A. Baum and J. E Singer, "Psychosocial Aspects of Health, Stress, and Illness," in *Cognitive Social Psychology*, ed. Albert H. Hastorf and Alice M. Isen (New York: Elsevier, 1982), 307–56.

25. Tina Maschi, "Trauma and Violent Delinquent Behavior Among Males: The Moderating Role of Social Support," *Stress, Trauma, and Crisis* 9, no. 1 (2006): 45–72, doi:10.1080/15434610500506233.

26. Ronald H. Aday, "Aging in Prison: A Case Study of New Elderly Offenders," *International Journal of Offender Therapy and Comparative Criminology* 38, no. 1 (1994): 79–91, doi:10.1177/0306624x9403800108; Maschi, Viola, and Morgen, "Unraveling Trauma and Stress, Coping Resources, and Mental Well-Being Among Older Adults in Prison," 857–67.

27. Jordan Picken, "The Coping Strategies, Adjustment, and Well-Being of Male Inmates in the Prison Environment," *Internet Journal of Criminology* (2012): 1–29, https://www.semanticscholar.org/paper/THE-COPING-STRATEGIES%2C-ADJUSTMENT-AND-WELL-BEING-OF-Picken/a8ba4e2b9bf027e969f7702c3d7aebf433834763.

28. Miriam D. Sealock and Michelle Manasse, "An Uneven Playing Field: The Impact of Strain and Coping Skills on Treatment Outcomes for Juvenile Offenders," *Journal of Criminal Justice* 40, no. 3 (2012): 238–48, doi:10.1016/j.jcrimjus.2012.02.002.

29. Aday, "Aging in Prison," 79.

30. Ariel Eytan, "Religion and Mental Health During Incarceration: A Systematic Literature Review," *Psychiatric Quarterly* 82, no. 4 (2011): 287–95, doi:10.1007/s11126-011-9170-6.

31. R. S. Allen, L. L. Phillips, L. L. Roff, R. Cavanaugh, and L. Day, "Religiousness/Spirituality and Mental Health Among Older Male Inmates," *The Gerontologist* 48, no. 5 (2008): 692–97, doi:10.1093/geront/48.5.692.

32. Carlos Osório, Thomas Probert, Edgar Jones, Allan H. Young, and Ian Robbins, "Adapting to Stress: Understanding the Neurobiology of Resilience," *Behavioral Medicine* 43, no. 4 (2016): 307–22, doi:10.1080/08964289.2016.1170661.

33. Osório, Probert, Jones, Young, and Robbins, "Adapting to Stress."
34. Osório, Probert, Jones, Young, and Robbins, "Adapting to Stress," 309.
35. Osório, Probert, Jones, Young, and Robbins, "Adapting to Stress," 310.
36. Osório, Probert, Jones, Young, and Robbins, "Adapting to Stress," 310.
37. Maschi, "Trauma and Violent Delinquent Behavior Among Males," 45; Maschi, Morgen, Leibowitz, and Rees, "Exploring the Relationship Between Cumulative Trauma and Recidivism Among Older Adults, 11; Edward Zamble and Frank Porporino, "Coping, Imprisonment, and Rehabilitation," *Criminal Justice and Behavior* 17, no. 1 (1990): 53–70, doi:10.1177/0093854890017001005.

5. Trauma, Mental Health, and Medical Concerns of Older Adults in the Prison System

1. Gergő Baranyi, Megan Cassidy, Seena Fazel, Stefan Priebe, and Adrian P Mundt, "Prevalence of Posttraumatic Stress Disorder in Prisoners," *Epidemiologic Reviews* 40, no. 1 (2018): 134–45, doi:10.1093/epirev/mxx015.
2. Tina Maschi, Keith Morgen, George Leibowitz, and Jo Rees, "Exploring the Relationship Between Cumulative Trauma and Recidivism Among Older Adults: Does Race and Offense History Matter?," *Traumatology* 25, no. 1 (2019): 11–20, doi:10.1037/trm0000167.
3. Maria Böttche, Philipp Kuwert, and Christine Knaevelsrud, "Posttraumatic Stress Disorder in Older Adults: An Overview of Characteristics and Treatment Approaches," *International Journal of Geriatric Psychiatry* 27, no. 3 (2011): 230–39, doi:10.1002/gps.2725; Substance Abuse and Mental Health Services Administration, *Trauma -Informed Care in Behavioral Health Services* (Rockville, Md.: Substance Abuse and Mental Health Services Administration, 2014), 57.
4. O. Frans, P.-A. Rimmo, L. Aberg, and M. Fredrikson, "Trauma Exposure and Post-Traumatic Stress Disorder in the General Population," *Acta Psychiatrica Scandinavica* 111, no. 4 (2005): 291–90, doi:10.1111/j.1600-0447.2004.00463.x.
5. Carsten Spitzer, Sven Barnow, Henry Volzke, Ulrich John, Harald J. Freyberger, and Hans Joergen Grabe, "Trauma and Posttraumatic Stress Disorder in the Elderly," *Journal of Clinical Psychiatry* 69, no. 5 (2008): 693–700, doi:10.4088/jcp.v69n0501; Substance Abuse and Mental Health Services Administration, *Trauma-Informed Care in Behavioral Health Services*, 4.
6. Amy L. Byers, Kristine Yaffe, Kenneth E. Covinsky, Michael B. Friedman, and Martha L. Bruce, "High Occurrence of Mood and Anxiety Disorders Among Older Adults," *Archives of General Psychiatry* 67, no. 5 (2010): 489, doi:10.1001/archgenpsychiatry .2010.35.
7. Walter Busuttil, "Presentations and Management of Post Traumatic Stress Disorder and the Elderly: A Need for Investigation," *International Journal of Geriatric Psychiatry* 19, no. 5 (2004): 429–39, doi:10.1002/gps.1099; Leann Kimberly Lapp, Catherine Agbokou, and Florian Ferreri, "PTSD in the Elderly: The Interaction Between Trauma and Aging," *International Psychogeriatrics* 23, no. 6 (2011): 858–68, doi:10.1017/s1041610211000366.
8. Keith Morgen, *Substance Use Disorders and Addictions* (Thousand Oaks, Calif.: Sage, 2017).
9. Joan M. Cook and Stephanie Dinnen, "Exposure Therapy for Late-Life Trauma," in *Treatment of Late-Life Depression, Anxiety, Trauma, and Substance Abuse*, ed. P. A. Areán (Washington, D.C.: American Psychological Association, 2019), 133–61; Cynthia Lindman Port, Brian Engdahl, and Patricia Frazier, "A Longitudinal and Retrospective

Study of PTSD Among Older Prisoners of War," *American Journal of Psychiatry* 158, no. 9 (2001): 1474–79, doi:10.1176/appi.ajp.158.9.1474.

10. Clara Martinez-Clavera, Sarah James, Eva Bowditch, and Tarun Kuruvilla, "Delayed-Onset Post-Traumatic Stress Disorder Symptoms in Dementia," *Progress in Neurology and Psychiatry* 21, no. 3 (2017): 26–31, doi:10.1002/pnp.477.

11. Bernice Andrews, Chris R. Brewin, Rosanna Philpott, and Lorna Stewart, "Delayed-Onset Posttraumatic Stress Disorder: A Systematic Review of the Evidence," *American Journal of Psychiatry* 164, no. 9 (2007): 1319–26, doi:10.1176/appi.ajp.2007.06091491.

12. Rachel Yehuda, Guiqing Cai, Julia A. Golier, Casey Sarapas, Sandro Galea, Marcus Ising, and Theo Rein et al., "Gene Expression Patterns Associated with Posttraumatic Stress Disorder Following Exposure to the World Trade Center Attacks," *Biological Psychiatry* 66, no. 7 (2009): 708–11, doi:10.1016/j.biopsych.2009.02.034.

13. Lapp, Agbokou, and Ferreri, "PTSD in the Elderly," 858; Yuval Palgi, Amit Shrira, Sharon Avidor, Yaakov Hoffman, Ehud Bodner, and Menachem Ben-Ezra, "Understanding the Long-Term Connections Between Posttraumatic Stress, Subjective Age, and Successful Aging Among Midlife and Older Adults," *European Journal of Psychotraumatology* 10, no. 1 (2019): article 1583523, doi:10.1080/20008198.2019.1583523.

14. Zahava Solomon, Hedva Helvitz, and Gadi Zerach, "Subjective Age, PTSD and Physical Health Among War Veterans," *Aging & Mental Health* 13, no. 3 (2009): 405–13, doi:10.1080/13607860802459856.

15. Sharon Avidor, Yael Benyamini, and Zahava Solomon, "Subjective Age and Health in Later Life: The Role of Posttraumatic Symptoms," *The Journals of Gerontology Series B: Psychological Sciences and Social Sciences* 71, no. 3 (2014): 415–24, doi:10.1093/geronb/gbu150.

16. Yuval Palgi, "Subjective Age and Perceived Distance-to-Death Moderate the Association Between Posttraumatic Stress Symptoms and Posttraumatic Growth Among Older Adults," *Aging & Mental Health* 20, no. 9 (2015): 948–54, doi:10.1080/13607863.2015.104 7320.

17. Yaakov Hoffman, Amit Shrira, and Ephraim S. Grossman, "Subjective Age Moderates the Immediate Effects of Trauma Exposure Among Young Adults Exposed to Rocket Attacks," *Psychiatry Research* 229, nos. 1–2 (2015): 623–24, doi:10.1016/j.psychres .2015.07.080.

18. Palgi, Shrira, Avidor, Hoffman, Bodner, and Ben-Ezra, "Understanding the Long-Term Connections Between Posttraumatic Stress, Subjective Age, and Successful Aging," 150.

19. Robert Granfield and William Cloud, "Social Context and 'Natural Recovery': The Role of Social Capital in the Resolution of Drug-Associated Problems," *Substance Use & Misuse* 36, no. 11 (2001): 1543–70, doi:10.1081/ja-100106963.

20. William, Cloud and Robert Granfield, "Conceptualizing Recovery Capital: Expansion of a Theoretical Construct," *Substance Use & Misuse* 43, nos. 12–13 (2008): 1971–86, doi:10.1080/10826080802289762.

21. James K. Boehnlein, "Culture and Society in Posttraumatic Stress Disorder: Implications for Psychotherapy," *American Journal of Psychotherapy* 41, no. 4 (1987): 519–30, doi:10.1176/appi.psychotherapy.1987.41.4.519.

22. Ron Acierno, Kenneth J. Ruggiero, Dean G. Kilpatrick, Heidi S. Resnick, and Sandro Galea, "Risk and Protective Factors for Psychopathology Among Older Versus Younger Adults After the 2004 Florida Hurricanes," *The American Journal of Geriatric Psychiatry* 14, no. 12 (2006): 1051–59, doi:10.1097/01.jgp.0000221327.97904.b0.

23. Glenda L. Wrenn, Aliza P. Wingo, Renee Moore, Tiffany Pelletier, Alisa R. Gutman, Bekh Bradley, and Kerry J. Ressler, "The Effect of Resilience on Posttraumatic Stress

Disorder in Trauma-Exposed Inner-City Primary Care Patients," *Journal of the National Medical Association* 103, no. 7 (2011): 560–66, doi:10.1016/s0027-9684(15)30381-3.

24. National Center for PTSD, "Understanding PTSD: A Guide for Family and Friends," May 2019, https://www.ptsd.va.gov/publications/print/understandingptsd_family_booklet .pdf.

25. Emily J. Ozer, Suzanne R. Best, Tami L. Lipsey, and Daniel S. Weiss, "Predictors of Posttraumatic Stress Disorder and Symptoms in Adults: A Meta-Analysis," *Psychological Bulletin* 129, no. 1 (2003): 52–73, doi:10.1037/0033-2909.129.1.52.

26. Lisa M. Lajavits, Donna Ryngala, Sudie E. Back, Elisa Bolton, Kim T. Mueser, and Kathleen T. Brady, "Treatment of PTSD and Comorbid Disorders," in *Effective Treatments for PTSD: Practice Guidelines From the International Society for Traumatic Studies*, 2nd ed., ed. E. B. Foa, T. M. Keane, M. J. Friedman, and J. A. Cohen (New York: Guilford Press, 2009), 606–13.

27. Dan G. Blazer, "Depression in Late Life: Review and Commentary," *FOCUS* 7, no. 1 (2009): 118–36, doi:10.1176/foc.7.1.foc118.

28. Cecilio Álamo, Francisco López-Muñoz, Pilar García-García, and Silvia García-Ramos, "Risk-Benefit Analysis of Antidepressant Drug Treatment in the Elderly," *Psychogeriatrics* 14, no. 4 (2014): 261–68, doi:10.1111/psyg.12057.

29. Ramzy Yassa, Vasavan Nair, Christine Nastase, Yves Camille, and Lise Belzile, "Prevalence of Bipolar Disorder in a Psychogeriatric Population," *Journal of Affective Disorders* 14, no. 3 (1988): 197–201, doi:10.1016/0165-0327(88)90035-3.

30. Erkki Isometsä, Martti Heikkinen, Markus Henriksson, Hillevi Aro, and Jouko Lönnqvist, "Recent Life Events and Completed Suicide in Bipolar Affective Disorder. A Comparison with Major Depressive Suicides," *Journal of Affective Disorders* 33, no. 2 (1995): 99–106, doi:10.1016/0165-0327(94)00079-0.

31. Andrew T. A. Cheng, Tony H. H. Chen, Chwen-Chen Chen, and Rachel Jenkins, "Psychosocial and Psychiatric Risk Factors for Suicide," *British Journal of Psychiatry* 177, no. 4 (2000): 360–65, doi:10.1192/bjp.177.4.360.

32. Erkki Isometsä, Markus Henriksson, Hillevi Aro, Martti Heikkinen, Kimmo Kuoppasalmi, and Jouko Lönnqvist, "Suicide in Psychotic Major Depression," *Journal of Affective Disorders* 31, no. 3 (1994): 187–91, doi:10.1016/0165-0327(94)90028-0.

33. Emily A. P. Haigh, Olivia E. Bogucki, Sandra T. Sigmon, and Dan G. Blazer, "Depression Among Older Adults: A 20-Year Update on Five Common Myths and Misconceptions," *American Journal of Geriatric Psychiatry* 26, no. 1 (2018): 107–22, doi:10.1016/j.jagp .2017.06.011.

34. Gary S. Moak, "Discharge and Retention of Psychogeriatric Long-Stay Patients in a State Mental Hospital," *Psychiatric Services* 41, no. 4 (1990): 445–47, doi:10.1176/ ps.41.4.445; Yassa, Nair, Nastase, Camille, and Belzile, "Prevalence of Bipolar Disorder in a Psychogeriatric Population," 197.

35. Annemiek Dols, Ralph W Kupka, Anouk van Lammeren, Aartjan T. Beekman, Martha Sajatovic, and Max L. Stek, "The Prevalence of Late-Life Mania: A Review," *Bipolar Disorders* 16, no. 2 (2013): 113–18, doi:10.1111/bdi.12104.

36. J. M. Hegeman, R. M. Kok, R. C. van der Mast, and E. J. Giltay, "Phenomenology of Depression in Older Compared with Younger Adults: Meta-Analysis," *British Journal of Psychiatry* 200, no. 4 (2012): 275–81, doi:10.1192/bjp.bp.111.095950.

37. Orestes Vicente Forlenza, Leandro Valiengo, and Florindo Stella, "Mood Disorders in the Elderly: Prevalence, Functional Impact, and Management Challenges," *Neuropsychiatric Disease and Treatment* 12 (2016): 2105–14, doi:10.2147/ndt.s94643.

38. Forlenza, Valiengo, and Stella, "Mood Disorders in the Elderly."

39. Alka A. Subramanyam, Jahnavi Kedare, O. P. Singh, and Charles Pinto, "Clinical Practice Guidelines for Geriatric Anxiety Disorders," *Indian Journal of Psychiatry* 60, no. 3 (2018): S371–82.

40. Catherine Ayers, Katrina Strickland, and Julie Loebach Wetherell, "Evidence-Based Treatment for Late-Life Generalized Anxiety Disorder," in *Treatment of Late-Life Depression, Anxiety, Trauma, and Substance Abuse*, ed. P. A. Areán (Washington, D.C.: American Psychological Association, 2015), 103–31.

41. Eric J. Lenze, Joan C. Rogers, Lynn M. Martire, Benoit H. Mulsant, Bruce L. Rollman, Mary Amanda Dew, Richard Schulz, and Charles F. Reynolds, "The Association of Late-Life Depression and Anxiety with Physical Disability: A Review of the Literature and Prospectus for Future Research," *American Journal of Geriatric Psychiatry* 9, no. 2 (2001): 113–35, doi:10.1097/00019442-200105000-00004; J. Schuurmans, H. C. Comijs, A. T. F. Beekman, E. Beurs, D. J. H. Deeg, P. M. G. Emmelkamp, and R. Dyck, "The Outcome of Anxiety Disorders in Older People at 6-Year Follow-Up: Results from the Longitudinal Aging Study Amsterdam," *Acta Psychiatrica Scandinavica* 111, no. 6 (2005): 420–28, doi:10.1111/j.1600-0447.2005.00531.x.

42. Annelieke M. Roest, Marij Zuidersma, and Peter de Jonge, "Myocardial Infarction and Generalised Anxiety Disorder: 10-Year Follow-Up," *British Journal of Psychiatry* 200, no. 4 (2012): 324–29, doi:10.1192/bjp.bp.111.103549.

43. Francis J. Kane, John Strohlein, and Robert G. Harper, "Nonulcer Dyspepsia Associated with Psychiatric Disorder," *Southern Medical Journal* 86, no. 6 (1993): 641–46, doi:10.1097/00007611-199306000-00010.

44. John M. Hettema, Jonathan W. Kuhn, Carol A. Prescott, and Kenneth S. Kendler, "The Impact of Generalized Anxiety Disorder and Stressful Life Events on Risk for Major Depressive Episodes," *Psychological Medicine* 36, no. 6 (2006): 789–95, doi:10.1017/s0033291706007367.

45. Morgen, *Substance Use Disorders and Addictions*, 10.

46. Sébastien Grenier, Josien Schuurmans, Maria Goldfarb, Michel Préville, Richard Boyer, Kieron O'Connor, Olivier Potvin, and Carol Hudon, "The Epidemiology of Specific Phobia and Subthreshold Fear Subtypes in a Community-Based Sample of Older Adults," *Depression and Anxiety* 28, no. 6 (2011): 456–63, doi:10.1002/da.20812.

47. Keith Morgen, Tina Maschi, Deborah Viola, and K. Zgoba, "Substance Use Disorder and the Older Offender," Vistas Online, 2013, https://www.counseling.org/docs/default -source/vistas/substance-use-disorder-and-the-older-offender.pdf?sfvrsn=6;D.D.Sartre, "Treatment of Older Adults," in *Addictions: A Comprehensive Guidebook*, 2nd ed., ed. B. S. McCrady and E. E. Epstein (New York: Oxford University Press, 2013), 742–57.

48. Substance Abuse and Mental Health Services Administration, *Trauma-Informed Care*, 57.

49. Nancy H. Liu and Jason M. Satterfield, "Screening, Brief Intervention, and Referral to Treatment (SBIRT) for Substance Abuse in Older Populations," in *Treatment of Late-Life Depression, Anxiety, Trauma, and Substance Abuse*, ed. Patricia A. Areán (Washington, D.C.: American Psychological Association, 2015), 181–210.

50. Center for Substance Abuse Treatment, "Substance Abuse Among Older Adults" (Rockville, Md.: Substance Abuse and Mental Health Services Administration, 1998), no. 26.

51. Kristine E. Pringle, Frank M. Ahern, Debra A. Heller, Carol H. Gold, and Theresa V. Brown, "Potential for Alcohol and Prescription Drug Interactions in Older People," *Journal of the American Geriatrics Society* 53, no. 11 (2005): 1930–36, doi:10.1111/j.1532 -5415.2005.00474.x.

52. Lawrence Schonfeld and Nicole S. MacFarland, "Relapse Prevention Treatment for Substance Abuse Disorders in Older Adults," in *Treatment of Late-Life Depression,*

Anxiety, Trauma, and Substance Abuse, ed. Patricia A. Areán (Washington, D.C.: American Psychological Association, 2015), 211–34.

53. Harold E. Doweiko and Amelia L Evans, *Concepts of Chemical Dependency*, 9th ed. (Stamford, Conn.: Cengage Learning, 2015).

54. Linda Simoni-Wastila and Huiwen Keri Yang, "Psychoactive Drug Abuse in Older Adults," *American Journal of Geriatric Pharmacotherapy* 4, no. 4 (2006): 380–94, doi:10.1016/j.amjopharm.2006.10.002.

55. Li-Tzy Wu and Dan G. Blazer, "Illicit and Nonmedical Drug Use Among Older Adults: A Review," *Journal of Aging and Health* 23, no. 3 (2010): 481–504, doi:10.1177/0898264310386224.

56. American Psychiatric Association, *Diagnostic and Statistical Manual of Mental Disorders: DSM-5* (Arlington, Va.: American Psychiatric Association, 2013).

57. Salah U. Qureshi, Mary E. Long, Major R. Bradshaw, Jeffrey M. Pyne, Kathy M. Magruder, Timothy Kimbrell, Teresa J. Hudson, Ali Jawaid, Paul E. Schulz, and Mark E. Kunik, "Does PTSD Impair Cognition Beyond the Effect of Trauma?," *Journal of Neuropsychiatry* 23, no. 1 (2011): 16–28, doi:10.1176/appi.neuropsych.23.1.16.

58. Kristine Yaffe, Eric Vittinghoff, Karla Lindquist, Deborah Barnes, Kenneth E. Covinsky, Thomas Neylan, Molly Kluse, and Charles Marmar, "Posttraumatic Stress Disorder and Risk of Dementia Among US Veterans," *Archives of General Psychiatry* 67, no. 6 (2010): 608, doi:10.1001/archgenpsychiatry.2010.61.

59. Vonetta M. Dotson, May A. Beydoun, and Alan B. Zonderman, "Recurrent Depressive Symptoms and the Incidence of Dementia and Mild Cognitive Impairment," *Neurology* 75, no. 1 (2010): 27–34, doi:10.1212/wnl.0b013e3181e62124.

60. Sherry A. Beaudreau and Ruth O'Hara, "Late-Life Anxiety and Cognitive Impairment: A Review," *American Journal of Geriatric Psychiatry* 16, no. 10 (2008): 790–803, doi:10.1097/jgp.0b013e31817945c3.

61. Robert G. Falter, "Selected Predictors of Health Services Needs of Inmates over Age 50," *Journal of Correctional Health Care* 6, no. 2 (1999): 149–75, doi:10.1177/107834589900600202.

62. Laura M. Maruschak, "Medical Problems of Prisoners," U.S. Department of Justice, 2008, https://bjs.gov/content/pub/pdf/mpp.pdf.

63. Ronald H. Aday, *Aging Prisoners* (Westport, Conn.: Praeger, 2003).

64. Doris J. James and Lauren E. Glaze, "Mental Health Problems of Prison and Jail Inmates," Bureau of Justice Statistics Special Report, September 2006, rev. December 14, 2006, https://www.bjs.gov/content/pub/pdf/mhppji.pdf.

65. Lee Hyer and Steven James Sohnle, *Trauma Among Older People* (Philadelphia, Penn.: Brunner-Routledge, 2001).

66. Andy Hochstetler, Daniel S. Murphy, and Ronald L. Simons, "Damaged Goods: Exploring Predictors of Distress in Prison Inmates," *Crime & Delinquency* 50, no. 3 (2004): 436–57, doi:10.1177/0011128703257198.

67. Cindy Struckman-Johnson and David Struckman-Johnson, "A Comparison of Sexual Coercion Experiences Reported by Men and Women in Prison," *Journal of Interpersonal Violence* 21, no. 12 (2006): 1591–1615, doi:10.1177/0886260506294240.

68. Ronald H. Aday, "Aging Prisoners' Concerns Toward Dying in Prison," *OMEGA—Journal of Death and Dying* 52, no. 3 (2006): 199–216, doi:10.2190/chtd-yl7t-r1rr-lhmn.

69. C. J. Mumola and Margaret E. Noonan, *Deaths in Custody Statistical Tables* (Rockville, Md.: U.S. Department of Justice, 2009).

70. Aday, "Aging Prisoners' Concerns Toward Dying in Prison," 199.

71. Tina Maschi, Deborah Viola, and Keith Morgen, "Unraveling Trauma and Stress, Coping Resources, and Mental Well-Being Among Older Adults in Prison: Empirical Evidence Linking Theory and Practice," *The Gerontologist* 54, no. 5 (2013): 857–67, doi:10.1093/geront/gnt069.
72. Maschi, Viola, and Morgen, "Unraveling Trauma and Stress."
73. Tina Maschi, Deborah Viola, and Lindsay Koskinen, "Trauma, Stress, and Coping Among Older Adults in Prison: Towards a Human Rights and Intergenerational Family Justice Action Agenda," *Traumatology* 21, no. 3 (2015): 188–200, doi:10.1037/trm0000021.
74. Maschi, Viola, and Morgen, "Unraveling Trauma and Stress," 857.
75. Elizabeth P. Shulman and Elizabeth Cauffman, "Coping While Incarcerated: A Study of Male Juvenile Offenders," *Journal of Research on Adolescence* 21, no. 4 (2011): 818–26, doi:10.1111/j.1532-7795.2011.00740.x.
76. Kristine A. Johnson and Shannon M. Lynch, "Predictors of Maladaptive Coping in Incarcerated Women Who Are Survivors of Childhood Sexual Abuse," *Journal of Family Violence* 28, no. 1 (2012): 43–52, doi:10.1007/s10896-012-9488-3.
77. Shannon M. Lynch, April Fritch, and Nicole M. Heath, "Looking Beneath the Surface," *Feminist Criminology* 7, no. 4 (2012): 381–400, doi:10.1177/1557085112439224.
78. Maschi, Viola, and Morgen, "Unraveling Trauma and Stress," 858.
79. Aday, "Aging Prisoners' Concerns Toward Dying in Prison," 200.
80. Maschi, Viola, and Morgen, "Unraveling Trauma and Stress," 859.
81. Ronald Aday, "Golden Years Behind Bars: Special Programs and Facilities for Elderly Inmates," *Federal Probation* 58, no. 2 (1994): 45–54.
82. Karen Kopera-Frye, Mary T. Harrison, Josette Iribarne, Elizabeth Dampsey, Michelle Adams, Tammy Grabreck, Tara McMullen, Kenneth Peak, William G. McCown, and William O. Harrison, "Veterans Aging in Place Behind Bars: A Structured Living Program That Works," *Psychological Services* 10, no. 1 (2013): 79–86, doi:10.1037/a0031269.
83. Hans Selye, *The Stress of Life* (New York: McGraw-Hill, 1976).
84. Ron Acierno, Melba A. Hernandez, Ananda B. Amstadter, Heidi S. Resnick, Kenneth Steve, Wendy Muzzy, and Dean G. Kilpatrick, "Prevalence and Correlates of Emotional, Physical, Sexual, and Financial Abuse and Potential Neglect in the United States: The National Elder Mistreatment Study," *American Journal of Public Health* 100, no. 2 (2010): 292–97, doi:10.2105/ajph.2009.163089.
85. John Dawes, "Ageing Prisoners: Issues for Social Work," *Australian Social Work* 62, no. 2 (2009): 258–71, doi:10.1080/03124070902803475.
86. P. G. Coleman, "Creating a Life Story: The Task of Reconciliation," *The Gerontologist* 39, no. 2 (1999): 133–39, doi:10.1093/geront/39.2.133.
87. Glen H. Elder, Monica Kirkpatrick Johnson, and Robert Crosnoe, "The Emergence and Development of Life Course Theory," in *Handbook of the Life Course*, ed. Jeylan T. Mortimer and Michael J. Shanahan (New York: Kluwer Academic/ Plenum, 2003), 3–19.
88. Robert J. Sampson and John H. Laub, "Crime and Deviance over the Life Course: The Salience of Adult Social Bonds," *American Sociological Review* 55, no. 5 (1990): 609, doi:10.2307/2095859.
89. Leonard I. Pearlin, Scott Schieman, Elena, M. Fazio, and Stephen C. Meersman, "Stress, Health, and the Life Course: Some Conceptual Perspectives," *Journal of Health and Social Behavior* 46, no. 2 (July 2005): 205–19, at 205.
90. L. A. Teplin, "The Prevalence of Severe Mental Disorder Among Male Urban Jail Detainees: Comparison with the Epidemiologic Catchment Area Program," *American Journal of Public Health* 80, no. 6 (June 1990): 663–69, doi:10.2105/ajph.80.6.663.

91. Tina Maschi, Sandy Gibson, Kristen M. Zgoba, and Keith Morgen, "Trauma and Life Event Stressors Among Young and Older Adult Prisoners," *Journal of Correctional Health Care* 17, no. 2 (2011): 160–72, doi:10.1177/1078345810396682.

92. Acierno, Hernandez, Amstadter, Resnick, Steve, Muzzy, and Kilpatrick, "Prevalence and Correlates of Emotional, Physical, Sexual, and Financial Abuse," 292.

93. Syd Hiskey, Michael Luckie, Stephen Davies, and Chris R. Brewin, "The Phenomenology of Reactivated Trauma Memories in Older Adults: A Preliminary Study," *Aging & Mental Health* 12, no. 4 (2008): 494–98, doi:10.1080/13607860802224367.

94. Hiskey, Luckie, Davies, and Brewin, "The Phenomenology of Reactivated Trauma Memories in Older Adults."

95. Leigh A. Neal, Nicholas Hill, Julian Hughes, Aisla Middleton, and Walter Busuttil, "Convergent Validity of Measures of PTSD in an Elderly Population of Former Prisoners of War," *International Journal of Geriatric Psychiatry* 10, no. 7 (1995): 617–22, doi:10.1002/gps.930100713.

96. Centers on Addiction, "Behind Bars II: Substance Abuse and America's Prison Population," February 2010, https://www.centeronaddiction.org/addiction-research /reports/behind-bars-ii-substance-abuse-and-america%E2%80%99s-prison-population.

97. Seena Fazel, Isabel A. Yoon, and Adrian J. Hayes, "Substance Use Disorders in Prisoners: An Updated Systematic Review and Meta-Regression Analysis in Recently Incarcerated Men and Women," *Addiction* 112, no. 10 (2017): 1725–39, doi:10.1111/add.13877.

98. Substance Abuse and Mental Health Services Administration, "TIP 44: Substance Abuse Treatment for Adults in the Criminal Justice System," September 2013, https:// store.samhsa.gov/product/tip-44-substance-abuse-treatment-for-adults-in-the -criminal-justice-system/sma13-4056.

99. Maschi, Gibson, Zgoba, and Morgen, "Trauma and Life Event Stressors Among Young and Older Adult Prisoners," 160.

100. U.S. Bureau of Justice Statistics, "Survey of Inmates in State and Federal Correctional Facilities, [United States], 2004," December 12, 2019, https://doi.org/10.3886 /ICPSR04572.v6.

101. Substance Abuse and Mental Health Services Administration, "TIP 44."

102. Tina Maschi and George S. Leibowitz, *Forensic Social Work*, 2nd ed. (New York: Springer, 2018).

103. Sartre, "Treatment of Older Adults."

104. American Psychiatric Association, *Diagnostic and Statistical Manual of Mental Disorders: DSM-4* (Arlington, Va.: American Psychiatric Association, 2000), 742.

105. Sartre, "Treatment of Older Adults"; Morgen, *Substance Use Disorders and Addictions*.

106. Maschi, Gibson, Zgoba, and Morgen, "Trauma and Life Event Stressors Among Young and Older Adult Prisoners," 161.

107. Andrew P. Wilper, Steffie Woolhandler, J. Wesley Boyd, Karen E. Lasser, Danny McCormick, David H. Bor, and David U. Himmelstein, "The Health and Health Care of US Prisoners: Results of a Nationwide Survey," *American Journal of Public Health* 99, no. 4 (2009): 666–72, doi:10.2105/ajph.2008.144279.

108. Maschi, Morgen, Leibowitz, and Rees, "Exploring the Relationship Between Cumulative Trauma and Recidivism Among Older Adults."

109. Tina Maschi and Ronald H. Aday, "The Social Determinants of Health and Justice and the Aging in Prison Crisis: A Call for Human Rights Action," *International Journal of Social Work* 1, no. 1 (2014): 15, doi:10.5296/ijsw.v1i1.4914.

110. Jill Levenson and Ryan T. Shields, "Sex Offender Risk and Recidivism in Florida," 2012, http://www.lynn.edu/about-lynn/news-andevents/news/media/2012/11/sex-offender -riskand-recidivism-in-florida-2012.

111. Levenson and Shields, "Sex Offender Risk and Recidivism in Florida."
112. American Civil Liberties Union, "At America's Expense: The Mass Incarceration of the Elderly," June 2012, https://www.aclu.org/report/americas-expense-mass-incarceration-elderly.

6. How Do We Co-Construct Community? A Conceptual Map for Reuniting Older Adults in Prison with Their Families and Communities

1. American Civil Liberties Union. (2012). *At America's Expense: The Mass Incarceration of The Elderly*. Retrieved from https://www.aclu.org/report/americas-expense-mass-incarceration-elderly; Human Rights Watch, "Old Behind Bars: The Aging Prison Population in the United States," January 2012, https://www.hrw.org/sites/default/files/reports/usprisons0112webwcover_0.pdf.
2. Tina Maschi, Deborah Viola, and Fei Sun, "The High Cost of the International Aging Prisoner Crisis: Well-Being as the Common Denominator for Action," *The Gerontologist* 53, no. 4 (2013): 543–54, doi:10.1093/geront/gns125.
3. Ronald H. Aday, *Aging Prisoners* (Westport, Conn.: Praeger, 2003).
4. American Civil Liberties Union, "At America's Expense: The Mass Incarceration of the Elderly," 2012, https://www.aclu.org/report/americas-expense-mass-incarceration-elderly.
5. Human Rights Watch, "Old Behind Bars."
6. Chad Kinsella, "Correctional Health Care Costs," January 2004, http://www.csg.org/knowledgecenter/docs/TA0401CorrHealth.pdf.
7. Ilora G. Finlay, "Managing Terminally Ill Prisoners: Reflection and Action," *Palliative Medicine* 12, no. 6 (1998): 457–61, doi:10.1191/026921698674823377; James Ridgeway, "The Other Death Sentence," 2012, https://www.motherjones.com/politics/2012/09/massachusetts-elderly-prisoners-cost-compassionate release/.
8. Edgar Barens, director, "Prison Terminal: The Last Days of Private Jack Hall" [documentary film], 2014, http://www.prisonterminal.com.
9. Maschi, Viola, and Sun, "The High Cost of the International Aging Prisoner Crisis," 543–54.
10. Bureau of Justice Statistics, "Mental Health Problems of Prison and Jail Inmates, " 2006, https://www.bjs.gov/content/pub/pdf/mhppji.pdf; Human Rights Watch, "Old Behind Bars."
11. Tina Maschi, Suzanne Marmo, and Junghee Han, "Palliative and End-of-Life Care in Prisons: A Content Analysis of the Literature," *International Journal of Prisoner Health* 10, no. 3 (2014): 172–97, doi:10.1108/ijph-05-2013-0024.
12. Maschi, Viola, and Sun, "The High Cost of the International Aging Prisoner Crisis," 543–54.
13. Bureau of Justice Statistics, "Mental Health Problems of Prison and Jail."
14. Bureau of Justice Statistics, "Mental Health Problems of Prison and Jail"; Kyung Yon Jhi and Hee-Jong Joo, "Predictors of Recidivism Across Major Age Groups of Parolees in Texas," *Justice Policy Journal* 6, no. 1 (2009): 1–28; Sharon Lansing, "New York State COMPAS-Probation Risk and Need Assessment Study: Examining the Recidivism Scale's Effectiveness and Predictive Accuracy," September 2012, http://www.criminaljustice.ny.gov/crimnet/ojsa/opca/compas_probation_report_2012.pdf; New York Department of Corrections and Community Supervision, "2009 Inmate Releases Three Year Post Release Follow-Up," June 21, 2019, http://www.doccs.ny.gov/Research/Reports/2017/2012_releases_3yr_out.pdf.

15. Justice Policy Institute, "[REPORTS 2018] The Ungers, 5 Years and Counting: A Case Study in Safely Reducing Long Prison Terms and Saving Taxpayer Dollars," November 15, 2018, http://www.justicepolicy.org/research/12320.

16. Maschi, Viola, and Sun, "The High Cost of the International Aging Prisoner Crisis," 543–54; Maschi, Marmo, and Han, "Palliative and End-of-Life Care in Prisons," 172–97.

17. Maschi, Marmo, and Han, "Palliative and End-of-Life Care in Prisons," 172.

18. Maschi, Viola, and Sun, "The High Cost of the International Aging Prisoner Crisis," 543–54; Maschi, Marmo, and Han, "Palliative and End-of-Life Care in Prisons," 172–97.

19. David M. Chavis and Grace M. H. Pretty, "Sense of Community: Advances in Measurement and Application," Journal of Community Psychology 27, no. 6 (1999): 635–42, doi:10.1002/(sici)1520-6629(199911)27:6<635::aid-jcop1>3.0.co;2-f.

20. Maschi, Viola, and Sun, "The High Cost of the International Aging Prisoner Crisis," 543–54; Maschi, Marmo, and Han, "Palliative and End-of-Life Care in Prisons," 172–97.

21. Sheldon Cohen, Benjamin H. Gottlieb, and Lynn G. Underwood, "Social Relationships and Health," in Social Support Measurement and Intervention: A Guide for Health and Social Scientists, ed. S. Cohen, L. G. Underwood, and B. H. Gottlieb (New York: Oxford University Press, 2000), 3–25; Sheldon Cohen and Thomas A. Wills, "Stress, Social Support, and the Buffering Hypothesis," Psychological Bulletin 98, no. 2 (1985): 310–57, doi:10.1037/0033-2909.98.2.310.

22. Cohen, Gottlieb, and Underwood, "Social Relationships and Health," 3–25.

23. Maschi, Marmo, and Han, "Palliative and End-of-Life Care in Prisons," 172–97.

24. Jim Ife, Human Rights and Social Work: Towards a Rights-Based Practice (Melbourne, Australia: Cambridge University Press, 2012).

25. Tina Maschi, Thalia MacMillan, Keith Morgen, Sandy Gibson, and Matthew Stimmel, "Trauma, World Assumptions, and Coping Resources Among Youthful Offenders: Social Work, Mental Health, and Criminal Justice Implications," Child and Adolescent Social Work Journal 27, no. 6 (2010): 377–93, doi:10.1007/s10560-010-0211-z.

26. Tina Chiu, "It's About Time: Aging Prisoners, Increasing Costs, and Geriatric Release," Vera Institute, 2010, https://www.vera.org/publications/its-about-time-aging-prisoners-increasing-costs-and-geriatric-release.

27. Eric A. Coleman, "Falling Through the Cracks: Challenges and Opportunities for Improving Transitional Care for Persons with Continuous Complex Care Needs," Journal of the American Geriatrics Society 51, no. 4 (2003): 549–55, doi:10.1046/j.1532-5415.2003.51185.x; Mary D. Naylor, Linda H. Aiken, Ellen T. Kurtzman, Danielle M. Olds, and Karen B. Hirschman, "The Importance of Transitional Care in Achieving Health Reform," Health Affairs 30, no. 4 (2011): 746–54, doi:10.1377/hlthaff.2011.0041.

28. National Association of Clinical Nurse Specialists, "Definitions of Transitional Care," https://nacns.org/professional-resources/toolkits-and-reports/transitions-of-care/definitions-of-transitional-care.

29. Susan C. Reinhar and Keith D. Lind, "Public Policy Implications for Pathways Through Transitions: The Rise of the Transitional Care Concept," Annual Review of Gerontology and Geriatrics 31, no. 1 (2011): 209–29, doi:10.1891/0198-8794.31.209.

30. Maschi, Viola, and Sun, "The High Cost of the International Aging Prisoner Crisis," 543–54; Brie Williams and Rita Abraldes, "Growing Older: Challenges of Prison and Reentry for the Aging Population," in Public Health Behind Bars: From Prisons to Communities, ed. R. B. Greifinger (New York: Springer, 2007), 56–72.

31. Maschi, Marmo, and Han, "Palliative and End-of-Life Care in Prisons," 172–97.

7. "Coming Out" of Prison: LGBTQ+ Older Adults' Experiences Navigating the Criminal Justice System

1. Allen J. Beck, Marcus Berzofsky, Rachel Caspar, and Christopher Krebs, "Sexual Victimization in Prisons and Jails Reported by Inmates, 2011–12," May 2013, https://www.hivlawandpolicy.org/sites/default/files/Sexual%20Victimization%20in%20Prisons%20and%20Jails%20Reported%20by%20Inmates%202011%20to%202012.pdf.
2. Valerie Jenness, Cheryl L. Maxson, Kristy N. Matsuda, and Jennifer Macy Sumner, "Violence in California Correctional Facilities: An Empirical Examination of Sexual Assault," May 16, 2007, https://ucicorrections.seweb.uci.edu/files/2013/06/PREA_Presentation_PREA_Report_UCI_Jenness_et_al.pdf.
3. Jody Marksamer and Harper Jean Tobin, "Standing with LGBT Prisoners: An Advocate's Guide to Ending Abuse and Combating Imprisonment," National Center for Transgender Equality, 2014, https://transequality.org/sites/default/files/docs/resources/JailPrisons_Resource_FINAL.pdf.
4. Tina Maschi, Samantha L. Sutfin, and Brendan O'Connell, "Aging, Mental Health, and the Criminal Justice System: A Content Analysis of the Literature," *Journal of Forensic Social Work* 2, nos. 2–3 (2012): 162–85, doi:10.1080/1936928x.2012.750254.
5. Tina Maschi, Deborah Viola, Mary T. Harrison, William Harrison, Lindsay Koskinen, and Stephanie Bellusa, "Bridging Community and Prison for Older Adults: Invoking Human Rights and Elder and Intergenerational Family Justice," *International Journal of Prisoner Health* 10, no. 1 (2014): 55–73, doi:10.1108/ijph04-2013-0017.
6. Samia Addis, Myfanwy Davies, Giles Greene, Sara MacBride-Stewart, and Michael Shepherd, "The Health, Social Care and Housing Needs of Lesbian, Gay, Bisexual and Transgender Older People: A Review of the Literature," *Health & Social Care in the Community* 17, no. 6 (2009): 647–58, doi:10.1111/j.1365-2524.2009.00866.x.
7. Richard Saenz, Kara Ingelhart, and Andrea J. Ritchie, "The Impact of the Trump Administration's Federal Criminal Justice Initiatives on LGBTQ People & Communities and Opportunities for Local Resistance," Barnard Center for Research on Women, 2018, https://www.lambdalegal.org/sites/default/files/publications/downloads/the_impact_of_the_trump_administrations_federal_criminal_justice_initiatives_on_lgbtq_people_communities_and_opportunities_for_local_resistance.pdf.
8. Addis, Davies, Greene, MacBride-Stewart, and Shepherd, "The Health, Social Care and Housing Needs of Lesbian, Gay, Bisexual and Transgender Older People," 647–58.
9. Substance Abuse and Mental Health Services Administration, "Einstein Expert Panel: Medication-Assisted Treatment and the Criminal Justice System," September 10, 2013, https://www.samhsa.gov/sites/default/files/mat-criminal-justice-panel-2011.pdf.
10. Laura S. Brown and David Pantalone, "Lesbian, Gay, Bisexual, and Transgender Issues in Trauma Psychology: A Topic Comes Out of the Closet," *Traumatology* 17, no. 2 (2011): 1–3, doi:10.1177/1534765611417763; Brian S. Mustanski, Robert Garofalo, and Erin M. Emerson, "Mental Health Disorders, Psychological Distress, and Suicidality in a Diverse Sample of Lesbian, Gay, Bisexual, and Transgender Youths," *American Journal of Public Health* 100, no. 12 (2010): 2426–32, doi:10.2105/ajph.2009.178319; Organization for Economic Co-operation and Development, "OECD Factbook," 2010, https://www.oecd-ilibrary.org/economics/oecd-factbook-2010_factbook-2010-en.
11. Ronald Hellman and Eileen Klein, "A Program for Lesbian, Gay, Bisexual, and Transgender Individuals with Major Mental Illness," *Journal of Gay & Lesbian Mental Health* 8, no. 3 (2004): 67–82, doi:10.1080/19359705.2004.9962380.

12. Rainbow Heights, "Rainbow Heights Club," 2015, revised 2019, http://www.rainbowheights .org/.
13. Rainbow Heights, "Rainbow Heights Club."
14. Lana Sue I. Ka'Opua, Amanda Petteruti, R. Nalani Takushi, James H. Spencer, Soon H. Park, Tressa P. Diaz, Shalia K. Kamakele, and Kaipo C. Kukahiko, "The Lived Experience of Native Hawaiians Exiting Prison and Reentering the Community: How Do You Really Decriminalize Someone Who's Consistently Being Called a Criminal?," *Journal of Forensic Social Work* 2, nos. 2–3 (2012): 141–61, doi:10.1080/1936928x.2012.746766.
15. Substance Abuse and Mental Health Services Administration, "Guidelines for a Trauma Informed Approach," 2014, https://s3.amazonaws.com/static.nicic.gov/Library/028436.pdf.

8. A Caring Justice Partnership Paradigm: Transforming the World from the Inside Out

1. Rollin McCraty, *Science of the Heart: Exploring the Role of the Heart in Human Performance*, 2nd ed. (Boulder Creek, Calif.: HeartMath Institute, 2015).
2. McCraty, *Science of the Heart.*
3. UNICEF UK, "Skin-to-Skin Contact," 2019, https://www.unicef.org.uk/babyfriendly /baby-friendly-resources/implementing-standards-resources/skin-to-skin-contact/.
4. Carl R. Rogers and Eugene T. Gendlin, *The Therapeutic Relationship and Its Impact* (Madison: University of Wisconsin Press, 1967).
5. Melissa McInnis Brown, Rachel B. Thibodeau, Jillian M. Pierucci, and Ansley Tullos Gilpin, "Supporting the Development of Empathy: The Role of Theory of Mind and Fantasy Orientation," *Social Development* 26, no. 4 (2017): 951–64, doi:10.1111 /sode.12232; Jason Marsh, "The Limits of David Brooks' 'Limits of Empathy'," October 4, 2011, https://greatergood.berkeley.edu/article/item/the_limits_of_david_brooks_limits _of_empathy.
6. Emma Seppala, "Compassionate Mind, Healthy Body," July 24, 2013, https://greatergood .berkeley.edu/article/item/compassionate_mind_healthy_body.
7. Mario Beauregard, Jérôme Courtemanche, Vincent Paquette, and Évelyne Landry St-Pierre, "The Neural Basis of Unconditional Love," *Psychiatry Research: Neuroimaging* 172, no. 2 (2009): 93–98, doi:10.1016/j.pscychresns.2008.11.003.
8. Beauregard, Courtemanche, Paquette, and St-Pierre, "The Neural Basis of Unconditional Love," 93.
9. Merriam-Webster's Collegiate Dictionary, "Justice," accessed XXXX, https://www .merriam-webster.com/dictionary/justice.
10. John Rawls and Erin I. Kelly, *Justice as Fairness* (Cambridge, Mass.: Harvard University Press, 2003).
11. Rawls and Kelly, *Justice as Fairness.*
12. Tina Maschi and George Stuart Leibowitz, *Forensic Social Work: Psychosocial and Legal Issues Across Diverse Populations and Settings* (New York: Springer, 2017).
13. Jerome Carl Wakefield, "Psychotherapy, Distributive Justice, and Social Work, Part 1: Distributive Justice as a Conceptual Framework for Social Work," *Social Service Review* 62, no. 2 (1988): 187–210, doi:10.1086/644542.
14. Maschi and Leibowitz, *Forensic Social Work.*
15. Tina Maschi and Robert Youdin, *Social Worker as Researcher: Integrating Research with Advocacy* (Boston, Mass.: Pearson, 2012).

16. Janet L. Finn and Maxine Jacobson, *Just Practice: A Social Justice Approach to Social Work*, 2nd ed. (Peosta, Iowa: Eddie Bowers, 2008).

17. Kathleen Akins, "Lost the Plot? Reconstructing Dennett's Multiple Drafts Theory of Consciousness," *Mind & Language* 11, no. 1 (1996): 1–43, doi:10.1111/j.1468-0017.1996.tb00027.x; John R. Anderson, *The Architecture of Cognition* (Cambridge, Mass.: Harvard University Press, 1983); Tim Bayne, *The Unity of Consciousness* (New York: Oxford University Press, 2010).

18. Carl Gustave Jung, *Collected Works*, Vol. 12: *Psychology and Alchemy* (Princeton, N.J.: Princeton University Press, 1953), 188.

19. Carl Gustave Jung, "The Phenomenology of the Spirit in Fairytales," in *The Archetypes and the Collective Unconscious*, Vol. 9, Part 1, trans. R. F. C. Hull (London: Routledge, 1948), 207–54.

20. Jung, "The Phenomenology of the Spirit in Fairytales."

21. Michelle S. Phelps, "Rehabilitation in the Punitive Era: The Gap Between Rhetoric and Reality in U.S. Prison Programs," *Law & Society Review* 45, no. 1 (2011): 33–68, doi:10.1111/j.1540-5893.2011.00427.x; Curtis Blakely, "American Criminal Justice Philosophy Revisited," *Federal Probation Journal of Correctional Philosophy and Practice* 72, no. 1 (2008): 4–5.

22. Mike Materni, "Criminal Punishment and the Pursuit of Justice," 2 *British Journal of American Legal Studies* 263 (2013), https://www.semanticscholar.org/paper/Criminal-Punishment-and-the-Pursuit-of-Justice-Materni/36c274dde75c64b126e80976730201b689f743a3.

23. Phelps, "Rehabilitation in the Punitive Era," 33–68; Blakely, "American Criminal Justice Philosophy Revisited," 4–5; Albert W. Alschuler, "The Changing Purposes of Criminal Punishment: A Retrospective on the Past Century and Some Thoughts About the Next," *University of Chicago Law Review* 70, no. 1 (2003): 1–22, doi:10.2307/1600541; Materni, "Criminal Punishment and the Pursuit of Justice."

24. Phelps, "Rehabilitation in the Punitive Era," 33–68; Blakely, "American Criminal Justice Philosophy Revisited," 4–5; Alschuler, "The Changing Purposes of Criminal Punishment," 1–22.

25. Materni, "Criminal Punishment and the Pursuit of Justice."

26. Francisco Fernflores, *Einstein's Mass-Energy Equation* (New York: Momentum Press, 2018).

27. Jung, "The Phenomenology of the Spirit in Fairytales," 207–54.

28. Deepak Chopra, *Everyday Immortality: A Concise Course in Spiritual Transformation* (La Jolla, Calif.: Random House, 1999); Beverly Rubik, David Muehsam, Richard Hammerschlag, and Shamini Jain, "Biofield Science and Healing: History, Terminology, and Concepts," *Global Advances in Health and Medicine* 4, no.1, suppl. (November 2015): 8–14, doi:10.7453/gahmj.2015.038.suppl.

29. Otto Dann, "Gleichheit," in *Geschichtliche Grundbegriffe*, ed. V. O. Brunner, W. Conze, and R. Koselleck (Stuttgart: Klett-Cotta, 1975), 997; Albert Menne, "Identität, Gleichheit, Ähnlichkeit," *Ratio* 4 (1962): ff.44; Peter Westen, *Speaking Equality* (Princeton, N.J.: Princeton University Press, 1990), 39, 120.

30. Office of Juvenile Justice and Delinquency Prevention, "Effectiveness of Restorative Justice Principles in Juvenile Justice: A Meta-Analysis," 2019, https://www.ncjrs.gov/pdffiles1/ojjdp/grants/250872.pdf; Edward Gumz and Cynthia Grant, "Issues in Criminal, Social and Restorative Justice," *Contemporary Justice Review* 15, no. 4 (November 2012): ebi, doi: 10.1080/10282580.2012.749591.

31. Catherine Beyer, "Geometric Shapes and Their Symbolic Meanings," July 8, 2019, https://www.learnreligions.com/geometric-shapes-4086370.

9. Accepting the Gift of Life: Incarcerated Older Adults' Prescription for Living Longer, Happier, and Healthier Lives

1. Rudolf Steiner, *Initiation and Its Results: A Sequel to* The Way of Initiation, trans. Clifford Baz (Chicago, Ill.: Occult, 1910); M. P. Pandit, *Kundalini Yoga*, 5th ed. (Madras: Ganesh, 1972); Mandira Ghosh, *Shiva-Shakti in Indian Mythology* (Gurgaon, India: Shubhi, 2007).
2. Liz McCaughey, "Etheric Body and Health," Kumara Hub, February 26, 2015, http://kumarahub.com/etheric-body-and-health/.
3. Steiner, *Initiation and Its Results.*
4. McCaughey, "Etheric Body and Health."
5. Eduardo Kulcheski, "O Duplo Etérico," accessed August 27, 2019, https://www.ippb.org.br/textos/especiais/editora-vivencia/o-duplo-eterico.
6. Steiner, *Initiation and Its Results.*
7. David R. Hawkins, *Power vs. Force: The Hidden Determinants of Human Behavior* (New York: Hay House, 2002), 282.
8. United Nations Office on Drugs and Crime, "Introductory Handbook on the Prevention of Recidivism and the Social Reintegration of Offenders," 2012, https://www.unodc.org/documents/justice-and-prison-reform/crimeprevention/Introductory_Handbook_on_the_Prevention_of_Recidivism_and_the_Social_Reintegration_of_Offenders.pdf.
9. Maia Duerr, "A Powerful Silence: The Role of Meditation and Other Contemplative Practices in American Life and Work," The Center for Contemplative Mind in Society, 2004, http://www.contemplativemind.org/admin/wp-content/uploads/2012/09/APS.pdf.
10. Marino Bruce, Kia Skrine Jeffers, Jan King Robinson, and Keith Norris, "Contemplative Practices: A Strategy to Improve Health and Reduce Disparities," *International Journal of Environmental Research and Public Health* 15, no. 10 (2018): 2253, doi:10.3390/ijerph15102253; Sujit Chandratreya, "Yoga: An Evidence-Based Therapy," *Journal of Mid-Life Health* 2, no. 1 (2011): 3, doi:10.4103/0976-7800.83251; Paul M. Lehrer, Robert L. Woolfolk, and Wesley E. Sime, *Principles and Practice of Stress Management* (New York: Guilford Press, 2009); National Center for Complementary and Integrative Health, "Meditation: In Depth," 2019, https://nccih.nih.gov/health/meditation/overview.htm#refs.
11. Joseph J. Loizzo, "The Subtle Body: An Interoceptive Map of Central Nervous System Function and Meditative Mind-Brain-Body Integration," *Annals of The New York Academy of Sciences* 1373, no. 1 (2016): 78–95, doi:10.1111/nyas.13065.
12. National Center for Complementary and Integrative Health, "Meditation: In Depth."
13. Ephrat Livni, "Use These Mantras to Start, Power Through, and Finish Your Day," 2019, https://qz.com/quartzy/1685501/use-these-mantras-to-start-power-through-and-finish-your-day/.
14. Nóra Kerekes, Cecilia Fielding, and Susanne Apelqvist, "Yoga in Correctional Settings: A Randomized Controlled Study," *Frontiers in Psychiatry* 8 (2017), doi:10.3389/fpsyt.2017.00204.
15. Elke Smeets, Kristin Neff, Hugo Alberts, and Madelon Peters, "Meeting Suffering with Kindness: Effects of a Brief Self-Compassion Intervention for Female College Students," *Journal of Clinical Psychology* 70, no. 9 (2014): 794–807, doi:10.1002/jclp.22076.
16. Beverly Engel, "Healing Your Shame and Guilt Through Self-Forgiveness," 2017, https://www.psychologytoday.com/us/blog/the-compassion-chronicles/201706/healing-your-shame-and-guilt-through-self-forgiveness.

17. RESTORE Programme, 2019, https://www.theforgivenessproject.com/restore-programme.

18. H. Simon, "Giving Thanks Can Make You Happier," 2019, https://www.health.harvard.edu/healthbeat/giving-thanks-can-make-you-happier.

19. Martin E. P. Seligman, Tracy A. Steen, Nansook Park, and Christopher Peterson, "Positive Psychology Progress: Empirical Validation of Interventions," *American Psychologist* 60, no. 5 (2005): 410–21, doi:10.1037/0003-066x.60.5.410.

20. Simon, "Giving Thanks Can Make You Happier."

21. Liberation Prison Project, 2019, http://www.liberationprisonproject.org/.

22. Claudia Battaglia, Alessandra di Cagno, Giovanni Fiorilli, Arrigo Giombini, Federica Fagnani, Paolo Borrione, Marco Marchetti, and Fabio Pigozzi, "Benefits of Selected Physical Exercise Programs in Detention: A Randomized Controlled Study," *International Journal of Environmental Research and Public Health* 10, no. 11 (2013): 5683–96, doi:10.3390/ijerph10115683.

23. Paul Clements, "The Rehabilitative Role of Arts Education in Prison: Accommodation or Enlightenment?," *International Journal of Art & Design Education* 23, no. 2 (2004): 169–78.

24. United Nations Office on Drugs and Crime, "Introductory Handbook on the Prevention of Recidivism and the Social Reintegration of Offenders."

25. Julia Lutsky, "Mentally Ill Prisoners in the New Jersey Prison System," *Prison Legal News*, February 15, 2001, https://www.prisonlegalnews.org/news/2001/feb/15/mentally-ill-prisoners-in-the-new-jersey-prison-system/.

26. Lewis Mehl-Madrona, "Qualitative Assessment of the Impact of Implementing Reiki Training in a Supported Residence for People Older Than 50 Years with HIV/AIDS," *The Permanente Journal* 15, no. 3 (2011): 43–50, doi:10.7812/tpp/10-152.

27. Melissa Li, "From Prisons to Communities: Confronting Re-Entry Challenges and Social Inequality," March 2018, https://www.apa.org/pi/ses/resources/indicator/2018/03/prisons-to-Communities; United Nations Office on Drugs and Crime, "The Nelson Mandela Rules," accessed September 1, 2019, https://www.un.org/en/events/mandeladay/mandela_rules.shtml; American Psychological Association, "Consensus Workgroup Policy Recommendations to the 115th Congress and Trump Administration on Behavioral Health Issues in the Criminal Justice System," 2017, https://www.aacap.org/App_Themes/AACAP/docs/Advocacy/transition_documents/Policy-Recommendations-to-the-115.pdf.

28. American Psychological Association, "Consensus Workgroup Policy Recommendations to the 115th Congress"; United Nations Office on Drugs and Crime, "Introductory Handbook on the Prevention of Recidivism and the Social Reintegration of Offenders."

29. To learn from other countries, investigate some of these sources: https://voxeu.org/article/incarceration-can-be-rehabilitative; https://www.ncjrs.gov/App/Publications/abstract.aspx?ID=82004; https://www.themarshallproject.org/2018/12/20/out-from-the-holocaust; and https://pdfs.semanticscholar.org/ec06/9c9d66890259a686d0a-3a6edd08e595a139f.pdf.

30. United Nations Office on Drugs and Crime, "Introductory Handbook on the Prevention of Recidivism and the Social Reintegration of Offenders."

31. Prison of Peace website, accessed September 1, 2019, http://www.prisonofpeace.org/.

32. Howard Zehr and Harry Mika, *Fundamental Concepts of Restorative Justice* (Akron, Penn.: Mennonite Central Committee, 1997).

33. Lisa, M. Najavits, "Seeking Safety" [video], 2002, https://www.treatment-innovations.org/seeking-safety.html.

34. Nina Esaki, Joseph Benamati, Sarah Yanosy, Jennifer S. Middleton, Laura M. Hopson, Victoria L. Hummer, and Sandra L. Bloom, "The Sanctuary Model: Theoretical

Framework," *Families in Society: The Journal of Contemporary Social Services* 94, no. 2 (2013): 87–95, doi:10.1606/1044-3894.4287.

35. Judith Landau, Mona Mittal, and Elizabeth Wieling, "Linking Human Systems: Strengthening Individuals, Families, and Communities in the Wake of Mass Trauma," *Journal of Marital and Family Therapy* 34, no. 2 (2008): 193–209, doi:10.1111/j.1752-0606.2008.00064.x.

36. Landau, Mittal, and Wieling, "Linking Human Systems."

37. Julia J. A. Shaw, "Compassion and the Criminal Justice System: Stumbling Along Towards a Jurisprudence of Love and Forgiveness," *International Journal of Law in Context* 11, no. 1 (2015): 92–107, doi:10.1017/s174455231400038x.

10. Realizing a Caring Justice World: Promising Global Practices for Justice-Involved Older Adults

1. Nick Le Mesurier, "Supporting Older People in Prison: Ideas for Practice," Age UK, June 2011, http://www.ageuk.org.uk/documents/en-gb/for-professionals/government -and-society/older%20prisoners%20guide_pro.pdf?dtrk=true.

2. Human Rights Watch, "Old Behind Bars: The Aging Prison Population in the United States," January 2012, https://www.hrw.org/sites/default/files/reports/usprison-so112webwcover_0.pdf; Katie Stone, Irena Papadopoulos, and Daniel Kelly, "Establishing Hospice Care for Prison Populations: An Integrative Review Assessing the UK and USA Perspective," *Palliative Medicine* 26, no. 8 (October 2011): 969–78, https://doi.org /10.1177%2F0269216311424219.

3. Doris J. James and Lauren E. Glaze, "Mental Health Problems of Prison and Jail Inmates," Bureau of Justice Statistics Special Report, December 14, 2006, https://www .bjs.gov/content/pub/pdf/mhppji.pdf.

4. Tina Maschi, Jung Kwak, Eunjeong Ko, and Mary B. Morrissey, "Forget Me Not: Dementia in Prison," *The Gerontologist* 52, no. 4 (2012): 441–51, doi:10.1093/geront /gnr131; Lorry Schoenly, "Perfect Storm Looming: Inmate Dementia Is on the Horizon," June 17, 2010, http://www.correctionsone.com/correctional-healthcare/articles/2083910 -Perfect-storm-looming-Inmate-dementia-is-on-the-horizon/; John Wilson and Sharen Barboza, "The Looming Challenge of Dementia in Corrections," *Correct Care* 24, no. 2 (2010): 12–14, https://www.ncchc.org/filebin/images/Website_PDFs/24-2.pdf.

5. Maschi, Kwak, Ko, and Morrissey, "Forget Me Not: Dementia in Prison," 441–51.

6. Mary T. Harrison, "True Grit: An Innovative Program for Elderly Inmates," *Corrections Today* 68, no. 7 (2006): 46–49, http://www.aca.org/fileupload/177/prasannak/Stewart _dec06.pdf.

7. Maschi, Kwak, Ko, and Morrissey, "Forget Me Not: Dementia in Prison," 441–51.

8. Maschi, Kwak, Ko, and Morrissey, "Forget Me Not: Dementia in Prison."

9. Jo-Ann Brown, "Living with Dementia in Prison,"https://www.churchilltrust.com.au /media/fellows/Brown_J_2015_Living_with_dementia_in_prison.pdf; Maschi, Kwak, Ko, and Morrissey, "Forget Me Not: Dementia in Prison," 441–51.

10. Brown, "Living with Dementia in Prison"; Maschi, Kwak, Ko, and Morrissey, "Forget Me Not: Dementia in Prison."

11. New York State Department of Corrections and Community Supervision, 2018, http:// www.doccs.ny.gov/.

12. Kristin G. Cloyes, Susan J. Rosenkranz, Katherine P. Supiano, Patricia H. Berry, Meghan Routt, Sarah M. Llanque, and Kathleen Shannon-Dorcy, "Caring to Learn

and Learning to Care," *Journal of Correctional Health Care* 23, no. 1 (2017): 43–55, doi:10.1177/1078345816684833.

13. Cloyes, Rosenkranz, Supiano, Berry, Routt, Llanque, and Shannon-Dorcy, "Caring to Learn and Learning to Care."

14. Elisabeth Thornton, Joan Welch, and April Holmes, "Chronic Disease Self-Management Education in Virginia's Prisons" [Powerpoint slides], Southern Gerontological Society Annual Meeting, April 17, 2015, https://d2mkcg26uvg1cz.cloudfront.net/wp-content /uploads/23-Virginia-Presentation-CDSME-in-Prisons-2015.pdf.

15. California Department of Corrections and Rehabilitation, "Long-Term Offender Program," 2018, https://www.cdcr.ca.gov/.

16. Kevin E. McCarthy, "State Initiatives to Address Aging Prisoners," OLR Research Report, March 4, 2013, https://www.cga.ct.gov/2013/rpt/2013-R-0166.htm.

17. James Baldwin and Jasmine Leete, "Behind Bars: The Challenge of an Ageing Prison Population," *Australian Journal of Dementia Care* 1, no. 2 (August/September 2012): 16–19, http://journalofdementiacare.com/wp-content/uploads/2014/04/AJDC-Prisons -Aug-Sept-2012.pdf.

18. United Nations Office on Drugs and Crime, "Assessing Compliance with the Nelson Mandela Rules," 2017, https://www.unodc.org/documents/justice-and-prison-reform /UNODC_Checklist_-_Nelson_Mandela_Rules.pdf.

19. Nick Le Mesurier, "Older People in Prison: A Monitoring Guide for IMBs," Age UK, 2011, http://ageactionalliance.org/wordpress/wp-content/uploads/2014/03/ID10735-IMB -Guide-Older-People-In-Prison.pdf.

20. Matthew Davies, "The Reintegration of Elderly Prisoners: An Exploration of Services Provided in England and Wales," *Internet Journal of Criminology* 1 (2011): 1–32, https://www.semanticscholar.org/paper/THE-REINTEGRATION-OF-ELDERLY -PRISONERS%3A-AN-OF-IN-Davies/7e3f0dee24e4a944d1a1ff185e016056bf591f61.

21. Tina Maschi, George Leibowitz, Joanne Rees, and Lauren Pappacena, "Analysis of US Compassionate and Geriatric Release Laws: Applying a Human Rights Framework to Global Prison Health," *Journal of Human Rights and Social Work* 1, no. 4 (2016): 165–74, doi:10.1007/s41134-016-0021-0; Brie Williams and Rita Abraldes, "Growing Older: Challenges of Prison and Reentry for the Aging Population," in *Public Health Behind Bars: From Prisons to Communities*, ed. R. Greifinger (New York: Springer, 2007), 56–72.

22. Brown, "Living with Dementia in Prison"; Mesurier, "Supporting Older People in Prison."

23. Tina Maschi, Deborah Viola, and Fei Sun, "The High Cost of the International Aging Prisoner Crisis: Well-Being as the Common Denominator for Action," *The Gerontologist* 53, no. 4 (2013): 543–54, doi:10.1093/geront/gns125; Samuel K. Roberts, *Aging in Prison: Reducing Elder Incarceration and Promoting Public Safety* (New York: Center for Justice at Columbia University, 2015), http://centerforjustice.columbia.edu /files/2015/10/AgingInPrison_FINAL_web.pdf.

24. Brown, "Living with Dementia in Prison"; Adam Wisnieski, "'Model' Nursing Home for Paroled Inmates to Get Federal Funds," Connecticut Heath I-Team, April 25, 2017, http://c-hit.org/2017/04/25/model-nursing-home-for-paroled-inmates-to-get-federal -funds/.

25. Baldwin and Leete, "Behind Bars," 16–19.

26. Asian and Pacific Conference of Correctional Administrators, "A Program That Works with and Treats Elderly and Infirm Offenders in the Pacific Region" [Newsletter], 2000, http://www.apcca.org/Pubs/news11/#item15.

27. Jack Stewart, "The Reintegration Effort for Long-Term Infirm and Elderly Federal Offenders (RELIEF) Program," *Forum on Corrections Research* 12, no. 3 (September 2000): 35–38, https://www.ncjrs.gov/App/Publications/abstract.aspx?ID=185853.

28. Bayview Senior Services, "Senior Ex-Offender Program," accessed June 20, 2018, https://bhpmss.org/senior-ex-offender-program/.

29. Prison Reform Trust, "Doing Time: The Experiences and Needs of Older People in Prison," 2008, http://www.prisonreformtrust.org.uk/Portals/0/Documents/Doing%20Time%20the%20experiences%20and%20needs%20of%20older%20people%20in%20prison.pdf.

30. RECOOP, "Transition 50+ Resettlement," 2018, www.recoop.org.uk/pages/services/transition-50-resettlement.php.

31. HM Chief Inspector of Prisons for England and Wales, "Annual Report 2012–13," October 23, 2013, http://www.justice.gov.uk/publications/corporate-reports/hmi-prisons.

32. Prison Reform Trust, "Doing Time."

33. Restore Support Network, 2018, http://www.restoresupportnetwork.org.uk/.

34. National Association of Area Agencies on Aging, "Supporting America's Aging Prisoner Population: Opportunities & Challenges for Area Agencies on Aging," 2017, https://www.n4a.org/Files/n4a_AgingPrisoners_23Feb2017REV%20(2).pdf.

35. National Association of Area Agencies on Aging, "Supporting America's Aging Prisoner Population."

36. Maschi, Kwak, Ko, and Morrissey, "Forget Me Not: Dementia in Prison," 441–51.

37. Families Against Mandatory Minimums, "About Us," accessed May 9, 2018, https://famm.org/about-us/.

38. National Association of Area Agencies on Aging, "Supporting America's Aging Prisoner Population."

39. Gina Barton, "Release Programs for Sick and Elderly Prisoners Could Save Millions, but States Rarely Use Them," https://projects.jsonline.com/news/2018/4/18/release-programs-for-sick-elderly-prisoners-could-save-millions.html.

40. Lindsey E. Wylie, Alexis K. Knutson, and Edie Greene, "Extraordinary and Compelling: The Use of Compassionate Release Laws in the United States," *Psychology, Public Policy, and Law* 24, no. 2 (2018): 216–34, doi:10.1037/law0000161.

41. Maschi, Leibowitz, Rees, and Pappacena, "Analysis of US Compassionate and Geriatric Release Laws," 165–74.

42. U.S. Department of Justice, Federal Bureau of Prisons, "Compassionate Release/Reduction in Sentence: Procedures for Implementation of 18 U.S.C. §§ 3582(c)(1)(A) and 4205(g)," Program Statement No. 5050.49, 2013, https://www.bop.gov/policy/progstat/5050_049_CN-1.pdf.

43. Wylie, Knutson, and Greene, "Extraordinary and Compelling," 216–34.

44. Christie Thompson, "Frail, Old and Dying, but Their Only Way Out of Prison Is a Coffin," *New York Times*, March 7, 2018, https://www.nytimes.com/2018/03/07/us/prisons-compassionate-release-.html.

45. National Association of Area Agencies on Aging. "Supporting America's Aging Prisoner Population."

46. Lesley Emerson, Karen Orr, and Paul Connolly, "Evaluation of the Effectiveness of the Prison to Peace: Learning from the Experience of Political Ex-Prisoners' Educational Programme," Centre for Effective Education, Queen's University Belfast, October 2014, https://www.executiveoffice-ni.gov.uk/publications/evaluation-effectiveness-%E2%80%98prison-peace-learning-experience-political-ex-prisoners.

47. Tomris Atabay, "Handbook on Prisoners with Special Needs," United Nations Office on Drugs and Crime, 2009, https://www.unodc.org/pdf/criminal_justice/Handbook_on _Prisoners_with_Special_Needs.pdf.
48. Atabay, "Handbook on Prisoners with Special Needs."
49. Dietrich Oberwittler and Sven Höfer, "Crime and Justice in Germany," *European Journal of Criminology* 2, no. 4 (2005): 465–508, doi:10.1177/1477370805056058.

Appendix 1

1. Don A. Dillman, Jolene D. Smyth, and Leah Melani Christian, *Internet, Mail, and Mixed-Mode Surveys: The Tailored Design Method*, 3rd ed. (Hoboken, N.J.: Wiley, 2009).
2. Leslie M. Tutty, Michael A. Rothery, and Richard M. Grinnell, *Qualitative Research for Social Workers* (Boston, Mass.: Allyn and Bacon, 1996).
3. Matthew B. Miles and A. Michael Huberman, *Qualitative Data Analysis: An Expanded Sourcebook*, 2nd ed. (Thousand Oaks, Calif.: Sage, 1994).

Appendix 2

1. Leslie M. Tutty, Michael A. Rothery, and Richard M. Grinnell, *Qualitative Research for Social Workers* (Boston, Mass.: Allyn and Bacon, 1996).
2. Matthew B. Miles and A. Michael Huberman, *Qualitative Data Analysis: An Expanded Sourcebook*, 2nd ed. (Thousand Oaks, Calif.: Sage, 1994).

INDEX